Praise for *Why Are We Bad at Picking Good Leaders?*

"Every CEO has to make tough, heart-wrenching decisions about his or her organization's talent. Who stays, who goes, who gets promoted? And there is no time to waste. With *Why Are We Bad at Picking Good Leaders?* Cohn and Moran provide an ingenious, yet down-to-earth guide that will help any CEO or hiring manager find and keep the kind of people that truly make a difference. I also highly recommend it to all motivated professionals who want to understand what their organizations are looking for before big promotions are handed out. This book is a great resource for rising stars who are serious about keeping their career trajectories on track."

—**Peter Löscher,** president and CEO, Siemens

"How many of us have had a boss we didn't like? And how many have lent our support to a potential leader who fell short? We all have. Why? Because zeroing in on real leadership potential is more art-form than process. Cohn and Moran demystify this process by providing a clear, entertaining, and insightful way of thinking about leaders and assessing their potential."

—**Jon R. Katzenbach,** coauthor, *Leading Outside the Lines,* and senior vice president, Booz & Company

"An enjoyable, very practical, and fresh perspective on some of the most important decisions organizations make."

—**Joseph L. Badaracco Jr.,** John Shad Professor of Business Ethics, Harvard Business School

"Large, global law firms like Allen & Overy need to take succession planning very seriously. Clearly we hire only outstanding lawyers. But equally important is leadership potential. Cohn and Moran nail it in their discussion of what to look for and how to find it when evaluating future leaders. I would advise anyone, especially those who manage professional service firms, to read this book."

—**Wim Dejonghe,** global managing partner, Allen & Overy

WHY ARE WE BAD AT PICKING GOOD LEADERS?

A BETTER WAY TO EVALUATE
LEADERSHIP POTENTIAL

JEFFREY COHN AND **JAY MORAN**

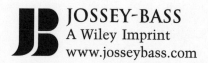

JOSSEY-BASS
A Wiley Imprint
www.josseybass.com

Published by Jossey-Bass
A Wiley Imprint
989 Market Street, San Francisco, CA 94103-1741—www.josseybass.com

Library of Congress Cataloging-in-Publication Data

Cohn, Jeffrey.
    Why are we bad at picking good leaders? a better way to evaluate leadership potential / Jeffrey Cohn, Jay Moran.—1st ed.
        p. cm.
    Includes bibliographical references and index.
    ISBN 978-0-470-60194-5 (hardback); ISBN 978-1-118-06218-0 (ebk);
ISBN 978-1-118-06219-7 (ebk); ISBN 978-1-118-06220-3 (ebk)
        1. Leadership. 2. Leadership—Case studies. I. Moran, Jay, 1968-   II. Title.
HM1261.C64 2011
658.4'092—dc22

                                                                          2011007467

Printed in the United States of America
FIRST EDITION
HB Printing   10 9 8 7 6 5 4 3 2 1

Contents

WHY ARE WE BAD AT PICKING GOOD LEADERS?

Introduction

Let's face it, we are lousy at picking leaders. Time and again, we complain about the quality of the men and women who run our companies, organizations, and governments. We bemoan their incompetence, their detachment, their lack of urgency. Inevitably we get rid of these leaders and move on to the next ones, usually with a bit of hope and excitement. Unfortunately the pattern repeats, and we find ourselves right back where we started, shaking our heads.

Why does this happen? Why don't we do a better job of picking effective leaders? For starters, because selecting the right people can be very, very hard.

Imagine yourself in the following situation.

You are the chairperson of the board of directors of a large technology company. Three months ago, the CEO of the company suffered a nonfatal heart attack and abruptly resigned. The company did not have a CEO succession plan in place, and as a result, the board has spent the past several weeks looking for the right person to take over the reins.

Choosing the next CEO is an extremely important decision. The company has more than forty-five thousand employees, and their monthly incomes, pensions, and benefits depend on its continued success. Tens of thousands of shareholders are also invested in the company's future, as are the customers who rely on the company's products every day.

After three months, the board has narrowed its CEO search to two candidates: Jim and Steve. Jim is forty-one years old, confident, bright, and highly driven. For the past three years, he has been running a billion-dollar division of a Fortune 100 company. His record for leading growth and profitability is impeccable, and his name regularly appears on many "who's who" lists of up-and-coming corporate stars.

The other candidate, Steve, now fifty-eight years old, is an industry veteran. As chief operating officer at one of the company's top competitors, he has steadily moved up through the ranks for two decades. It is hard to imagine someone who knows the company's line of business better than Steve does. In fact, he is known as an efficiency expert who is adept at cutting costs, and he has participated in several important acquisitions.

At the succession meeting to decide which candidate to choose, it quickly becomes clear that the board is divided. Half of the board members are firmly aligned in favor of Jim, and the other half are just as enthusiastic about Steve. Everyone feels the urgency to make the right decision, and emotions are high.

"Jim looks like he just got out of college!" one board member exclaims, and this is not the first time that the issue has been raised. "People aren't going to take him seriously. He doesn't have enough experience. We need someone with more gravitas, more depth. And that's Steve. Steve won't need any on-the-job training. He instantly commands respect."

Others jump to Jim's defense, quick to point out an obvious area in which he outshines Steve—his energy, his charisma. "Gravitas?" one of his supporters counters. "When Jim walks in the room, the entire place lights up. He's electric! He is *exactly* what we need. Someone who has the magnetism and passion to take our company to the next level."

The arguments continue like this for hours. Jim is dynamic, bold, brilliant, absolutely driven to succeed. Or—depending on your point of view—he's raw, untested, a fish out of water when it comes to the company's industry. Steve is seasoned, accomplished, respected, a veteran who knows what it takes to lead. Or he's too conventional, subdued, lacking inspiration, not the kind of guy who will move the company in new directions.

At the end of the night, the board is deadlocked, split down the middle. Half want to hire Jim, and an equal number want Steve. As chair, you will be casting the decisive vote.

The company's fate rests on the next words that you will say. You take one final look at each candidate's detailed résumé, background, and references. You try to picture how each candidate would fare at this very table after arriving on the first day.

Who will you choose? *How* will you choose?

. . . .

How often have you said or heard any of the following:

- "Our president is doing a terrible job."
- "Corporate leaders care only about stuffing their own pockets."
- "Those guys on Wall Street are ruining the economy."
- "Our local school system is a mess because we have a lousy superintendent."
- "My favorite sports team would be undefeated if it had a better coach."
- "The head of my department is nice, but she just can't get everyone to work from the same page."
- "Congress is out of touch with the people."
- "My organization's strategy is not working. I wish we had better decision makers at the top."

And the perennial favorite:
- "I wish I worked for a better boss."

If you have said or heard these, you're not alone. In fact, according to a 2010 poll, almost 70 percent of Americans believe that there is a "crisis in leadership" in the United States.[1] Whether it's another corporate scandal, government gridlock, soaring deficits, mass layoffs, broken school systems, lack of progress on pressing issues like climate change, multimillion-dollar severance packages for executives of companies that are now defunct: increasingly people are frustrated and wondering why it is that we can't find better people to get the job done.

If this trend is surprising, it is because most leaders look good on paper. They are long on credentials. They are confident, they work hard, and they're smart. Certainly we expect them to do well.

So why are so many of the people we depend on failing to succeed? In order to answer this question, we need to turn it around. Instead of looking at the issue in terms of *their* failure, let's ask ourselves what role *we* play. Why aren't we choosing better leaders?

The tempting answer is that we don't have better choices; that when it comes to candidates, we are faced with a weak slate. Whether at the ballot box or in the boardroom, the argument goes, the right people just aren't willing to lead.

This argument doesn't hold—we can't keep passing the buck. And even if this explanation were true, doesn't it mean that we are promoting the wrong people through the system? If the only candidates with experience are simultaneously not qualified to lead, how did they get in the running for leadership positions?

The answer lies with us: we put them in positions of authority, and with that comes responsibility. We need to own up to our part, and the truth is that we don't do a competent job of selecting the men and women who have what it takes to lead. What exactly is it that enables someone to do that? What qualities are essential for leadership success? And how do we know if the leaders we choose possess these attributes? These are the real questions everyone should be asking—and we provide the answers in this book.

· · · · · · · · ·

For the past two decades, the two of us have been dedicated to understanding what makes great leaders great. As part of various succession planning or leadership development initiatives, we have advised hundreds of organizations on how to evaluate and groom their best talent.

As specialists in leadership assessment, we are regularly called on to help Fortune 500 and large, international companies identify their high-potential leaders. Using customized, multilayered techniques, we help them distinguish between above-average professionals and those who have the potential to lead at the highest level. Boards and hiring managers have learned that relying on traditional evaluation methods is not enough. In fact, those methods can even be dangerous. Traditional evaluation techniques too often rely on "gut feel" and promote people based on charisma, confidence, academic achievement, experience, technical skills, and—sadly—an ability to interview well. This is not the way to identify good leaders.

That's where we come in. We consistently help organizations cut through the window dressing and focus on the leadership attributes that matter.

Of course, when we started out nearly two decades ago, we didn't know what makes great leaders great; we were just as curious and puzzled as everyone else. Like many others, we figured it was due to intelligence or personality or maybe old-fashioned good luck.

The true genesis of this book started with our extensive search for answers in the academic world. For years we studied and worked alongside scholars at Harvard, Yale, INSEAD, IMD, and other top-notch universities. We helped design CEO workshops, participated in executive education programs, and pressed our academic colleagues and mentors for the best of their ideas.

We found that leadership scholarship is all over the map. Some academics assert that leadership is a matter of judgment or character. Some say vision. Some say passion. Others pinpoint resilience or charisma. Today's top scholars tend to place a laser-like focus on individual leadership traits, and they have written entire volumes devoted to narrow themes. Certainly these books are interesting and insightful, but they are almost always incomplete. For starters, how can leadership be reduced to a single attribute? The people we know, not to mention the great leaders of history, are much more complicated than that.

More important, *description* doesn't go far enough. It doesn't provide enough information to know how to choose better leaders. Even if we could agree that effective leadership comes down to character and judgment, for example, how do we know that we are picking leaders who possess these traits? How do we spot integrity during an interview or debate, or test for good judgment?

From the academy, we went to the executive suite. We figured that the men and women who run today's best organizations would have a good idea of what it takes to lead. We talked to the heads of Fortune 500 companies, nonprofit groups, sports teams, schools, think tanks, and government leaders at the state and federal levels. We asked them directly, "What criteria do you look for in your future leaders?" "What qualities does it take to succeed?" Each answered by saying how critical it is to find and groom the right talent. Yet like their counterparts in the academy, these executives gave us scattershot answers. Some looked for strategic thinkers. Some said innovators. Others pointed to great motivators of teams.

Almost every one of these responses made sense, but none was particularly clear or complete. The executives had trouble defining leadership in any consistent and coherent way. For all their talents, most of them were not able to satisfactorily explain why *they* were effective leaders, much less how to identify that potential in others. Instead, what they gave us often amounted to stock answers or familiar cliché. It almost felt as if they were regurgitating the latest magazine article that they happened to be reading. (One CEO even quoted the headlines off the magazine on his desk, seemingly unaware of what he was doing.)

This is the backdrop against which we began to develop a leadership model to fill in the gaps. Increasingly the executives we spoke with wanted to know more. They were eager to hear what ideas we had gleaned from their peers. They also wanted to learn what our colleagues and friends in top executive education programs were doing to help develop leadership talent. They'd ask, "What are they doing at Harvard? What are they doing at IMD [a top European business school]? What competencies are other companies looking for? How do they find it? How do they measure it?"

From this collective experience, we developed the leadership framework described in this book. It didn't happen all at once, of course. It was a dynamic process, and we had a lot of help. But over time, we were able to bridge our academic and professional training in a way that made breakthrough sense.

• • • • • • • • •

What we learned from two decades of shuffling between executive offices and the ivory tower is that seven leadership attributes, which pop up over and over again, are the most vital: integrity, empathy, emotional intelligence, vision, judgment, courage, and passion. These are the attributes that academics seize on, decipher, and blend. They are the traits repeatedly cited in business journals and biographies. Hiring managers insist that many of these qualities are what they seek in candidates, even if the how or why of finding them is something few hiring managers truly comprehend.

What we have discovered is how to decode and connect these attributes. We have determined how they fit together. Our breakthrough insight is an overall framework for making leadership selection decisions.

In a way, these qualities are like the DNA of every good leader. They are the building blocks of overall success. Unlike DNA, however, these attributes are not innate and mostly can be learned. They are fundamental pieces; taken individually or even in small sets, they provide only a partial picture and do not mean much. In fact, if any one of these attributes is missing, a person who is called on to lead will eventually fail.

These seven qualities must be taken as a whole to capture the essence of leadership. They form a powerful, defining structure, and an individual equipped with all seven has enormous potential; he or she is a superstar in waiting who, given the right training and opportunity, will be poised to accomplish great things.

The trick is knowing what these attributes mean and how to spot them. Until now, we have kept our framework as part of our private consulting work behind closed doors. It has served us well and consistently helped many organizations identify their best talent.

We wrote this book to help others find better leaders in their businesses, governments, nonprofits, military, schools, churches, teams, unions, and local clubs. Our hope is that the leadership model we have developed will form part of a broader discussion. The time has come to stop complaining about bad leadership from the sidelines, as if we were a bunch of disappointed and helpless fans. Instead we need to take action and reevaluate the role that each of us plays in deciding who gets to step onto the field.

We also hope that individual readers will use the insights in this book to reflect on their own leadership development opportunities. If there is one thing that we have learned in the long journey toward this book, it is that no one is perfect. Every leader has weaknesses, sometimes glaring ones. Richard Nixon was a master strategist with severe flaws in his character. Former Disney chief Michael Eisner could dazzle with his vision, but he suffered from an outsized ego and notorious temper. Nobel prize winner Al Gore Jr. is a leading voice in the campaign against global warming, but as a presidential candidate, he had difficulty connecting with the people.

This pattern of weak spots holds for all leaders. Just as important, however, is the fact that all great leaders are constantly trying to improve. They realize that they can do better. To this end, our leadership assessment work with companies includes custom-tailored feedback to help candidates pinpoint areas that are not their natural strengths. Armed with this knowledge, they are in a position to develop better self-awareness or improve their social skills, for example. Along the same lines, we hope that this book will help readers better understand which aspects of their leadership might be holding them back.

· · · · · · · · ·

This book devotes an entire chapter to each of the seven attributes. We explain what each attribute means in the context of leadership and why it matters. We also provide effective techniques for identifying these qualities. Because connections are important too, throughout the book we highlight how the attributes fit together. Appendix B summarizes how these attributes enable leaders to fill important organizational needs—what makes a great innovator, strategist, communicator, change agent, and the like. This appendix should be particularly interesting for boards, CEOs, human resource managers, executive search firms, and others who regularly interview candidates for leadership positions.

This book is full of examples and stories. Many feature CEOs and other leaders whom we have met through our professional practice. We interviewed over a hundred individuals for this book, and we drew on a vast reservoir of research and contacts that ran much deeper than that.

Although we have focused each chapter around one leader who exemplifies that attribute, no single leader holds the exclusive key to understanding what each attribute means and how it works. Therefore, we have also sprinkled in scores of other anecdotes and vignettes from leaders in a variety of different fields—including George Steinbrenner, Bono, Jeff Bezos, and Hall of Fame basketball coach Mike "Coach K" Krzyzewski, to name a few. We were fascinated by their stories, and we think you will be too. Although some of these people are quite famous, try not to have any preconceived notions as you read each chapter. Throw out what you know about someone—his or her personality, charm, age, race, religion, education, and family connections. When judging leadership potential, none of that distinguishes a below-average leader from someone who is great.

Leadership potential starts with integrity. No leader can be effective without it, regardless of his or her strengths. In fact, without integrity, leaders can be downright dangerous. Witness the undoing of Enron. At its height in 2001, Enron was the seventh largest company in America. Its leaders, Jeff Skilling and Ken Lay, were celebrated as champion innovators, the darlings of Wall Street. Yet lurking beneath the accolades were two men whose passion burned in the form of hubris and greed. They lacked integrity and an ethical balance. In Chapter One, we revisit the Enron story and highlight several positive examples, including Ryder CEO Greg Swienton, to explain how critical this attribute can be.

In addition to integrity, it is not possible to lead others without also knowing what makes them tick. A good leader is in touch with the emotions and needs of followers, and this person handles social relations wisely. Without empathy, he just won't click with his team. In Chapter Two, we talk with Jerry Colangelo and Coach K, the two men who brought the U.S. Men's Olympic Basketball Program back to glory with the kind of social savvy that all leaders should emulate.

People like Colangelo and Coach K make their mark by interacting with others, but it is also true that leadership starts from within. Great leaders know themselves: they are aware of their own blind spots, emotions, biases, and temper. They have the maturity to seek advice. In Chapter Three we explain what emotional intelligence means and why it is such a critical attribute for leaders to master. Delos "Toby" Cosgrove, CEO of the world-famous Cleveland Clinic, shows what it is like to move from the operating room to the executive suite—and how emotional intelligence fostered greater confidence and trust in him from his staff, his board, and even his patients.

No matter what a person's strengths, why would anyone follow her if she had no idea where she wanted to go? Leadership requires vision—the kind of imagination and inspiration that pushes others toward future goals. In Chapter Four, we profile a visionary leader who also happens to be a rock star—Bono, front man of U2. Bono is perhaps best known for his chart-topping ballads and leather jacket, but he's working to change the world in more significant ways. His "melody line" is something to inspire the masses. In Chapter Four, we tell you all about it, including the lessons his story contains.

It's important to have vision, even if not enough leaders do. But what good is a vision without the means to get there? Leadership requires a plan to get from point A to point B, and that requires an ability to chart a course and make tough decisions. Effective leaders know they can't do everything, and great leadership involves evaluating difficult trade-offs and focusing on what's most important for the team. In a word, it means having judgment. In Chapter Five, we begin our examination of judgment with Siemens CEO Peter Löscher. In the wake of a massive bribery scandal, Löscher needed a strategy for turning the German engineering giant around. His decision making put Siemens back on the right track, and in Chapter Five, we shed light on why good judgment is so crucial.

The attributes we've touched on so far are a potent combination, but a person needs more in order to withstand the pressures of leadership. To lead is to be on the front line, to face criticism, attack, unforeseen setbacks, and the efforts of saboteurs who do not want this person to succeed. In short, it takes courage—the kind of courage personified by Judith Mackay, arguably the world's leading voice in the antismoking movement. For over thirty years she has taken on Big Tobacco. During that time, she has received death threats and been ostracized by peers and vilified in public, all while working for little or no pay. She has visited countries in the midst of civil war. Her efforts have changed the landscape for a new generation of advocates, and in Chapter Six, we highlight her experience in our broader discussion about courage.

Finally, all leaders need passion. Amazon founder and CEO Jeff Bezos is a pioneer in online commerce. His company has revolutionized the way people around the world shop and read. What people don't always realize is just how much Bezos had to persevere to get Amazon where it is today. During the dot-com crash, many experts thought the company was finished, that the online bookstore would never last. Bezos had the determination to prove them all wrong, however, and his story is a lesson for everyone: leaders are ambitious and spirited people. In Chapter Seven, we take a closer look at Bezos's roller-coaster ride at Amazon to show how only leaders with passion can drive organizations through difficult times and even create new industries.

Altogether, these seven attributes—integrity, empathy, emotional intelligence, vision, judgment, courage, and passion—form the backbone of effective leadership. Each is an essential piece. Take away just one, and you're likely to end up with someone entirely different. You might end up with a fraud like Jeff Skilling, a leader of many strengths whose lack of integrity did him in.

Chapter Eight addresses a question that is on the plate of virtually anyone that has to make an important hiring decision: How do you put all the pieces together? How do you use the attributes and assessment techniques described in this book to find or groom the right person for a critical leadership role? In Chapter Eight, we provide a road map that explains how the world's top organizations conduct assessments and then link the results to leadership development initiatives, including coaching, mentoring, customized workshops, off-site programs, and the creation of special cross-functional teams, to name only a few. Linking assessment and development activities ensures that rising stars have every possible chance to blossom into great leaders. It also attracts other talent to the organization. If done correctly, this approach becomes a powerful competitive advantage for the organization, and one that is hard to replicate.

What about communication? Innovation? Strategic thinking? Crisis management? In other words, how did we narrow our attribute list down to the seven in this book?

The answer is actually simple: the seven leadership attributes in this book are the basic building blocks. Other aspects of leadership, like good communication skills, flow from these seven. For example, communication skills flow out of vision and empathy. The same two attributes, plus courage, are the keys to innovation. In sum, many of these other qualities are leadership competencies. They focus more on what leaders *do* rather than the underlying attributes that allow them to do it. Leadership assessment, however, requires focusing on the seven fundamental qualities. When a leader goes awry, one or more of these is missing.

Along the same lines, other commonly used (and misused) leadership labels are either part of our seven attributes or false predictors of leadership success. For example, some readers might wonder why we haven't included "honesty" or "strong ethics" in our framework. Actually we have. These qualities are part of integrity, which we discuss in Chapter One. Similarly, characteristics such as "even-tempered" or "analytical" are part of emotional intelligence (Chapter Three) and judgment (Chapter Five), respectively. Other qualities, such as charisma, are not reliable indicators of effective leadership. We provide an extensive list of synonyms, misnomers, competencies, and other leadership labels in Appendix A, which should serve as a useful reference guide for many readers.

• • • • • • • • •

We began this Introduction with an inside look at a key hiring decision. In the choice between Jim and Steve, the board was divided. Its members had some pretty strong opinions about which candidate possessed the right qualities to lead. Half seized on Jim's dynamism, citing his charm, brains, and energy. Others were convinced that Steve's experience, know-how, and level-headedness made him the candidate most likely to succeed.

In the heat of the discussion, however, the board neglected to consider another critical attribute: integrity. For all their debate about age, experience, passion, and vision, they failed to see how this fundamental aspect of leadership affected who the right candidate might be.

Would it surprise you to learn that the person they eventually chose, Steve, ended up disappointing in the end? Steve's problems didn't stem from a lack of energy or personal allure, however. Instead, Steve's leadership suffered from a fundamental aspect of character: he didn't always tell the truth. Steve had a habit of covering his tracks or spinning the facts to make him look good. As CEO, he used a company veteran as a scapegoat for his own mistakes, and later he became embroiled in a series of fudged expense reports that were part of a self-dealing scheme. After only two years, the board had to start their search all over again to find the company a new leader.

Unfortunately, as advisors to boards of directors, we see this kind of situation more than we would like. Too often, hiring decisions are made without a careful consideration of this essential leadership trait, integrity. Take away any one of these seven leadership attributes, and the leader will ultimately stumble. Yet among the seven attributes, integrity is the foundation. Without it, no candidate will truly excel, or likely even last, in a leadership role.

How can we evaluate someone's integrity? Is it even possible? How can we know if they are likely to succeed and make the right calls in what would be, to them, unprecedented situations? Let's get started.

Integrity

One of the truly famous leaders of our time became president of a Fortune 500 company when he was only forty-four. At an age when most people are still struggling for professional recognition, he had reached the top. People called him a genius. A rainmaker. A superstar.

His story didn't start that way, however. He wasn't born with a silver spoon. The son of a machine-parts salesman, he spent his youth in blue-collar towns. He was a rather nerdy child, a self-described loner who earned good grades. He worked hard; as a teenager, he saved fifteen thousand dollars at an after-school job. Later he won an engineering scholarship to Southern Methodist University and then distinguished himself as a junior bank officer in Texas. Everyone who knew him agreed that this man possessed great passion. He was definitely determined to get ahead.

He earned an M.B.A. from Harvard Business School, where he again distinguished himself by graduating with honors. In the classroom, he showed a special interest in free markets. From there, he moved to McKinsey & Company, a premiere consulting practice, and became one of the youngest partners in the firm's history.

Here was a person whose intellectual horsepower was beyond question. People described him with words such as "incandescently brilliant" and "the smartest guy I ever met." He was a visionary too. A paradigm changer. The kind of person who sees the world differently than the rest of us do. He could sift through data, recognize trends, uncover hidden opportunities.

His specialty was the energy business, in particular the labyrinthine market for natural gas. He came up with novel ideas for how to transform the industry. His innovative thinking showed no end.

He later left the consulting firm to join a major client, and the next several years were a meteoric rise to the top. He created new business units, discovered untapped revenue streams, and almost single-handedly revolutionized the energy sector. Magazine covers lauded him. They celebrated his leadership and marveled at his ambitious ideas. During the span of a decade, his company's market capitalization increased from $4 billion to over $100 billion, and he became a very wealthy man.

Today he is retired and leads a quiet life in Englewood, Colorado, where he is serving a twenty-four-year prison sentence for mass fraud.

The person we just described is Jeffrey Skilling, the former CEO of Enron. His story is well documented, and most of the world immediately associates his name with crime. And yet until the sudden collapse of Enron, he displayed the passion, intellect, and vision of a great leader. What went wrong?

INTEGRITY IS THE FOUNDATION

Integrity is the fundamental leadership attribute. Nobody can lead effectively without it. Former Wyoming senator Alan Simpson once said, "If you have integrity, nothing else matters. If you don't have integrity, nothing else matters."[1]

Simpson's words aren't exactly true; other aspects of leadership are critically important as well. But if you need to make a list, integrity belongs at the very top. It's where you start. It's what holds everything else together.

Integrity is like the foundation of a house. It's not the first thing people notice, yet without it, all the granite countertops and wood floors don't have a place to stand. In fact, without integrity, all those amenities are merely a waste of money. Other aspects are important, to be sure: no one would want to live in a house with poor heating or faulty plumbing, for instance, and a leaky roof is an energy killer and a real nuisance. These problems, however, can be fixed. When a house lacks a solid foundation, on the other hand, you might as well tear the place apart and start over. Otherwise you're likely to be crushed beneath the rubble when it all comes crashing down.

The same is true in leadership. Integrity is the fundamental attribute that keeps everything else secure. A leader who possesses integrity but lacks vision or passion, for example, will at worst be incompetent. He might muddle through or create temporary setbacks. By contrast, be wary of leaders who dazzle the world with brainpower or charisma at the expense of deeper ethics. These people might lie, cheat, and steal their path to the top. And like Jeff Skilling at Enron, they might destroy the organization along the way.

As a concept, integrity is a complex part of human character. Most of us have a vague sense of what it means, although we might have difficulty describing how it works in practice. In essence, integrity boils down to honesty, consistency, and solid ethics. Leaders who possess integrity follow up on their promises. They match their words with deeds. They eschew deception. They treat people consistently and apply rules evenly. Finally, leaders with integrity don't unfairly jeopardize others in order to advance their own agendas.

Of these characteristics, honesty may seem to be the most straightforward, but it means a lot more than just telling the truth. Mere silence is not enough. Honest leaders are accountable and own up to their mistakes. They are capable of delivering bad news even though doing so might be painful. This includes holding others accountable too. Imagine the boss who avoids having a tough conversation with an underperforming employee. Instead, she puts off the discussion until any remedial steps are too late. That's not acting with integrity.

The most common problem with honesty is when leaders believe that it is limited to avoiding outright lies. According to this way of thinking, omissions of truth are acceptable, and it is okay to deceive. But as we like to point out to colleagues and friends, another word for deceive is *mislead.*

To be sure, there are times when leaders must be cautious about what they say. The president of the United States, for example, must take steps to avoid the onset of public euphoria or panic. Sometimes this means bending or omitting segments of the truth. But this is discretion, done with the group's welfare in mind. Deceit, by contrast, is undertaken to protect individual interest. Usually the person who operates this way parses words as a stratagem for self-preservation. He finds loopholes. He rationalizes the bad outcomes of others. He tells himself, *It's not my fault if they didn't read between the lines,* or, *I didn't lie—they just weren't clever enough to work out all the possible ramifications.* This isn't the way to lead a group of people. Whenever we meet someone who deflects questions like a trial lawyer, we know that candidate would not make for an effective leader.

This potential for deceit also underscores why a lack of integrity is so dangerous in the hands of those who are intellectually gifted and can use their impressive cognitive skills in dramatic, undetectable ways. Given their access to power and information, they are in a unique position to exploit organizational interests. But effective leaders do not conduct themselves in this manner. Their sense of integrity does not permit it. For them, transparency and leadership are one and the same.

GOOD LEADERS ACT ETHICALLY

Of course, honesty by itself does not constitute integrity. A criminal might be perfectly forthcoming, but we wouldn't want him to lead. With this in mind, people with integrity also know the difference between right and wrong. They treat others fairly, consistently, and with a just hand.

They begin by living up to their promises. Leaders with integrity stay true to their commitments. They never back-pedal to serve their immediate needs. Watch out for people who constantly claim, "Circumstances have changed," or "I wouldn't have said that if I had known," or "That's not what I meant," only to leave others hanging. Good leaders deliver on their word.

When it comes to other issues of right and wrong, good leaders exercise strong ethics. Some people claim that the concept of ethics is too vague and leaves too much room for personal interpretation. According to this view, fairness is in the eyes of the beholder. "One person's terrorist is another's freedom fighter" is this argument's familiar refrain. So how can we expect leaders to adhere to any definable standard?

Although it's true that no universal sense of right or wrong is readily apparent with respect to abstract human issues (such as the meaning of equality or the proper role of the state), this fact does not mean that we have to throw ethics out the window and resort to nihilism. On the contrary, most of the practical problems that leaders face every day are amenable to a rather straightforward ethical rule: one's own interests cannot count for more than the interests of others. Stated differently, treat others the way you would expect to be treated. In other words, follow the Golden Rule, a principle that has stood the test of time in different cultures around the world. For example, the wisdom of the Golden Rule was rediscovered by Jesus and Confucius; by the Stoic philosophers of the Roman Empire; by

Leviticus and the Mahabharata; by social contract theorists such as Hobbes, Rousseau, and Locke; and by moral philosophers such as Kant in his categorical imperative.[2]

If this litany is a little too rich for your blood, consider what we in the business community often refer to as the "newspaper" or "mother" test. Would you be comfortable if what you are doing were printed on the front page of the *Wall Street Journal*, with all the facts laid out for everyone to see? Would you be comfortable if your mother knew the truth behind your decision? Viewed in this light, most ethical issues that leaders face aren't as difficult as they might appear.

Let's consider a couple of common examples. Is it okay to punish one employee for breaking company policy while permitting another to escape with a lesser decree? Obviously not. Each should be treated consistently. If you were in their shoes, you would expect the same. Is it okay to accept special favors from vendors knowing that it might create bias with respect to a future procurement decision? What would your shareholders expect? Would they react favorably knowing that their investment is subject to this kind of influence? As a leader, would you feel okay having such information printed on the front page of your annual report?

Toys-R-Us CEO Jerry Storch told us that this last issue is something that his company pays especially close attention to: "We have a zero-tolerance policy towards even slight gifts from a vendor. If there is something that trades hands, then there needs to be an invoice and compensation for it."[3] For Storch, this rule is critical for fostering an ethical culture. Moreover, he believes that making it stick occurs only if direction comes from the top. "The first year I got here," he told us, "the auditors said, 'Hey, do you and your wife want to go to the U.S. Open tennis tournament?' They were nice guys, so I said sure. But I also said that I have to pay for the tickets. They agreed, although they told me they weren't thinking that because they were sponsors of the event. So then I received the tickets, and they were some ridiculous price, like a thousand dollars apiece.

So I wrote a personal check for two thousand dollars, or whatever it was." Hearing this story, we couldn't help but tell Storch that we hoped he at least ended up with good seats. "They were good seats," he laughed. "I would never have paid that on my own, but I did."

For many professionals, distinguishing between appropriate and inappropriate offerings can be a particularly difficult lesson to learn. Perhaps due to inexperience, they see kickbacks as a legitimate part of moving up the corporate ladder, and they are eager for all the perks that might come their way. The stories they've heard from friends or colleagues who enjoy VIP treats fan the fire by making such splurges seem like standard fare. Rising professionals, especially successful ones, can easily be lured into thinking that they too are entitled.

But this is a dangerous path because it is easy to lose sight of the fact that not all perks are the same. When a middle manager's company sends her on a training conference to Las Vegas, this is different from accepting special favors from a vendor or other third party, a situation that poses a potential conflict of interest. The manager might feel a sense of indebtedness that is not easy to shake.

Top leaders should be particularly wary of believing that they deserve special treatment. This kind of thinking can severely cloud their judgment. And the risk is compounded by the fact that it is a common trap for people in positions of authority. Simply stated, power can corrupt, and leaders who are not grounded with a strong sense of integrity often end up traveling down a slippery slope. They create their own shifting, internal calculus until nothing is off limits—first U.S. Open tickets, then a private jet, then perhaps the corporate treasury.

When Dennis Kozlowski was CEO of Tyco International from 1992 to 2002, he funded much of his lavish lifestyle at company expense. He used $5 million of Tyco money to buy his second wife's wedding ring, and on her fortieth birthday, the company paid for a toga party on the Italian island of Sardinia, complete with a private concert by Jimmy Buffett and a giant ice sculpture of Michelangelo's *David* with vodka flowing out of its penis. Tyco spent almost $17 million on a luxury eighteen-room Manhattan apartment in Kozlowski's name, plus an extra $12 million for furnishings (including a six thousand dollar gold shower curtain). Yet through it all, Kozlowski never thought that he was doing anything wrong because there was no cover-up, no criminal intent. He simply felt he deserved these perks because he was the CEO.

At Enron, executive behavior was even worse. Top brass there resorted to elaborate schemes in order to cover up the company's real financial condition. Once all the smoke cleared following bankruptcy, a complex web of offshore accounts and phony partnerships appeared. Enron had been falsifying records. Its CFO, Andy Fastow, used shell companies to hide massive losses from Enron's financial statements. In theory, these companies were supposed to be independent, but Fastow worked both sides of every transaction. Even worse, he cut out a piece for himself and put it in his pocket. All in all, he defrauded Enron shareholders out of tens of millions of dollars this way. This number pales in comparison to the amount that Enron illegally shifted, however: at the height of Enron's debt, its balance sheet showed that it owed nothing, when in reality it owed $30 billion.

LEADERS WITH INTEGRITY GET RESULTS

The Enron and Kozlowski examples are extreme cases, but (sadly) not as surprising as they should be. As a society, we are accustomed to leaders with big egos, and we often expect them to act in self-absorbed ways. In fact, we almost believe they *should* display a certain degree of swagger. The truth is that most of us like a little bit of rock star in our leaders. We respond to their magnetism, their celebrity. Unfortunately, a variety of research shows that by placing too much emphasis on these other qualities and not enough on integrity, we are doing ourselves a great disservice. Leaders who possess integrity get results, and the organizations they lead consistently outperform the rest.

From a commonsense standpoint, we all understand the personal benefits of dealing with someone who possesses integrity. We trust and respect them. They are the kind of people we want as relatives, colleagues, neighbors, friends. But what about at the organizational level? Does integrity translate into a quantifiable difference at the bottom line? Or is it just some touchy-feely concept? How do we know that integrity *works*?

Tony Simons, a professor at Cornell University who studies organizational behavior and leadership, researched these questions and tested whether staying true to one's word and treating others fairly is correlated with higher company performance. The kind of person he had in mind was Stan Myers, CEO of SEMI, a global semiconductor industry association. Many years ago when Myers was CEO of Mitsubishi Silicon America, the company decided to move its headquarters from the San Francisco Bay Area to Dallas. Employees were offered an option: relocate to Dallas and stay with Mitsubishi, or accept a severance package consisting of eight months of salary. A year after the move, Myers learned that a former employee named Alan had left the company without receiving his severance. The company never cut him a check, and Alan never asked for one. Instead, each party had simply gone its separate way. Without hesitation, Myers immediately tracked down Alan and made sure that the company sent him a check. Then he visited Alan's new office and asked to meet with him in a conference room. When Alan arrived, he was confused.

"What are you doing here?" he asked. "I haven't seen you for a while."

"Yes, Alan, but I wanted to tell you that we forgot to pay you your severance."

Alan was overwhelmed, and *fifteen* years later, Myers heard from him again. Alan had become a successful entrepreneur, and he sought out Myers to present him with an engraved iPod Nano as thanks for his leadership and friendship.[4]

Obviously Myers's gesture made a lasting impact on Alan, but this story throws our question into stark relief: Was Myers an effective leader, or was he merely a Good Samaritan? Sure, he did the right thing, but did he advance Mitsubishi's interests? Many readers might conclude that he did not. After all, it seems likely that Alan would have forgotten about the unpaid check. In effect, Myers voluntarily issued it from the company treasury, a sum of money that Mitsubishi might have kept, along with the time and expense of Myers's trip to personally apologize to Alan. From Mitsubishi's standpoint, might those resources have been better spent if Myers had stayed in Dallas and worked on more pressing issues?

To test this hypothesis, Simons surveyed over sixty-five hundred employees at seventy-six Holiday Inn franchises. These surveys asked participants to anonymously rank the extent to which their managers' words and actions were aligned. Using a five-point scale, employees evaluated statements such as, "My manager delivers on his promises," and, "My manager practices what he preaches." Simons and his fellow researchers then correlated the results of the surveys with the hotels' customer satisfaction surveys, personnel records, and financial records. Controlling for other variables, they found that perceptions of managerial integrity had a profound effect on hotel performance. In fact, the link was so strong that a one-eighth-point difference in a hotel's score on the survey translated to an increase in profitability of 2.5 percent of revenues—or $250,000 annually per hotel.[5] No other aspect of managerial behavior that Simons's team measured had this big of an effect.

How exactly does this work? Why does integrity drive financial performance? In the best-run organizations, it flows from a culture in which workers know that they can rely on others to follow the rules and get things done. Kroger CEO Dave Dillon likens integrity to the way in which our faith in a traffic system permits us to move around the city. "You know," he said, "that when the light is green, you can go because people who want to go the other way are stopped at red. If you didn't have that in an organization, on every transaction you would have to start over."[6] In other words, you might take integrity for granted, but things break down fast when it goes away. "Integrity allows you to assume important characteristics about how things work," Dillon continued. "Without it, you'd have to expend extra energy on every issue, just like you'd have to stop at every corner if the traffic system didn't operate the way it does."

Basically it all comes down to trust. Integrity fosters trust, which leads to higher productivity. When employees trust their leaders, they don't have to worry that their work won't be rewarded, that promises won't be met, that the organization will go bankrupt, or that executives will milk all the profits for personal benefit. Like the driver who has faith in the traffic system, employees can hit the gas and get from point A to point B.

For decades, leadership experts Jim Kouzes and Barry Posner have been conducting extensive research to identify which leadership qualities are most important for business and government executives. As part of this effort, they ask the following open-ended question: "What values (personal traits or characteristics) do you look for and admire in your leader?"

After administering a questionnaire to over seventy-five thousand people around the world, the same result comes up year after year: honesty consistently ranks as the most desired leadership trait. More than competence, intelligence, inspiration or even vision, followers want a leader who tells the truth. For example, in 1987, 1995, 2002, and 2007, 83, 88, 88, and 89 percent of respondents, respectively, indicated that honesty was the most desired trait. These figures compare with 43, 40, 47, and 49 percent, respectively, who said intelligence was what they wanted most.[7] According to this extensive survey, honesty was twice as important as intelligence!

"When people talk to us about the qualities they admire in leaders," Kouzes and Posner reported, "they often use 'integrity' and 'character' as synonymous with honesty. No matter what the setting, everyone wants to be fully confident in their leaders, and to be fully confident they have to believe that their leaders are people of strong character and solid integrity."[8]

One organization that understands this dynamic is Ryder System, a Fortune 500 company based in Miami, Florida. Leaders at the company place an emphasis on creating a culture where everyone is up-front and treated fairly. As one of the nation's largest providers of transportation and supply chain management services, Ryder employs roughly thirty thousand workers across North America, Europe, and Asia and generates more than $7 billion in annual revenue.[9]

When CEO Greg Swienton took over the top post in 2001, he discovered a company that had all the pieces to succeed but was still coming up short because the different pieces of the organization didn't operate together. "We were like the Chicago Cubs," he explained to us.[10] "We had good players, but we didn't win very much."

A big reason for Ryder's inability to fully gel as a team was its tradition of insularity. People didn't share information or ideas much across business units and they didn't feel comfortable stepping forward to admit that something might be amiss. They were terrified of reporting bad news to their superiors, and as a result, they hunkered down in silos, allowing what would have been otherwise manageable problems to escalate.

Swienton set out to change all this. He knew that in order to see improvement, Ryder needed a corporate culture with more openness. People had to come to terms with the idea that honesty, accountability, and organizational success go hand in hand.

"The truth will set you free. But first it will make you miserable" was Swienton's early mantra. He knew the job wouldn't be easy.

Convincing people to adjust their mind-set never is. He made it absolutely clear to everyone at Ryder that there would be no negative repercussions if they shared bad news—only if they kept it to themselves. Slowly, employees began to open up and trust him. But more than just taking his word, they saw firsthand that he meant what he said.

In the early days of his tenure, Swienton recognized that there was a problem with the company's asset management program. As a transportation and logistics company, Ryder had a large fleet of trucks and vehicles across the United States. Ensuring the company efficiently managed these assets, as well as the financing to procure, distribute, and maintain them, was an important priority, and one that Wall Street closely scrutinized.

As a new CEO, Swienton needed someone with more knowledge of the asset management program to explain the problem to the company's board. Consequently, he asked an executive with hands-on experience to accompany him and give a presentation at the next board meeting. In effect, Swienton was asking the manager to deliver the bad news. The manager, Swienton told us, turned white as a ghost.

Swienton reassured the manager that the latter was the only person who knew enough about the problem to give the board an honest hearing. He also told the manager, "Look, I'll make you a deal. If the board appreciates your story, I'll give you the credit. If they have a problem with it, I'll take the blame." The main thing was to get the situation out in the open so the organization could deal with it. "You see," Swienton said to the employee, "if we don't share this information with the board, here's what will happen. We're both screwed if the problem gets worse and it turns out we kept the board in the dark. Or if we fix it, we won't get credit because they will not have known that there was a problem in the first place." In the end, he convinced the manager, who took the lead in giving the board a full appraisal, as he knew that Swienton had his back. The board, while not pleased, still congratulated both of them for their transparency, provided several good ideas, and a solution was found.

If Swienton hadn't led with integrity—if his style had been to issue threats, for example, or show an obsession with self-preservation—this result almost certainly would not have happened. The manager would never have even been invited to the board meeting. Instead, the manager provided full disclosure, and, following Swienton's lead, learned firsthand that a system of accountability, transparency, and trust enables everyone to get ahead.

This kind of behavior sets an important precedent and has a cascade effect. The manager took this lesson back to his team, who passed it on to their coworkers, and so on. After a while, the entire organization had a new framework for how to act.

According to Greg Greene, Ryder's chief administrative officer and director of the company's human resource function, Swienton's leadership encouraged integrity in others. In 2011, Green told us that Ryder was a much more open, cordial, productive place to work where people felt comfortable airing their views. There was a sense that everyone was traveling along the same path and that organizational results mattered more than individual triumphs. Greene told us that people outside the organization were aware of the change too. More and more, he said, he was receiving calls from professionals who wanted to work at Ryder because of its positive culture. "What counts is being allowed to get the job done right and to take pride in what you do. People everywhere really respond to that."[11]

INTEGRITY IS CONTAGIOUS

For years psychologists and sociologists have been intrigued by the change in human behavior that occurs when people move from an individual to a group setting. In particular, the tendency of large numbers of people to act in the same way at the same time has fueled intense intellectual debate. Freud called this the "herd" or mob mentality, and it manifests in many ways. We see it in apparel trends, for example, and the consumer craze that sometimes accompanies the introduction of a new product such as the iPad. When kids get together, they often converse in their own language or act out special games. University students engage in binge drinking.

An especially disturbing brand of the herd mentality is a group's propensity for unruliness. Anyone who has witnessed a World Cup or Super Bowl celebration knows what we mean. During such outbreaks, pandemonium is often set loose. Individuals who are otherwise docile in the privacy of their homes seem to change personalities altogether. They may shout, fight, burn, cry, loot, even kill, when they see others doing the same.

No one can explain exactly why people act this way. But in the 1960s, Stanley Milgram, a psychologist at Yale University, conducted an experiment to determine how far individual behavior might deviate from the norm. Milgram's focus was slightly different from the herd mentality: he wanted to test the effect of authority on individual behavior. Specifically, he set out to determine the extent to which participants would be willing to administer an electric shock to complete strangers if an authority figure told them that this is what they were required to do.

Here is how the experiment worked. Two strangers arrived in a waiting area. When the experimenter entered, the strangers were asked to draw lots to determine who would be the "teacher" and who would be the "learner." Unbeknown to the person with the teacher role, both lots said the same thing. But the learner was a professional actor who played along by giving himself the learner designation. With their roles determined, the participants separated into two rooms. In one room were the teacher and experimenter (who wore a white doctor's coat to contribute to the impression of authority). The actor-turned-learner went to another room.

There was no way to see from one room to the next. Instead the teacher was instructed to sit in front of a console that contained what he believed was an electroshock generator and an intercom. The teacher was further instructed to ask a series of questions to the learner. When the learner made an error, the teacher was required to "penalize" the former by administering an electric shock in increasing increments of 15 volts. Of course, the shock wasn't real at all. But the teacher believed it was real because the actor responded through the intercom with prerecorded protests and demonstrations of pain. The greater the indicated voltage, the more dramatic the response was. Some actors feigned heart problems or loss of consciousness. They cursed, banged on walls, even screamed.

What is striking is that although the teachers believed they were causing severe harm to the learners, they continued to administer what they thought were shocks. Many giggled nervously. Although at some point all participants expressed a desire to stop and check on the learner, they continued administering shocks if the experimenter said that he would take responsibility and that the experiment required the teachers to continue. Only one of the forty participants steadfastly refused to administer shocks below the 300 volt level. More frightening, 65 percent of the participants were willing to continue until the maximum 450 volts, a fatal level.[12]

Milgram's study has been used to explain atrocities under Nazi Germany and during the My Lai massacre in Vietnam in 1968. But it has practical applications for everyday leadership as well, in that people in organizations look to the leader for guidance on how to act. This includes deciding what is right and what is wrong. When a leader sets the tone for what is ethically permissible, the tone is contagious. Group members will naturally permit their own sense of integrity to follow. They might even rationalize severe deviations in ethical conduct. They might tell themselves that they are merely "cogs in a wheel" or "this is how things are done." So long as the leader is willing to take responsibility, the thinking goes, "What can I do?"

Revisiting the Enron example, it seems fair to conclude that this type of thinking spread across the organization because of what was being said and done at the top. Skilling and Enron founder Kenneth Lay sent a clear message to everyone that the company's culture was one based solely on dollars and cents, kill or be killed. Enron's performance review system mandated that employees be graded on a scale from 1 to 5 every six months, with the further stipulation that 10 percent had to be fired after the review. This system, which came to be known as "rank and yank," benchmarked employees in categories such as teamwork and communication. Yet insiders report that the only factor that really mattered was how much money someone brought in. If an employee brought in business, it didn't matter if he was a jerk. The performance review system also devolved into a smoke screen for cronyism as senior executives manipulated the process to make room for their friends.[13]

Management's obsession with Enron's stock price also provided employees with a clear signal of what mattered most. A giant stock ticker was placed in the lobby, and TV monitors showing CNBC were displayed in all the elevators. At meetings, employees were constantly reminded of the central importance placed on a fast-rising stock price, and in 1998, when the stock hit fifty dollars a share, Skilling and Lay handed out fifty-dollar bills to every employee. Indeed, it seemed that for Skilling, the organization's only measure of value was what came out of Wall Street. When traveling on the road, he phoned in several times a day to inquire about the stock price. Salaries, bonuses, even the right to keep one's job, were all tied to that magic number. Any concern for collegiality, serving customers, public goodwill, or creating long-term institutional value were minor concerns at best.

Against this backdrop, it is no surprise that Enron's traders conducted themselves so despicably when the California energy crisis hit in 2000: they were merely carrying out what they had been led to do. In fact, the crisis wasn't actually a crisis at all, but rather an artificial electricity shortage created when companies such as Enron used their control over vast energy grids to interrupt the normal flow of service. In effect, the company shut down plants and exported power from California. When the price spiked, the company sent the power back in. Rolling blackouts drove California residents and businesses into a frenzy, and Enron made billions in the process.

Back at Enron headquarters, traders secretly caught on tape were overjoyed. As a summer heat wave in California stoked wildfires and sent the price of energy soaring, they exclaimed, "Burn, baby, burn!" and "That's a beautiful thing!" As news accounts showed Californians trapped in elevators and elderly citizens unable to pay their bills, the traders joked, "All that money you guys stole from those poor grandmothers in California," and "The best thing that could happen is a fucking earthquake, let that thing float out in the Pacific."[14]

This complete breakdown in ethics issued from the top. Leaders must possess integrity, and Skilling and Lay clearly did not. Despite their brilliance, vision, hard work, and ambition, they were unable to offer effective leadership. In the end, everyone lost, from the CEO all the way down to the line worker whose decades of savings and pension accruals disappeared almost overnight.

Just as striking, Enron's contagious culture spread far beyond the walls of its corporate office. The company's accounting firm, Arthur Andersen, which was complicit in letting it record dubious cash streams, collapsed soon after Enron's bankruptcy. Numerous banks came under legal and ethical scrutiny for allowing Enron to cook the books. Subsequent investigation showed that financial institutions lent Enron money under bogus deals merely to keep their investment banking fees flowing. Skilling and Lay's brand of leadership spawned a vast web of fraud, deception, and greed.

Good leaders know that they have the power to raise or lower ethical standards across the organization. Leaders like Greg Swienton at Ryder leverage their influence by setting a positive example based on integrity and acting with openness, consistency, and candor. The trust they foster leads to greater efficiency and cooperation. In the end, individual and group behavior reinforces the organization's long-term interest, and everyone wins.

ZEROING IN ON INTEGRITY

In our own executive assessment practice, we always start with integrity. No one can offer effective leadership without it. But how do you tell if a person has integrity?

Without a doubt, this is one of the most difficult attributes to pinpoint in others. Unlike passion or analytical ability, for example, integrity is not always obvious or easily quantified. Moreover, a person who lacks integrity will have no qualms about lying to persuade you that he or she has it. But most of us don't judge someone's integrity based on superficial comments anyway. Rather, an opinion about someone's integrity is typically based on years of observation, or at least with first-hand knowledge of how that person behaved in a specific situation.

Nor does glancing at a résumé reveal much about a person's character. Past experience is more likely to reveal whether that person has resilience, judgment, even vision, than it is to answer difficult questions about integrity. This is because we are usually unaware of the ethical trade-offs that people might make. Past interests and decisions are hidden. True motives remain unclear.

When evaluating a potential employee, many organizations rely on references to assess integrity. They ask former colleagues generic questions, such as "Tell me about Terry. Is she pleasant to work for? Do you trust her? Does she treat people fairly?"

These are important questions, to be sure, but alone they are insufficient, as evidenced by the number of character cases that slip through the cracks. A distressing number of leaders—such as former Refco CEO Phillip Bennett, former Qwest Communications CEO Joe Nacchio, and former Illinois governor Rod Blagojevich—caused enormous damage with their ethical lapses. A cursory review of peer referencing does not go far enough to identify these potential character issues before they start to brew.

Another reason that integrity is hard to assess is that people are often hesitant to say bad things about others. They give others the benefit of the doubt. After all, it is difficult to critically appraise someone else's character. We are more aware of deficiencies within ourselves. There is also a confidentiality issue associated with making sensitive statements about others. People naturally fear that full disclosure might come back to bite them. As a result, traditional 360-degree referencing, while very important, has significant limitations.

Almost every interviewer also has a personal approach for gauging integrity in others, a strategy that relies more on instinct than anything else. The interviewer thinks, "He seems like a straight shooter" or "I can get along with her."

We all want to find a personal comfort zone with the people we interview, but one of the problems with this approach is that it lacks consistency. It is also rather unsophisticated. If, when addressing character issues, an organization relies merely on the ad hoc efforts of a rotating slate of interviewers, the results will be mixed at best.

When we assess leaders, we combine 360-degree referencing and traditional interview questions with a technique designed to test for ethical awareness. We pose several hypothetical situations to see if the people we are interviewing can recognize subtle ethical issues where no clear rules or boundaries exist. The idea is that no amount of interview preparation can let them massage the facts. Our approach also maintains consistency by giving us a benchmark with which to compare a variety of candidates across a variety of fields.

We ask candidates to read a short case containing a potential problem. We also give them some background information and key facts or ideas to consider. We then ask the candidate how she might go about addressing the situation. Our goal is to gain a better understanding of how the leader thinks about a potential ethical dilemma. Does she recognize hidden issues involving trust, consistency, or transparency? Does she perceive how circumstances might unfairly affect others? Can she draw a connection between integrity issues and overall organizational performance?

Here is an example of the type of hypothetical situation we pose to someone we are interviewing for a leadership position:

You are the CEO of a medium-sized public company.

One day an employee walks into your office with some bad news regarding a company-organized social activity that occurred last month.

It seems that several members of the finance team were out for dinner to celebrate the end of a good quarter. Joe, a promising vice president, had a few too many drinks. He made some lewd comments, and he touched a junior employee, Susan, in an inappropriate way. The CFO (as head of the finance team) was at the dinner, although he did not witness these events; rather, he heard about it from Susan the following Monday morning.

You immediately call the CFO to your office to hear what happened. You learn that on the Monday following the dinner, the CFO and head of HR talked with Joe, who basically confirmed Susan's story. He was contrite and he personally apologized to everyone. HR also conducted a thorough investigation and determined that this incident does not pose a liability risk to the company.

Based on these developments, the CFO believes that the company should not take any further action. The CFO emphasizes that Joe is a "rising star" and probably the most valuable member of the finance team.

"I think it's water under the bridge now," he says. "What do you think?"

What follows are two actual responses that we have received. We have selected these answers because they are representative of two common—albeit different—ways of thinking about this leadership scenario. Candidate A responded:

Well, this is a difficult situation. I'd like to talk personally with the head of HR just to make sure I get all the facts straight. I'd also speak immediately with our legal counsel to confirm that we aren't facing potential liability.

As for Joe's conduct, obviously it's not acceptable even if he is a star performer, and we can't have this behavior at our company. It sounds like we were lucky this time, and that the incident passed with sincere apologies and Joe was up-front that he made a mistake. That's reassuring.

But we need to make sure this doesn't happen again. I'd order a review of our corporate code of ethics and training on sexual harassment. Joe has likely learned his lesson, but maybe we aren't doing enough as an organization to make sure that employees understand the seriousness of what he did.

Candidate B responded:

First of all, this situation is not water under the bridge. If you consider it from Susan's point of view, she is a relatively power-less junior employee, and many of her bosses are probably men. Even if she says she accepts Joe's apology, there is a good chance that she still feels taken advantage of. It's also very likely that many others in our organization have heard about the event, and probably people outside of our company too. This incident is serious.

With this in mind, Joe's termination might be warranted. What is our company's official policy? If we follow the CFO's suggestion and do nothing, I'm worried what effect that will have on other people in our company, especially Susan. Will they think that the rules work one way for some people and another way for others? I don't know how our employees will trust senior management if that is the message we are sending, and this could have a serious long-term effect on our organization.

Finally, I'm also troubled by the CFO's handling of this situation. The fact that he didn't tell me about it raises questions about his judgment. The fact that he doesn't appreciate the seriousness of Joe's conduct is also highly worrisome. What kind of signals is he sending? He might need some type of counseling, as well as other disciplinary action.

Notice that candidate B, who provided a much more astute answer, started off by explicitly recognizing the effect on Susan, whereas candidate A glossed over this point. Candidate B was not unduly influenced by Joe's star status. By contrast, candidate A called Joe's behavior unacceptable "even if he is a star," but these words rang hollow because the candidate showed almost no concern for Susan. Picking up on subtle clues in the words that a candidate uses (or does not use) is a valuable part of the assessment process.

Candidate B also demonstrated that he understood why this type of issue is so critical for the company. He could connect integrity and strong ethics with overall organizational success. Candidate A asserted that Joe's actions were "not acceptable" and that "we can't have this behavior at our company," but it was not clear that he truly grasped why.

Finally, notice that candidate B also seized on the CFO's behavior. For him, the fact that the CFO so easily dismissed the situation (he didn't even mention it to the CEO) pointed to a larger leadership question. Although this might seem obvious after lengthy consideration, a candidate who is reading the case for the first time may well gloss over it. By contrast, strong candidates are quick to zero in on such issues.

In total, these answers suggest that the two candidates had different levels of ethical awareness, and exploring this further would be necessary. The answer that candidate A gave would cause us to pay extra attention (and custom-tailor our inquiries) to peer referencing that might shed light on his integrity.

It is important to emphasize that we are not trying to predict conclusively whether a candidate has integrity. The nature of the process does not lend itself to that kind of wholesale task. But our approach does test for ethical awareness in a way that traditional interviewing or 360-degree referencing can't. Also, when a candidate's response is compared with those given by several hundred high-potential leaders, clear patterns emerge. The ones with real ethical awareness stand out above the rest.

We conclude this chapter with another hypothetical situation that we like to ask executive candidates. Imagine that you are the one being interviewed, and then determine what you would do in this situation:

You have just been hired as CEO of a major multinational electronics manufacturer. A significant portion of the company's manufacturing base is located in eastern Europe and Asia, and you are making your first visit to the region to learn more about the company's operations.

You have a meeting with Jack Smith in his office in Sofia, Bulgaria. Jack is in charge of European and Asian operations, which he runs from that office. Jack is a ten-year veteran of the company. You are very impressed with him, as well as the extent of the company's reach in that region of the world.

Near the end of your meeting, you say to Jack, with a chuckle and almost as a throwaway comment, "How do you keep away from the mafia over here?"

With a straight face, he answers, "We pay 'em."

When you ask for clarification, he explains that payments are routinely, and secretly, made to local mafia groups, and probably some terrorist groups, throughout areas of eastern

Europe, Russia, and China. "They threaten to blow up our factories or kill our workers," Jack explains. "And forget the police—the mafia own them," he adds. "So we pay them. That's what everyone does over here."

On the plane ride back to the United States, you consider what you have learned. What, if anything, should you do about it?

Empathy

"Invincible." "Unbeatable." "The greatest team ever."

Accolades like these emblazoned almost every major sports cover during the hot Barcelona summer of 1992. For the first time, professional basketball players from the National Basketball Association (NBA) were allowed to participate in the Olympic Games, and the United States had assembled a stunning roster of legendary talent: Earvin "Magic" Johnson, Michael Jordan, Larry Bird, (Sir) Charles Barkley, and Karl "the Mailman" Malone, to name only a few. Each man alone was a force, a superstar. Together, their collective alchemy constituted something else altogether. Soon they were being referred to simply as the Dream Team, and they coasted through the competition with an astonishing forty-four point average margin of victory. In the gold medal game, they demolished Croatia by thirty-two points, reducing the contest to a largely ceremonial affair. Fans everywhere went crazy. The players were treated like royalty. Team USA was a global phenomenon.

Twelve years later, there was a new U.S. team, also made up of NBA all-stars, including LeBron James, Dwayne Wade, Carmelo Anthony, Tim Duncan, and Allen Iverson, but their record reveals a different story. On August 15, 2004, at the Olympic Games in Athens, the U.S. team was pounded by Puerto Rico. *Puerto Rico*—that small tropical island with not quite 4 million inhabitants (and the score wasn't even close). Adding insult to injury, less than a week later, the U.S. team lost again, this time to Lithuania and then to Argentina. When the dust finally settled, the result was a bronze medal finish. Fans were embarrassed. Players and coaches were humiliated. The national basketball program was at an all-time low.

What went wrong? Why did the vaunted 2004 U.S. team, once again comprised of the best basketball players in the world, fare so poorly? More to the point, what could be done to turn things around?

The man assigned the difficult task of answering these questions was Jerry Colangelo, former owner of the Phoenix Suns. After the debacle in Athens, he was handpicked by NBA commissioner David Stern to revitalize the national team.

"David called me in January of '05, and asked me if I'd be interested in taking over the program," Colangelo recalled. "I said I would. I knew the program needed major changes, but I said that I would."[1] Colangelo plunged ahead, knowing that basketball fans everywhere were counting on him to succeed.

THE MAN FROM HUNGRY HILL

Colangelo grew up in the 1950s in the South Chicago suburb of Chicago Heights. His family lived in the section known as Hungry Hill, a working-class neighborhood named for its poverty and steep terrain.

Like many other immigrant enclaves of its day, Colangelo's neighborhood was a gritty place. Good jobs were scarce, and people struggled. His grandparents' first home had been a dilapidated wood shack made from two abandoned boxcars. To the people on the Hill, the wealth, privilege, and opportunity of Chicago's famed Michigan Avenue and Gold Coast might as well have been a million miles away.

The way to survive was to stick together. Families and neighbors stayed tight. An independent ego was something that the capricious Hill streets didn't easily abide. Instead, you had to see things from the other guy's shoes. "People in our neighborhood were welcome in our homes all the time," Colangelo told us. "If someone got into trouble, we helped them out. We always had their backs."

Colangelo is a relative unknown in mainstream America, and he likes it that way. A certain degree of anonymity is in keeping with his humble South Chicago roots. But when it comes to the sporting world, Colangelo is one of the most respected leaders around. In addition to being former owner of the Suns, he is the former owner of the Arizona Diamondbacks baseball team. *Sporting News* voted him one of the most powerful people in all of sports, and in 2004, he was elected to the Basketball Hall of Fame in Springfield, Massachusetts.

After America's ignominious performance in Athens, it was clear to Colangelo and others that talent alone did not constitute a decisive advantage for the U.S. team. The United States still possessed superior talent, but the rest of the world was catching up. Other teams were hungrier too, they had better chemistry, and they had figured out how to win. What Team USA needed was better leadership. Simply fielding a roster of superstars wouldn't suffice. Players needed motivation, a common purpose, a sense of unity.

Recognizing the importance of getting others to buy into this vision, the first thing Colangelo did was convene a large meeting of former coaches and players in Chicago. Altogether, about thirty men were there, including Dean Smith, Chuck Daley, John Thompson, Lenny Wilkens, Jerry West, Michael Jordan, Chris Mullen, and Danny Manning. (For basketball fans, it was a very special gathering.) Colangelo wanted to hear about their Olympic experiences. What did it mean to them? What did it feel like? How about team chemistry?

The next step was finding a new coach, a new bench leader. As former owner of the Suns, Colangelo recognized that this decision was the most important one he would make. He of course knew that he needed a solid tactician as well as someone with sufficient experience and a reputation for maintaining discipline. But he also knew that he needed to find a coach with something more. Colangelo was trying to change the dignity of the U.S. program, its perception. In 2004, several of the players had acted like prima donnas, seemingly more interested in their latest music videos, corporate endorsements, or personal statistics than the team. As a result, the team's public image had suffered. Colangelo wanted to change all that. He wanted to instill more humility in the program, with less "I" and more "we."

In order to reach these goals, Colangelo knew that above all else, he needed a players' coach—someone who understood the intangible human element of the game and could relate to the players' needs and emotions. In short, his primary concern in finding a coach was to select someone who understood what made everybody else tick.

He chose Mike Krzyzewski, long-time coach of the men's basketball program at Duke University and a Hall of Fame inductee. Aside from Coach K's impressive record (as of 2010, his teams had been to the Final Four eleven times and won four National Collegiate Athletic Association championships), Colangelo had known him for a long time. Both men grew up in Chicago, they both preached heart and character, and they shared the same language.

Kryzyzewski told us, "Jerry and I already had a friendship. And this gets back to our roots. Both Jerry and I have a similar upbringing and values. It's like your family when you're growing up—our parents would say we're going to church. We know what we're supposed to do and how to act at the dinner table. We have unwritten rules. We have tradition. We had a family culture."

Based on this common history, Colangelo knew that Kryzyzewski was the right man to get the job done. He could get the players to work together again. One of Coach K's mantras has always been:

"I believe in you." He places enormous emphasis on making sure that everyone is emotionally connected. From the head coach down to the last person off the bench, his philosophy is that the entire team's bond is what gives them strength.

Perhaps the greatest endorsement of Colangelo's choice came from the least likely of sources: Dean Smith, the coach of the men's basketball program at the University of North Carolina (UNC). The rivalry between Duke and UNC is by far the most intense in college basketball. The two universities are separated by a mere eight miles along Tobacco Road. If you are loyal to one of the schools, anything to do with the other is typically viewed with anathema. Yet at the early meeting of coaches and players in Chicago, Smith was one of Krzyzewski's biggest supporters. When members of the gathering started to nominate coaches, Smith stood up and announced to everyone that Coach K was the right guy for the job. He told them no one would form a tighter union with his players; no one would have a better chance of lifting Team USA back on top.

THE IMPORTANCE OF EMPATHY

In her book *Team of Rivals*, Pulitzer Prize–winning historian Doris Kearns Goodwin recounts how Abraham Lincoln once advised temperance advocates to avoid using too much vitriol when denouncing drinkers. People who took to whiskey, Lincoln knew, wouldn't respond well to that, and the result would be denunciation met with denunciation, "crimination with crimination and anathema with anathema," he wrote. Instead, if reformers wanted their opinion to count, they needed to see things from the other side's perspective. Lincoln had learned that when people are "shunned and despised," they naturally retreat into themselves, closing off all avenues to their hearts and heads. "Such is man, and so must he be understood by those who would lead him."[2]

Lincoln's story highlights another critical attribute of leadership: empathy, the capacity to share another person's emotions or feelings. Empathy is the ability to understand what someone else is experiencing. For example, if someone else is feeling disgust, pain, frustration, or anxiety, an empathic observer is able to pick up on that and experience the same emotion in a vicarious way.

Although experts disagree about where empathy comes from or how it works, most believe that it is tied to our imitative capabilities. Highly empathic individuals are able to detect an emotional state in others and then experience a reciprocal state in themselves. Some experts limit this ability to emotional understanding. Others believe there is a cognitive dimension too, as in the ability to imagine what someone else is thinking. Either way, empathy involves a fundamental ability to tune in to others. Usually this is done by appreciating subtleties in facial expression, tone of voice, demeanor, body language, and other signals.

Empathy works on many levels. The classic case involves two people who are in the same room. If a person is sitting near you on the sofa, for example, and she can truly understand your mood, almost all of us would say that she has empathy. But what if you are sitting on the other side of a two-way mirror? That same person can see you, but you can't see her. She notices your tone of voice, your posture, they way you shuffle your hands, the look on your face, and she understands what you are feeling. This too is empathy, even though the two of you may never have met.

Note that just because a person is empathic doesn't imply that she will act on it in any particular manner. Once action is involved, a host of other attributes come into play. For example, you might empathize with someone who has gambled away her life savings, but this doesn't mean you pity her or will do anything to help. Empathy is not the same as sympathy. With empathy, you feel *with* someone; with sympathy, you feel *for* someone. Similarly, someone might be attuned to another's sense of grievance and simultaneously decide that this emotional feeling isn't serious enough to stop everything and make others wait.

Empathy is critical for leadership for many reasons. Combined with integrity, it drives trust. It gives followers a sense that their interests are being looked after, and this creates positive energy. Followers who sense that a leader appreciates them are motivated to carry out their duties in a more committed way.

How does this work? Part of the reason is physiological. Research in neuroscience indicates that a person's behavior creates a connection that affects the brain chemistry of others around him or her. When one person laughs, for example, it sets off a chain reaction that continues back and forth and is carried on to others (listen for this next time you are in a movie theater watching a comedy).

Daniel Goleman, Richard Boyatzis, and Annie McKee call this phenomenon "mood contagion," and they have studied its implications for leadership. Their conclusion is that certain behaviors that make people feel good, such as laughing or smiling, also foster a positive social connection, or "resonance." Thus, leaders who facilitate this resonance contribute to the entire group's positive social interaction. Empathy is an important piece of this. When followers sense that their leader is attuned to what they are experiencing in the moment, they feel good; they feel connected. "Empathy, which includes listening and taking other people's perspectives, allows leaders to tune in to the emotional channels between people that create resonance," write Goleman, Boyatzis, and McKee.[3]

To understand how empowering empathy can be, think of some of your best relationships. We have all experienced a teacher or mentor who made us feel as though our particular needs were being heard. Remember how much you trusted that person? Remember how motivated you were to listen to her and follow her advice? Remember how hard you were willing to work because of this relationship?

TICK-AND-CLICK

For purposes of understanding how empathy affects leadership, it is useful to break it down into two separate parts. Often these parts work together, but not always.

The first is the ability to appreciate or understand the emotions of other people, wholly apart from what the others know or see. Imagine the same two-way mirror, with a leader sitting on one side of the mirror picking up on the emotions or needs of the person on the other side. We call this understanding one person has of another the "tick." A person with empathy is attuned to what makes other people tick in a given moment. He has good social awareness.

The second part is the "click": the response that a person makes to the signals that she receives. Consider two friends sitting together at lunch. One has just gone through a bitter breakup and is feeling quite sad. The empathetic friend understands what her friend is going through; she can "feel her pain." But she does more than just feel; part of her empathy includes her capacity to mirror a response. She is likely to adopt the same tone of voice, the same facial expression, the same posture as her friend has. In this way, the two of them feel connected.

Leaders with empathy draw on both the tick and click to make important gains.

TRUST AND RELATIONSHIPS

In terms of trust, the lesson of the two friends at lunch can be applied to a larger group. When employees, colleagues, and others sense that their leader understands them, they feel a connection. They listen more, are willing to open up, and view the leader with greater confidence and respect. Consider the following example from a 1992 presidential campaign event at the University of Richmond that included Bill Clinton, George H. W. Bush, and Ross Perot.

During a town-hall style of debate, the candidates heard questions from members of the audience and then took turns answering. At one point, the microphone was handed to a young woman who described how she was personally affected by the large national debt and poor economy. She knew friends who had lost jobs, she said, and who couldn't pay their mortgages. She wanted to know how each of the candidates was affected by the national debt, and if he wasn't, how he could possibly relate to the common person on the street.

President Bush seemed at a loss to understand the woman's question. He had trouble identifying with her concerns. The woman even dared to interrupt him, to try and help, saying, "How has it affected *you*?" But the president still didn't get it. Instead, with a blank expression on his face, he talked about "stimulating the export, investing more, better education systems." Both the substance and impersonal nature of his response seemed to miss the woman's emotional plea entirely.

When it was Clinton's turn, he walked right over toward the woman and stopped a few feet in front of the audience. He looked her straight in the eye and said, "Tell me how it's affected you again. You've known people who have lost their homes and jobs? Well, I've been governor of a small state for four years. I'll tell you how it's affected me. . . . In my state when people lose their jobs, there's a good chance I'll know 'em by their names. When a factory closes, I know the person who ran it. When the businesses go bankrupt, I know them. And I've been out here for thirteen months meeting in meetings just like this one, ever since October, with people like you all over America."[4]

Near the end of Clinton's remarks, the television camera panned to the woman. She was nodding her head up and down while she listened. The two of them wore identical facial expressions. The tone of Clinton's voice matched that of the concerned young woman. His demeanor and nonverbal cues were in perfect sync with hers.

Then the camera panned to President Bush. He seemed to be frozen in an unknowing grin, almost like the awkward uncle who isn't really sure what he should do with his nieces and nephews.

Bill Clinton isn't everyone's favorite politician, but no matter how you feel about the man or his politics, it's difficult to deny the importance of his exchange during the debate. It was a key moment of the campaign. Clinton's empathy, his emotional response, established a strong bond not just with the young woman but also with viewers across the nation.

Coach K uses that kind of empathy to build trust. For him, it is one of the essential ingredients of leadership success. "Leadership boils down to strong relationships," he told us. "The way you get teammates to play well with one another is to build trust from the very first day of practice, and sometimes even before they ever step on the basketball court. I try to understand my players as people. We all get together at my house, or some of the players actually like to cook, and we invite the whole team over. Before I can be an effective leader, I have to know the players, they have to get to know me, and we have to know and trust each other."[5]

This penchant for building relationships is what Colangelo was counting on when he hired Krzyzewski to coach Team USA. Based on his experience with the Suns as well as discussions with former Olympic coaches and players, he knew that the problem with Team USA wasn't technical; it wasn't a matter of skill or tactics in adjusting to international rules. The real difference lay in social interaction. What Team USA needed was a coach who could produce strong relationships, trust, and goodwill.

After establishing the roster for the new squad, both Coach K and Colangelo spent time getting to know the players off the court. Each day the team met in a special room at the Wynn Hotel in Las Vegas, where everyone was staying. This opportunity for individuals to get to know each other, and share goals, stories, and impressions was instrumental in building a solid bond.

In the business world, one leader who understands this as well as anyone else is Herb Kelleher, cofounder and former CEO of Southwest Airlines. Legend has it that Kelleher and a friend conceived of the idea for Southwest on a cocktail napkin while at a bar in San Antonio, Texas, in 1966. What they envisioned was a low-cost airline that circumvented the traditional ways of doing business while still providing high-quality service.

To get there, Kelleher fostered a corporate culture that catered to the needs of its employees as people. Southwest became a fun place to work. Employees were encouraged to take themselves lightly. They wore funny shirts and often sang the in-flight announcements. Kelleher himself participated in this collegial atmosphere. When he learned that mechanics on the graveyard shift found it difficult to participate in company picnics, he held a 2:00 A.M. barbecue, and he and the pilots were the cooks.[6]

For Kelleher, this kind of personal touch made people connect. "We try to value each person individually at Southwest and to be cognizant of them as human beings," Kelleher said. "We try to memorialize and celebrate and sympathize with and commemorate the things that happen to them in their personal lives. What we're really trying to say is, 'We value you as people apart from the fact that you work here.'"[7]

Kelleher had his eye on customers too. He knew that people want to have a good time when they travel. They don't want vacations to begin with grumpy clerks or shoddy service. And he knew that when employees feel appreciated, the feeling is contagious. "The way you treat your employees is the way they will treat your customers," said Kelleher.[8]

That culture at Southwest continues today. Leaders at the company place a big emphasis on making sure that employees feel appreciated, connected, and engaged. For example, CEO Gary Kelly travels extensively to make sure that high employee morale is maintained. During a trip in 2009, he visited Nashville after the area had just experienced severe flooding. Every employee in the city was told that he or she could come to a two-hour open meeting. The meeting was nothing fancy—they met out on the tarmac where bags are unloaded from conveyor belts and placed on carts. One employee, John, explained that he had lost his home due to the floods and was living in a hotel room. Kelly responded, "This company is here for you, and we are going to give you what you need."[9] Kelly immediately had Southwest send a home-care replacement package to John, complete with blankets, kitchen utensils, linens, and other essential supplies.

Kelly's emotional connection with employees doesn't end when he goes away either. During that same trip to Nashville, for example, the brother of a former employee stopped Kelly. He was crying. "My sister worked for ya'll," he told Kelly. "She recently passed away, and I can't thank you enough for what you guys did."

"We were caught off guard a little," recalled Ginger Hardage, senior vice president of communication and culture, who was traveling with Kelly. "But Gary handled the situation well. He can really relate to people. Five minutes later he was yukking it up with the flight crew."

This esprit de corps extends to a catastrophic fund, which each employee contributes to, that serves as a safety net in the event that one of them has a major problem. The employees are happy to contribute to it because, Hardage explained to us, "It makes our employees feel safe. Everyone knows that we are in this together and that we can make a difference if we act together."

Southwest also runs a program called Internal Customer Care, a group that keeps tabs on employees to make sure that company leadership is aware of important personal events in their lives. "Any time a major event happens, we want the leader to know," said Hardage.[10] "If it's a wedding, we send a wedding gift. If we know about it, then the employee gets a gift. And Gary [Kelly] usually sends it."

SOCIAL SAVVY

Besides fostering trust, empathy also equips leaders with a keen sense of social savvy that helps them sift through complex social dynamics and make good decisions.

Consider the following example. A school administrator is called on to make an important presentation at a public school system's governing board meeting. Because the presentation concerns a controversial plan to close down one of the local high schools, many interested parties are in attendance: parents, teachers, students, staff, the press, the superintendent of the school system, other local residents, and the full board.

Now let's imagine that just as the administrator is about to begin his presentation, new information surfaces. For a few moments, there is an argument among the board members. A couple of parents in the audience begin to shout. Newspaper cameras start clicking. When calm is finally restored, the administrator is instructed to proceed.

There are at least a hundred different ways this could turn out badly for both the administrator and his employer, the school system. At first glance, his task seemed easy enough: his boss, the superintendent, told him to appear at the meeting and report what he had learned about the plan. The truth, however, is that our administrator is going to need the deftness of a seasoned politician in order to accomplish what he came here to achieve.

Naturally he's going to be worried about doing his job right, and he wants to present his findings accurately. He is also surely concerned about pleasing his boss and looking good in front of the school board. But the board might be split into factions. Or members of the audience might ask questions that place the superintendent in a negative light. Or his own personal feelings as a member of the community might not square with what he is required to say as administrator. Or a surprise confrontation could emerge.

Without a strong sense of empathy, our administrator has almost no chance of succeeding. Leaders must be able to understand the shifting emotions of the people around them. They need to be able to walk into a room and instantly recognize underlying agendas at work. They need to understand how their words, even their facial expressions, will have an impact on what constituents think and say. They must consider how different people will react to one another. Will conflict erupt, or will harmony and cooperation prevail? Leaders must be able to do all of this in real time and in high-stakes public situations. Simply put, they need social savvy.

The capacity to maneuver this kind of situation is also sometimes referred to as social intelligence, a concept introduced in the 1920s by psychologist E. L. Thorndike. He defined it as the ability to handle social relations wisely. More recently, researchers such as Karl Albrecht have used the same term to express similar ideas.

Whichever label you prefer, empathy is an essential part of it. Empathic leaders possess the awareness needed to maneuver complex social situations. They use their emotional resonance to pick up important cues.

Social intelligence isn't limited to empathy alone, however. A good leader requires strong emotional intelligence and judgment as well (topics we cover in subsequent chapters). In our hypothetical situation about the school board, the administrator needs to maintain his composure at the meeting. Empathy won't be sufficient if he doesn't also possess self-control. He also needs a healthy dose of self-awareness in order to know how he comes across to others— the message his body language sends, for example. Finally, he needs excellent judgment. He has to be able to process unfolding events and anticipate how a particular comment might lead the group in one direction or another.

Social intelligence is a sticky area for many leaders. In 2003, for example, Howell Raines was at the top of his game. He held arguably the most prestigious job in journalism: executive editor of the *New York Times.* A veteran at the newspaper, he had moved steadily up the ranks since 1978, winning a Pulitzer in 1992. Peers applauded his editorial talent and aggressive investigation. The newspaper's 9/11 coverage represented a particularly big feather in Raines's cap, with the *Times* winning seven Pulitzers for its coverage.

But when one of the paper's reporters, Jayson Blair, was caught plagiarizing, Raines's leadership came under fire. For years, editors learned, Blair's work had contained a pattern of deception and misrepresentation. The entire incident was a huge embarrassment for the *Times.* Many thought Raines was derelict in his supervision, and in June 2003 he was forced out.

A closer look behind the scenes reveals that Raines was no scapegoat, however; there were early problem signs. Accusations of leadership indifference predated the Blair episode, and disgruntled staffers were the rule rather than the exception. People thought he was arrogant and inaccessible. After his resignation, it came out that one staffer had told Raines, "You don't listen, you intimidate, you play favorites." Someone said he was "the nastiest editor I've ever worked with."[11] Another charged, "This was very quickly not about Jayson Blair, but about Howell and the star system he created. The level of anger was just out of control."[12] Raines might have been a talented editor, but his lack of social savvy limited his leadership success.

The same might be said of Carly Fiorina. Looking for a savior to turn around its lagging business, Hewlett-Packard brought in the charismatic Fiorina as its new CEO in 1999. She lived up to her celebrity billing. Her face was a fixture in the media, and she appeared in television commercials alongside famous personalities like actor Matt Damon and the musician Sheryl Crow. She traveled the world in HP's corporate jet.

Unfortunately, her flashy ways didn't square with many inside HP. Several company veterans thought her style ran against the tradition of humility and camaraderie that characterized HP's culture. They thought she was out of touch, aloof, intimidating.[13] She rubbed people the wrong way. Fiorina defended herself by saying that she needed to shake things up. That's why she had been hired, she said. In the end, Fiorina might have been right, but the board lost faith in her. She was let go in early 2005.

When the Gulf oil crisis erupted in May 2010, former BP CEO Tony Hayward's social blunders exacerbated an already difficult situation. During an early interview, he claimed that the oil spill was "relatively tiny" compared with the "very big ocean," and he consistently underestimated the extent of the leak.[14] Obviously the spill wasn't tiny from the vantage point of the Gulf Coast fishermen who lived nearby.

Worse was the comment Hayward posted on Facebook to the effect that more than anyone else, he wanted the crisis to be over because, he said, "I want my life back." This quip was widely seen as insensitive to the men whose lives had been lost in the explosion. President Obama responded, "He wouldn't be working for me after any of those statements," and although his days were probably already numbered, that was the last straw.[15] Hayward lacked the social savvy to survive.

It is easy to criticize him with the benefit of hindsight, but Tony Hayward was not a rookie. Before the Gulf oil crisis, his performance at BP was impressive enough to scale the company ladder for twenty-eight years. In fact, if Deepwater Horizon had never exploded, most of us wouldn't know his name. Hayward might even have retired in quiet glory. Still, firing Hayward was the right thing to do. Certainly Deepwater Horizon was an unexpected crisis, but unexpected crises happen all the time (albeit not on the scale of a Gulf oil spill). And when they do, leaders need to be able to step in, take charge, and address touchy situations. Indeed, the value of empathic leadership is most evident during such crises. With this in mind, when we nominate, appoint, and elect top leaders, social savvy is not something that we can afford to second-guess.

TEAM BUILDING AND CHEMISTRY

Empathy also enables leaders to build better teams. It acts as a kind of superantenna with which the leader can gather important information and bolster a group's chemistry. "By being attuned to how others feel in the moment," write Goleman, Boyatzis, and McKee, "a leader can say and do what's appropriate, whether that means calming fears, assuaging anger, or joining in good spirits."[16] With empathy, leaders are able to match appropriate personalities and talent to achieve optimal team composition. They can choose people who will complement each other. For example, a leader who recognizes that many of the group members are naturally reserved can deliberately add a member who is good at rallying collective energy.

* * * * * * * * *

From the beginning, Colangelo worked closely with Coach K to select the right players for Team USA. The two of them carefully interviewed and assessed a large slate of athletes to make sure each was a good fit. Colangelo told us that he wanted to look each one in the eyes to gauge his character and commitment. Part of the problem with the 2004 squad was a lack of desire, discipline, and selflessness, which ultimately sapped team chemistry. By relying on the kind of empathy that he learned growing up in Hungry Hill and with Coach K at his side, Colangelo was able to put together a better roster. "I could see in the player's body language if he had a fire in his belly, whether he would clamp down his ego for the sake of the team," Colangelo told us.

Coach K agreed. An important part of his philosophy has always been about choosing the right players. "One time, when we were getting ready for practice, Kobe [Bryant] came in and sat down in my office," Coach K told us. "He said, 'Coach, I'm ready to do whatever it takes to win, but please let me guard the best player on the other team every night. I'll shut him down.'" During the first day of practice, Coach K told us, Bryant didn't take a single shot. "Here was the NBA scoring champion not shooting. Not once," Coach K said. "He wanted to send the entire team a message about unselfishness."

Colangelo and Coach K together had to make some difficult decisions behind closed doors, cutting many perennial NBA All-Stars to come up with a final roster for the 2008 Olympic basketball team. There were more than thirty players on the U.S. national squad, all of whom were eligible for the Olympics. Colangelo and Coach K cut this group to fourteen and ultimately to twelve. Not only had these men never before been cut from any team, for their entire lives—at the high school, college, or pro level—they were always the standout players on their respective teams, and many of them showed a strong desire to represent their country. But Colangelo and Coach K stood firm; they selected not only stars, but role players too, who would complement each other.

Once the roster was selected for Team USA, Coach K and Colangelo pushed for a three-year commitment to ensure continuity and team chemistry. This was quite a change from the past, when players would show up a few months before the Olympic Games. Colangelo told us, "These players are extremely busy, with plenty of distractions over sponsorships and the like, and not a lot of time for family."[17] Yet not a single player complained. To Colangelo and Coach K, this was another indicator that they were picking the right men for the team.

Once the daily practices were in full swing, Coach K used his empathy to make adjustments. He continually worked to make sure the unit gelled. We were able to watch (on the sidelines with the staff) a closed-door practice in Las Vegas at the University of Nevada campus in March 2008, and it is hard to imagine a coach having a better sense of his players. Coach K was constantly attuned to the ebb and flow of individual mood, energy, and the role that most fit a particular player's disposition. Coach K confided, "If we didn't have the right level of energy or we weren't communicating with one another on the court, I would get LeBron [James] in the game. He can't stop talking and moving. And in very tense situations, we need Kobe on the court because he just projects so much confidence that we are going to win no matter what." Jason Kidd's role, by contrast, was that of the "wily, steady veteran," which Coach K used as a calming influence for the younger players.

The result was a first-rate team that won the gold medal in the 2008 Olympics in Beijing. After the victory celebration, Colangelo told everyone that their mission wasn't finished, however. They still had more work ahead: "We'll see you back next summer to start practicing for the world championship games," he announced.

Team USA went on to win the 2010 FIBA World Championship, cruising past home-favorite Turkey in the final game. When we spoke with Colangelo, he reflected on the team's string of success with a feeling of pride and satisfaction. "Winning that tournament was important too. In some parts of the world, FIBA is as big as or bigger than the Olympics. We're back on top. We restored respect and dignity to the national program and learned how to win again. Before, other coaches thought we were arrogant prima donnas, but now they come up and congratulate us with a genuine level of respect. Times have changed," he beamed.

HOW TO FIND EMPATHIC LEADERS

Finding leadership empathy is not easy. As with the other leadership attributes, we use a multipronged approach, relying on different assessment techniques and data points before reaching a conclusion.

The first technique we use is 360-degree feedback. We talk to individuals who know the candidate well: colleagues, former bosses, subordinates, peers. People like to discuss empathy, so it's relatively easy to solicit information about this topic.

The key is to ask questions that touch on a candidate's ability to develop social connections and then to probe any unclear remarks. With this in mind, here are some of the kinds of questions we ask during a 360-degree review:

- How well does the person listen?
- How can you tell he really understands what you are saying?
- Does he probe beneath the surface?
- Does he read body language well? How can you tell?
- How long does it take him to size up people?
- Does he make other people feel as if they are on the same page?
- How does he handle interpersonal conflict?
- Does he nip potential conflict in the bud before it erupts into something more substantial?
- Do you feel that he understands your needs?
- Does he make you feel that you are a part of the decision-making process?
- How does he respond to conflict?
- Is he able to sense conflict before it arrives?
- Does he try to defuse it? How?
- Tell me about a situation where he had to convince others to adopt an idea that was initially resisted.
- Does he fine-tune his argument to meet the specific needs of different individuals?
- Can he walk into a conference room full of diverse constituents and quickly size up everyone's underlying agendas?
- Do you feel that he knows you as a person? Why do you say that?

For many people, a common challenge is the ability to listen. As Stephen Covey has written, "Most people do not listen with the intent to understand; they listen with the intent to reply. They're either speaking or preparing to speak. They're filtering everything through their own paradigms, reading their autobiography into other people's lives."[18]

With this in mind, we pay special attention to how others respond to questions that turn on a candidate's ability to listen. Probing is important because people often offer subtle clues. For example, people sometimes say generally, "He usually knows what he wants to do," or "She's very friendly," or "I've never had a problem." On the surface, each of these answers seems relatively benign. But they could be masking a serious problem underneath.

When we interview candidates, we also try to make a judgment about their empathy by the way they interact with us. Do they interrupt? Do they insist on plowing ahead with an answer even after we've hinted that we want to move on? These are minor details, but added to other feedback, these details can point to something bigger.

We view 360-degree feedback and traditional interviewing as just a start. They give a good indication of how a candidate behaves in a routine, one-on-one situation. But these techniques aren't very useful for evaluating leadership potential in complex social circumstances, however, making them a poor proxy for overall social intelligence.

To overcome this limitation, another technique we use in our leadership assessments is a simulation exercise, modeled on special workshops conducted at top business schools. Many executive education programs run crisis simulations to train executives to lead in difficult situations. For example, we participated in a crisis simulation at Harvard Kennedy School that was moderated by former national security advisor Samuel "Sandy" Berger. At issue in that exercise was what to do in response to a terrorist attack. Participants role-played various department heads, members of the military, elected leaders, and White House staff. New information was sent in on a rolling basis.

This kind of simulation can be quite intense. Participants are required to make decisions and communicate with others under strenuous conditions. Good judgment is at a premium. So is empathy. Emotional signals tend to bounce rapidly around the room. If one person gets unhinged, the whole group can fall apart. Observing how each participant acts usually reveals a lot about his or her social savvy. If a participant misses important social cues, for example, or has trouble getting a message across or listening, this is a warning sign that the person does not possess the kind of empathy necessary to lead a large group.

In our assessment work, we use similar simulations. Often we tailor the exercise to a company's particular business needs. We create case studies based on actual challenges facing the company and lead group discussions. The focus isn't always a crisis, but we are careful to craft a scenario that poses tough interpersonal dynamics. This is one of the best ways to observe in real time a candidate's social intelligence.

During the exercise, we look for answers to such questions as these:

- Do participants recognize the personal agendas that others have?
- Do they listen?
- Do they pick up emotional cues and signals?
- Do they exercise self-control?
- What kind of aura do they give off?
- Does their behavior encourage cooperation, or lead to unhealthy posturing and finger pointing?

If the scope of our assessment assignment does not permit a group simulation, we try to replicate the same experience in a one-on-one vignette. The point here is to assign the candidate a role, provide some facts, and ask how he or she would react in a group setting. For example, the following is a hypothetical situation that we present to a candidate to read and address:

You are a senior executive in the marketing division of a major company. In this role, you have direct responsibility for several product lines. Your boss, John, directly manages the other product lines.

You and John attended the same business school and have worked together for more than eight years. You have a collegial working relationship, and he treats you like a true co-manager of the marketing division.

In recent years, corporate financial results have been lackluster. As a result, the CEO has decided to cut costs by eliminating underperforming product lines, including all employees who work within those lines. To meet this objective, you and John have spent the past three weeks analyzing the firm's product portfolio. You have divided the portfolio into three groups: underperforming, borderline, and performing products. A board meeting has been set at which John will present your mutual findings, including a written report. During the meeting, it is anticipated that the CEO will request a vote to formally approve the product cuts that John proposes.

At the meeting, all is going as expected until John gets to the Zoom product line. Zoom is run by Zack, a man you personally hired. During your work with John to prepare for the meeting, the two of you concluded that the Zoom product line was a borderline case. At the board meeting, however, John asserts that Zoom is underperforming, and he has revised the written report to this effect. You can't help but think that the reason John moved Zoom to the underperforming category is that John suspects that Zack is gay. Over the years, John has made several remarks indicating a lack of tolerance in this area.

John has concluded his presentation, and the CEO asks if there is any additional information that should be considered before a vote is taken.

What do you do?

Most candidates have difficulty with this question. Whether a candidate admits it or not, the fact that Zack might be gay (and

John's apparent prejudice) elicits an emotional response, which is exactly what we are hoping for. We want to replicate the sense of unease that often occurs in social situations.

Zack's sexual orientation is also a bit of a red herring because it's not really pertinent to the central dilemma. Instead, the central dilemma is how to deal with John's unexpected behavior in a group setting. Many candidates feel compelled to "speak up" or "call John out" in front of the board. They assert that their conscience demands it. They tell us that they have to do "the right thing."

Having the courage of one's convictions is an admirable trait, but more careful consideration of this situation reveals that this response is not a very savvy way to proceed. How exactly is the candidate going to "call John out"? Is she going to announce to the board that she and John are not in agreement? Would she go as far as accusing John of deliberately changing the report in order to sabotage Zack? Is she going to air her belief that John is a bigot? What would the board's likely response be? How is the meeting likely to move forward from there? What is the candidate's working relationship with John going to be like after the meeting? Remember that John is the candidate's boss. Making him look bad in front of the board isn't a sound strategy for success. Nor is giving the board the impression that she and John are not operating from the same page.

Think about your own initial answer to this dilemma. Given the context, is this a constructive way to deal with John's action? What would you do?

3

Emotional Intelligence

History is full of men who might have conquered the world if only they could have conquered themselves. Napoleon was a military genius whose hubris led to bitter defeat. Henry VIII was a multitalented intellectual, but his lust, vanity, insecurity, and indulgence led to six marriages, binge-eating, wild mood swings, and near-disaster for the English treasury.

Modern leaders are just as likely to let their inner demons get the best of them. Nixon was undone by his own paranoia. Marion Barry Jr., who twice became mayor of Washington, D.C., saw his career marred by an addiction to cocaine. Arizona senator John McCain's reputation as a fiery maverick appealed to independent voters when he ran for president, but many others saw him as an erratic hothead who could not control his temper. And these are just a few of the most public examples. Privately, executives with anger management or substance abuse issues are quietly removed from their organizations every day.

Leaders need to understand their blind spots and weaknesses as much as their strengths. They need to be able to listen to others and expose themselves to new ideas. They need to evolve and adapt to new challenges. They need to work well with diverse personalities. These demands require a disciplined, mature mind, which is by no means easy. All of us are flawed and have room to grow, yet confronting our own flaws requires considerable effort.

Most of the time, personal flaws stay hidden from the public eye, getting played out in the dynamics of family or inhabiting our private thoughts. Even at work or in group settings, our emotional issues might not seem severe given the relatively limited amount of responsibility or pressure that we have.

Those in positions of leadership, however, operate under heightened scrutiny and face much greater demands. Consequently, the level of a leader's emotional intelligence, as it is commonly called, can have tremendous impact. Without it, all the passion, vision, and cognitive ability in the world are not enough to let a leader last.

· · · · · · · · ·

The Cleveland Clinic in Cleveland, Ohio, is one of the world's premiere medical centers. Its 150-acre campus is home to cutting-edge expertise in urology and rheumatology, among other fields, and in 2010, it had been ranked America's number one cardiac care facility for fifteen consecutive years. The first human face transplant was performed at the clinic in 2008, and its patients come from all fifty U.S. states and more than one hundred other nations to receive treatment.

CEO Delos "Toby" Cosgrove was trained in cardiology, and for most of his career, he was one of the best surgeons around. After joining the Cleveland Clinic in 1975, he performed heart surgery on more than twenty-two thousand patients. His specialty was valve repair, and during a span of thirty years, he published several books and hundreds of journal articles, and he personally filed thirty patents.

In autumn 2004, his career took a dramatic turn when the clinic's board of directors asked Cosgrove to become chief executive officer. It was an exciting opportunity, and Cosgrove looked forward to the transition after accepting the offer. "I was pretty confident in my ability to lead, and I certainly loved the institution," Cosgrove told us.

Not wasting any time, he quickly put together his idea of a strategic vision, outlining ambitious plans for new facilities, international expansion, and a shift in organizational culture. He scheduled meetings and took inventory of his new staff. Then reality sunk in: "I began to realize that I had no idea of the scope and magnitude of the challenge," he said. "I went over to the Parker Hannifin building, a place that I didn't even know existed [before]. . . . People were punching their computers, and I thought to myself, 'Now I'm responsible for *them*!' Previously I had only been responsible for one person at a time, [the one] on the operating table."

There was also a new business vocabulary for Cosgrove to learn: "There were all of these abbreviations and terms . . . issues with finance, HR responsibilities, advertising and marketing and political ramifications. It was like learning a new language in my spare time. I was overwhelmed," he admitted.[1]

People looked at him differently too. It was as if he carried the mantle of the Cleveland Clinic around his neck. Before, as surgeon, he was confident in the operating room and knew exactly what he needed to do. But now, as CEO, his responsibilities, and the expectations others had of him, weren't so clear-cut. "People were monitoring my every word and even how I looked at them, or the facial expressions I made. I realized that I had become a very public figure," Cosgrove told us. "I went to the store and was stopped four times before I got to the cash register. Blogs reported that I was at a Cavaliers game, chowing down on a hot dog. The CEO of the Cleveland Clinic—with a hot dog!" The extra scrutiny to his own habits aside, Cosgrove felt out of place, misunderstood, alone, and shocked at his inability to deal with leading a complex organization.

He didn't panic, though, or aggressively continue to push forward with his ambitious plans. He knew that if he pushed too hard and too fast, he would achieve nothing. Instead, he took a step back and turned a critical eye inward. He started to take inventory of himself, as much as of the facilities and people around him, to figure out what he needed to do to lead the clinic.

Using feedback from people within the clinic as well as outside experts, Cosgrove adjusted his style. He became more inclusive, transparent, and communicative. He learned to listen. He adjusted to the idea of not having immediate results. He accepted the fact that in order to perform this new job, he would have to cede a lot of control.

WHAT IS EMOTIONAL INTELLIGENCE?

Emotional intelligence basically refers to self-mastery skills—the ability to perceive, control, and improve the connection between what we feel and the way we act. The previous chapter focused on empathy—a person's ability to pick up on the emotional cues of others. Emotional intelligence, by contrast, refers to how well a person is attuned to himself or herself.

Emotional intelligence has received a lot of attention in recent decades. In fact, for some scholars, such as Daniel Goleman, it is the most important component of leadership.[2] Goleman analyzed competency models from 188 companies, including Lucent Technologies, British Airways, and Credit Suisse. What he found is that emotional intelligence is at least twice as important as other competencies, such as technical skills or cognitive ability, in terms of driving performance. Other experts who have studied emotional intelligence claim that the impact on performance is not as great.[3] Nevertheless, most generally agree that it is an important attribute of effective leadership,[4] and we have found in our assessment practice that emotional intelligence is a key predictor of leadership success.

In terms of leadership, what exactly must a person understand and master in order to succeed? How does he or she get to that point? What does it mean to say that a leader possesses emotional intelligence? The answers lie in three questions:

1. Do I know myself?
2. Can I control myself?
3. Do I look for ways to improve?

When we can look at someone and answer yes to each question, then we know that he or she has the emotional intelligence to effectively lead.

Do I Know Myself?

Self-awareness is difficult for a leader—or anyone else—to acquire. Most of us are not as attuned to ourselves as we would otherwise like to believe.

Part of this is common sense. Although no one else can ever truly appreciate the personal thoughts and emotions that we internalize every day, there is also a side to ourselves that we do not see. Our facial expressions, demeanor, nervous tics and habits, the extent to which we appear to listen: each of these is projected toward others. And who we are and what we project can be entirely different.

Think about how often you have been in a meeting and thought to yourself, *Karen always looks like she's about to lose her temper,* or, *Tom almost never looks me in the eye when he speaks,* or *Terri is a decent speaker, but she talks too quickly.* From a distance, we are able to formulate all kinds of impressions about others. These impressions might not always be accurate—Karen might be much happier than she seems—but as the old saying goes, perception is reality.

Because we do not share that level of detachment with respect to ourselves, it is much more difficult for us to know what kinds of signals we are sending. You might think that you radiate trust or confidence or open-mindedness to your colleagues, but the reality might be quite different.

Even viewed from an objective standpoint, the connection between human behavior and self-awareness is still quite difficult to explain. Some psychologists claim that our behavior is the product of deeply rooted repression. Others say we are conditioned by external stimuli or driven by a need to control our environment. Evolutionary psychologist Steven Pinker even claims that a tendency to delude ourselves is an innate part of human nature. According to Pinker, we have been biologically conditioned to trick ourselves into thinking that we are better than we are in order to appear more credible to others. "People consistently overrate their own skill, honesty, generosity, and autonomy," Pinker writes. "They overestimate their contribution to a joint effort, [and] chalk up their successes to skill and their failures to luck."[5]

None of these different theories implies that self-awareness is impossible, only that barriers exist. Truly knowing ourselves requires time and effort, which leads to the last major impediment to self-awareness: most of us get so busy that we don't take time to reflect in a meaningful way. We get caught up in social rules, responsibilities, and expectations. Many people expend so much effort worrying about their jobs, their children, the commute, soccer practice or piano lessons, the 401(k), professional training, paying the bills, and more, that they lose track of the bigger picture: whether they are happy, or fulfilled, or who they want to be.

We all need self-understanding, especially leaders. In his classic work, *On Becoming a Leader*, Warren Bennis wrote, " 'Know Thyself,' was the inscription over the Oracle at Delphi. And it is still the most difficult task any of us faces. But until you truly know yourself, strengths and weaknesses, know what you want to do and why you want to do it, you cannot succeed. . . . People begin to become leaders at that moment when they decide for themselves how to be."[6] Being honest with yourself means understanding who you are: your values, personal life story, strengths, weaknesses, and ambitions.

Self-awareness is important for leadership for many reasons. First, as we explain in Chapter Seven, knowing oneself is an essential part of unlocking personal passion. Leadership is hard work that requires enormous commitment and tenacity. Individuals who know what is most important to them are far more likely to find the right career track for releasing their energies.

Second, leaders who have a good understanding of their strengths and weaknesses, biases and blind spots, are more likely to have productive interaction with others. Bill George, former CEO of Medtronic, explains, "Those who are comfortable with themselves tend to be more open and transparent—which includes sharing their vulnerabilities."[7] When someone feels comfortable in his own skin, this sense of ease comes across to others.

Finally, self-awareness is essential for good judgment. Simply stated, a person who isn't cognizant of his or her own blind spots or weaknesses is more likely to make mistakes. Harvard leadership professor Ron Heifetz describes how this works by using his analogy of the "balcony" and the "stage."[8] According to Heifetz, a leader needs to be able to mentally switch between the two. Someone who is always the lead actor, always on the stage, will get caught up in her own performance; she won't be able to separate herself from the bigger picture. By moving to the balcony, she has a bird's-eye view; she can see how her interaction with others flows within the overall scene and can judge the audience reaction. Of course, if she's only in the balcony, she's just an observer, not a participant at all. By mentally switching back and forth, she is able to fine-tune her performance and make better decisions.

Cosgrove's initial challenges as the new CEO of the Cleveland Clinic tested his emotional intelligence. Faced with unfamiliar communications issues, for example, or the pressures attendant on being a public figure, he might have rushed forward with rash decisions, such as making wholesale changes to his staff. Many individuals who step into a new role are fearful of looking weak and feel compelled to demonstrate quickly that they have all the answers. As a result, they often sidestep the hard work of introspection.

Cosgrove took a different tack. Professionally he was confident and not accustomed to making mistakes, but he didn't suffer from arrogance. Before making any organizational changes, he decided to look within, and he realized that his experience as a first-rate heart surgeon didn't equip him with all that he needed to successfully lead. His tendency to make snap judgments, for example, did not mesh well in his larger role. As a surgeon, he was accustomed to technical work that required quick, clear, nonnegotiable decisions. His new role required more nuance. "I soon realized as CEO that I needed to slow down and listen more."

He also had to get used to non-immediate results. In surgery, it was clear at any moment whether his actions were successful. For CEOs, the flow of information requires a longer time line. "That was a huge change for me," Cosgrove admitted. "It was something I had to get my head around. Doctors are used to instant report cards. As CEO, feedback wasn't anything like that."

Another successful leader who demonstrates a high level of self-awareness is Facundo Bacardi, chairman of Bacardi Limited. A family-controlled private company, Bacardi Limited is one of the largest spirits makers in the world, with annual revenues in excess of $5 billion. In addition to the well-known Bacardi Superior brand and its aged dark rums, the company owns such labels as Dewar's whiskey, Grey Goose and Eristoff vodka, Martini vermouth, and Bombay Sapphire gin.

Bacardi is the great-great grandson of the company's founder, Facundo Barcardí i Massó, a Catalan wine merchant who emigrated to Cuba in 1830. For the past 180 or so years, the family has owned and operated the business, first in Santiago, then Havana, and eventually in Bermuda and the United States. With a storied history like that, you might expect the forty-three-year-old Bacardi to feel a sense of entitlement regarding his inherited leadership role, but he is refreshingly down-to-earth. "I've seen a number of CEOs who believe instinctively that they always know what to do, so they sort of shoot from the hip rather than taking the time to listen to others," he told us.[9]

Bacardi takes a more measured approach to his job. Working closely with the company's CEO, he didn't allow his famous name or insider status to let him get carried away. Instead, he kept a careful eye on how he could leverage his unique position to make the most difference. This sense of self-awareness enabled him to lead Bacardi Limited's complicated transition from a family company to a professional company—a journey that was not easy.

In 1991, the company employed sixty to seventy family members. By 2010, that number was down to about ten. "Before 1992 we were truly a family company, with five operating companies and family members on all the boards of directors. We were inward looking," Bacardi admits.

That all started to change with the Martini & Rossi acquisition in 1992. Fresh out of college, Bacardi was able to work on that deal and gain some perspective on the company and its competitive position. In 1993 he left to attend law school, but rejoined the company in 1997 after finishing his degree and working at a venture capital firm in Atlanta. Importantly, he came in as a nonexecutive director, allowing time to find his rhythm. He also supported the new direction the company seemed to be taking: "We had our first non-family CEO in '97. It was an important decision for us. We had been a rum company for 130 years. Beginning in 1992 with Martini and then in 1998 with the acquisition of Dewar's and Bombay, the company was growing quickly. We needed to bring in people with different skill sets than the ones we had."

That first stage turned out to be rocky. A shareholder rebellion ensued, and in 2000 the CEO was asked to leave. Although the family shareholders did not go back to a family member to exercise operating control of the company, a person who was close to many shareholders was selected to steer them through this challenging period. Finally, in 2005, the first external CEO without close ties to the family was appointed, Andreas Gembler; that was also the year that Bacardi became chairman. "That's when we really turned the corner in terms of having a different mind-set," Bacardi told us. "Before then we never really took a hard look at how we measured efficiency. At Philip Morris International, Andreas had that exposure, and drove it through the organization. [The year] 2005 [when Gembler came on] began the journey of getting to a place where we needed to be."

This is not to say that the journey was smooth. Bacardi admitted that when he became chairman, he still had a lot to learn. In particular, when he began to take a direct role in the supervision of the company's day-to-day business, he was struck by the degree to which regular board members were not aware of such critical issues such as infighting among the executive team. He knew that in order to move forward, the company needed to change—it needed an executive team with personalities and skill sets that were more complementary and who believed in the company's vision.

This situation put Bacardi in a difficult position, and he said, in retrospect, that at times he moved too fast: "What I failed to see early on is that there is a role for family members who maybe aren't the best at the traditional core business responsibilities. There are other means of participating that can have an intangible yet important impact. They can be brand advocates, for example, or develop relationships with consumers." The key, he says, is to remain inclusive. The company must give family members an opportunity to look at the process, to at least know that they have a stake in the game. Insiders have a place, but they also need to recognize the demands of a truly global business.

For Bacardi, this all started with keeping a critical eye trained on himself. "Being a family member and chairman is a tricky combination," Bacardi says. "On one hand, as a member of the family, there isn't anyone who is more dedicated and motivated to achieve great success for the company, and I know this company very well. At the same time, I learn so much from the perspectives and experiences of the board members and executives within the organization." Bacardi said that having people in the company who bring a variety of experience in the consumer goods sector made his life easier. They challenged him with new ideas, and by listening to them, he was better able to do his job.

As of 2010, Bacardi's formula for balancing the roles of ultimate family insider, honest broker, and leader of a global business had worked out well. During his tenure as chairman, the company enjoyed record growth every consecutive year. Without a person of Bacardi's emotional intelligence at the top, it is highly unlikely that the global spirits maker would have achieved this level of success.

Cosgrove and Bacardi are two leaders who were willing to learn and assess situations before they acted. By taking some time to reflect, Cosgrove avoided any rash decisions and realized that he needed to get accustomed to nonimmediate feedback. Bacardi learned that although some family members had to be moved to nontraditional roles, accomplishing this meant going at a measured pace. Bacardi also grew to understand that he must seek outside perspective, even though no one else knew more about the company than he did.

· · · · · · · · ·

What happens when leaders don't possess this kind of self-awareness and control? We worked with Sandy (name changed), an incredibly successful line manager for a global pharmaceutical company who had direct control and responsibility for $250 million worth of business. In her role as line manager, Sandy was known for her driven, meticulous style, and her boss affectionately referred to her as the company's "bulldog."

Sandy produced, and she was given a big promotion that put her in charge of the company's European business. Enthusiastically she jumped right in, eager to make her mark. She laid out impressive goals, gave speeches to her staff, and assiduously went about learning all aspects of the new position.

After just a few months, though, her region was in disarray, with almost all of the countries under her watch missing their targets. Just as worrisome, in a 360-degree review that included each of her subordinates and several colleagues, Sandy received harsh feedback. She was perceived as being an abrasive micromanager who refused to admit mistakes. People thought she overvalued her own ability and undervalued that of others. The new cross-cultural demands of the position didn't help, as Sandy's management and communication style had to be understood by professionals from several different countries. The company's CEO took notice, and with a few words to Sandy, he hoped that she might self-correct. She didn't. The truth is that she couldn't recognize her own deficiencies. She lacked the wherewithal to step back, look at herself in the mirror, and reflect. Instead, she dug in with the skills and routines that had worked very well for her in the past. She began to micromanage even more, taking her bulldog approach to another level, which had the effect of further alienating her from her staff.

Finally, the CEO took formal action. In line with our recommendation, he stepped in and set Sandy up with an executive coach. For the first time in her career, Sandy performed the hard work of deep and serious introspection. She learned that her prior strength was actually a weakness in her new role. Although her naturally meticulous style had served her well as a line manager, in her new leadership role it made her come across as a micromanager who lacked confidence in others.

After a year, Sandy showed marked improvement. She had an increased sense of self-awareness, and feedback indicated that it was making a difference: a 40 percent higher overall performance score on her annual 360-degree review. In addition, several of her colleagues reported that she was easier to work with than she had been in the past.

Do I Control Myself?

Jonathan Ornstein, CEO of Mesa Air Group, a regional air carrier based in Phoenix, has a notorious temper. His assistant once reported that he was in a bad mood "60 percent of the time" and that one of her tasks included tracking his mood and, if it was a bad one, warning other executives it might be better to stay away if necessary. "Sometimes he would come in to the office in a bad mood in the morning, and it would set the tone for the whole office," she said.[10] Scott Kirby, president of US Airways, offered, "I don't know that I've ever hung up on anyone in my life—except Jonathan. He's loud, volatile, insulting, doesn't listen to the other perspective."[11]

This reputation for hotheadedness did Ornstein no favors during the tough years of 2007 and 2008, when the company was locked in a dispute with the Air Line Pilots Association. Union leaders became so angry at his outbursts that they issued a no-confidence statement regarding him.[12] More damaging, during that period, the airline was losing an average of fifty pilots per month.[13] Jim Corridore, an industry analyst with Standard & Poor's, said he had never covered a company with such a widespread discontent with management.[14] Perhaps this record of behavior is one reason that Mesa Air filed for bankruptcy in January 2010.

Effective leaders control their emotions and bad habits. Some of the most tempestuous leaders don't seem to realize that they have a problem. But even if they do, recognition alone is not enough; a leader must be willing and able to take action and make changes. Failing to do so can be just as bad as not having self-awareness at all. What good is it to be aware of an explosive habit or disabling emotion if you don't control it?

Self-control issues usually emerge in times of great stress or pressure, and an inability to deal with these situations can produce widespread effects. When leaders can't control their emotions, they are bound to make mistakes. For example, a CEO who loses patience or composure during a tense merger negotiation, might overlook a critical fact or agree to terms that are unfavorable to his or her organization. Other leaders make poor decisions out of anger, passion, or vengeance. Bobby Knight, the legendary former basketball coach at Indiana University, threw a chair in a game (which didn't end his job) and was accused of hitting players (which did). His ouster still leaves Hoosier boosters feeling uneasy, and the basketball program has never fully recovered.

Finally, self-control is also a key factor in maintaining trust and strong professional relations. Colleagues and subordinates need to know that their leader is level-headed. Emotionally intelligent leaders are perceived as steady and reliable. Those who go off the rails, in contrast, can intimidate or even frighten their followers. Lyndon Johnson sometimes used his temper to good effect while in the Senate, where a flat power structure and arm-twisting could win colleague votes, but as president, it hurt him because it sometimes interrupted the flow of information from subordinates. His reputation for surliness prevented aides from telling him the truth, and others were scared away.

Those who depend on a steady leader also lose confidence when their leader is erratic. They begin to wonder what effect her behavior might have on the health of the entire organization. In 2010, General Stanley McChrystal lost his assignment as commander of U.S. forces in Afghanistan when an article published in *Rolling Stone* revealed his free-wheeling attitude. McChrystal had long been known as a bit of a loose cannon. He wasn't one to mince words or hold his breath. As a cadet at West Point, for example, he had received more than one hundred hours of demerits for drinking, partying, and insubordination, and when he took charge in Afghanistan in 2009, his outspokenness put the administration in an awkward position. In London, he publicly called Vice President Biden's counterterrorism strategy "shortsighted," and his own war policy review was leaked to the press in a way, many felt, that preempted President Obama from making a truly independent decision.[15]

The *Rolling Stone* article was the last straw, however. In it, McChrystal's aides portrayed their boss as someone who openly mocked the administration. "In private, Team McChrystal likes to talk shit about many of Obama's top people on the diplomatic side," wrote Michael Hastings, author of the piece. Apparently U.S. Ambassador Karl Eikenberry and Special Representative to Afghanistan Richard Holbrooke were frequent targets of McChrystal's scorn, and during a trip to Paris, McChrystal reportedly said to an aide, with a laugh, "Are you asking about Vice President Biden? Who's that?"[16]

When the White House learned about the *Rolling Stone* article, the general was summoned to Washington for a meeting in the Oval Office, at which time he was permitted to resign. Forcing McChrystal out was the right call, but the whole affair was unfortunate because McChrystal has a strong military mind and a career marked by several notable achievements. If he had been able to control his tongue, with a little more emotional intelligence, he could have contributed more.

George Steinbrenner, the late owner of the New York Yankees, is remembered for a lot of things, including his mercurial personality. Words commonly used to describe him include *blustery, bombastic, rash, commanding, tyrannical, jerk*—and these are the words we can print. Steinbrenner bought the Yankees in 1973 and was an active voice in the management of the club almost right up until his death in 2010. But his ownership story is really a tale of two lives.

In the 1970s and 1980s, he controlled the team with an iron fist. People who worked for him thought he was despotic and meddling.[17] Steinbrenner had a particularly nasty reputation for making frequent, impulsive personnel changes. He hired and fired manager Billy Martin a staggering five times, and in 1985 he promised Yankee legend Yogi Berra that the latter would manage the entire season "win or lose," only to turn around and fire Berra after just sixteen games. (Berra was so upset that he didn't return to Yankee Stadium for over a decade, until after Steinbrenner apologized to him.) "The Boss" also got into some trouble with the league. He was temporarily suspended from baseball in the early 1990s after paying a gambler money to dig up dirt on star outfielder Dave Winfield, and he caused several flare-ups with players over strict facial hair rules and other oddities.[18]

What people don't often mention is that the Yankees were relatively unsuccessful when Steinbrenner was actively micromanaging the team. Although the great Reggie Jackson teams of 1977 and 1978 brought home World Series crowns, these were the only two championships in Steinbrenner's first twenty-four years. The club missed the playoffs altogether from 1981 to 1995, the longest playoff drought in Yankees history.

In the 1990s, Steinbrenner began to mellow. Part of the reason might have been his temporary suspension. But former manager Gene Michael said that the boss of the 1990s and beyond was a different man. He gave his players and managers more leeway and more discretion. His outbursts diminished, and he no longer fired managers every year. When we spoke with Steinbrenner in 2007, he confided that his style had become more patient. He also told us that he learned to step out of the limelight and let players have center stage. "From a personal and a business perspective, I realized that it was about them getting the attention and me advising from more of a distance." He had recognized the importance of developing talent internally rather than relying exclusively on externally recruited stars. Local heroes such as Derek Jeter, Mariano Rivera, and Andy Pettitte were all groomed in the Yankees' farm system. "This awareness and change in attitude unleashed the potential of the team," Steinbrenner said.[19] Chicago White Sox owner Jerry Reinsdorf agreed: "Mr. Steinbrenner understood and embraced the power of the players, and he put this knowledge to good use in establishing the Yankees as one of sports world's most iconic brands."[20]

What is also interesting about the latter half of Steinbrenner's era is that his team started to win. A lot. The Yankees were in the playoffs every year from 1995 to 2007, and they won World Series crowns in 1996, 1998, 1999, 2000, and 2009.

Do I Look for Ways to Improve?

Good leaders know that leadership is always a work in progress. No one is perfect, and everyone can get better. Whether it's a matter of honing communications skills, building and motivating teams, or shaping an overall direction for the enterprise, every leader has a number of developmental areas worthy of extra care.

Looking for ways to improve is especially important in a new role or when the environment is quickly changing. Perhaps the number one reason most otherwise talented leaders fail is that they become prisoners of their past successes and cannot adapt to new situations. In fact, leaders need to be open to fresh ideas. They need to take remedial steps to deal with blind spots or weaknesses. They need to find ways to prevent stubbornness, complacency, ignorance, bias, familiarity, and other common habits from undermining the organization. Doing so not only improves a leader's personal skill set, it also often provides this person with an alternative set of solutions.

Finally, seeking ways to improve oneself helps to forge the important relationships that every leader needs to succeed, especially when in unfamiliar terrain. A new role means fresh faces and constituencies and leaning on others for support. Getting buy-in is critical. A leader who shows a willingness to open up, ask questions, and be vulnerable is most likely to succeed. Some people erroneously equate showing vulnerability with indecisiveness. On the contrary, a leader's willingness to let others know that she or he doesn't have all the answers is an effective way of bringing others into the process with important information. It also helps get advance support among the very people who will implement the ultimate decision.

In Cosgrove's case at the Cleveland Clinic, he worked with a team of advisors, coaches, and mentors to help him get up to speed. Among those he reached out to was Jack Welch, CEO of General Electric. "Welch told me early on to 'grab the microphone,'" Cosgrove told us. "He wanted to make sure I communicated a clear vision to the troops frequently and clearly. It was great early advice." Not all of us have access to luminaries like Welch, but we can identify experts we trust and respect.

Cosgrove also investigated various executive education programs and seminars and attended a "New CEO Workshop," at Harvard Business School. Although there are hundreds of M.B.A. courses for leaders, few courses and programs are tailored exclusively for current CEOs. One of the most respected is the Chief Executive Leadership Institute at the Yale School of Management, which conducts annual CEO conferences twice a year. (Disclosure: During the early 1990s, we cut our teeth in the leadership field by interviewing executives and helping to design workshops at this institute.) Top CEOs and leaders of other organizations from around the world attend because these conferences provide a rare opportunity to get extensive peer feedback. As Jeffrey Sonnenfeld, director of the institute as well as a senior associate dean and professor at the Yale School of Management, has told us numerous times, the CEO's office is a lonely spot, and leaders need to reach outside and make sure that they have a forum where healthy debate and self-discovery can take place.

Cosgrove also reached outside his inner circle, as well as the organization, and added new people to his executive team. "I needed to bring people in to complement my blind spots," Cosgrove told us. "I had no problem bringing smarter people on to my executive team. As a matter of fact, my philosophy is to hire only people smarter than me. That's helped me, and, more important, the clinic, over and over again." These experts have helped Cosgrove cover some of his blind spots, and they serve as a sounding board for new ideas.

Facebook CEO Mark Zuckerberg might be the only person in history who knows what it feels like to run a billion-dollar company at the age of twenty-three. His company revolutionized social media and earned him a personal fortune in the process, but the experience of running Facebook hasn't always been smooth for the young entrepreneur.

In early 2010, Facebook came under fire for its privacy controls. Users of the site complained that the company's policy for protecting personal information was unclear at best. Some wondered aloud if the company's business model actually *relied* on third-party access to user information in order to generate revenue. Zuckerberg tried to publicly address these concerns at the All Things Digital conference in San Francisco in June 2010. But when he was interviewed at the conference by two veteran journalists from the *Wall Street Journal,* Walt Mossberg and Kara Swisher, many observers thought Zuckerberg flopped. His answers came across as evasive, irritating, and rambling,[21] and his onstage sweating and overall sense of unease did not leave a positive impression. Zuckerberg's public image woes continued several months later with the release of the film *Social Network.* In the movie, Zuckerberg is depicted as someone who stole the idea for Facebook from two Harvard classmates, and he comes across as arrogant, vindictive, and socially inept. Altogether, these events created the perception that Facebook's CEO did not have a high level of emotional intelligence.

Regardless of whether this perception is true, it should be pointed out that the young billionaire took steps early on at Facebook to improve his leadership skills, starting with bringing outsiders onto his executive team. In particular, he and chief operating officer Sheryl Sandberg developed a positive working relationship. As part of her executive role, Sandberg helped to round out Zuckerberg's blind spots, including his tendency to come across as uncaring and aloof. The two met regularly to discuss a variety of issues, including each other, and Sandberg has served as a coach, mentor, and friend. According to Sandberg, "We agreed that we would give each other feedback every Friday."[22] In 2010, Zuckerberg still had a long way to go in terms of refining his leadership style and effectiveness, but he was still a young man and a very young CEO. Moreover, his willingness to work on issues of emotional intelligence was a positive sign that his leadership ability would continue to grow.

FINDING EMOTIONAL INTELLIGENCE

Emotional intelligence is perhaps most important to assess when leaders are moving into new roles with greater responsibility. In these situations, individuals often need to operate outside their comfort zones. For example, they might be called on to operate with constituencies with whom they have no experience. In other situations, they might have to maneuver a different culture or value system. Another case might involve moving between two organizations of different size, complexity, strategic challenge, or stages of development. Doing so requires emotional maturity, discipline, confidence, and a strong commitment to learn and grow. Failure to some degree is inevitable. How a leader deals with and learns from failure becomes paramount. Even the smartest and most ambitious people do not succeed without emotional intelligence.

Moreover, while other attributes such as judgment are also tested in new roles, emotional intelligence is harder for organizations to predict. Organizations often naively assume that a leadership candidate will excel in a different role simply because she or he has always excelled in prior roles. When the two of us talk to hiring managers or CEOs who have been stung by recent personnel decisions, emotional intelligence issues are most often the cause.

This is not surprising. Unpacking the emotional makeup of others is not a simple task. In the case of Sandy, her CEO rightly predicted that she had the cognitive skills to lead several European markets. Sandy's lack of emotional intelligence, however, was something he did not expect. By the time he was able to jump in and take corrective measures, a lot of time, resources and goodwill had already been wasted.

With all of this in mind, how can we assess emotional intelligence *before* making critical leadership appointments? Most organizations go about it in the wrong way (or fail to do so at all). Some believe that certain extroverted personality types are indicative of emotional intelligence and leadership success. This is simply not true.[23] Although it is always smart to avoid leaders with personality disorders such as extreme narcissism, history clearly shows that successful leaders come in a variety of shapes. Jack Welch, former CEO of General Electric, was known for his charisma, tough command, and up-or-out mentality. Herb Kelleher at Southwest Airlines used a friendlier, inclusive, more communal disposition to great effect. And each of these men has a personality much different from that of Bill Gates, who is known for being more focused, analytical, and temperamental. Yet all three have been highly successful CEOs.

Rather than concentrate on personality type, a hiring manager would do better to determine if a candidate understands his or her own personality and the potential downside of it.

Carl Diehl is the cofounder of Bar Method, a small national exercise company with thirty-five studios in nine states and a media company that sells exercise DVDs. In 2010, he was looking for new franchisees to support his expanding business. "I gave all our interviewees nine paragraphs corresponding to the nine personality types of the Enneagram—a system for understanding the human personality—and asked them which one seemed to fit them best."[24] Diehl's two finalists were the ones who made time for personal reflection, something not all that common.

Diehl wasn't looking for a particular personality type. Rather he wanted to see how aware each individual was of his or her own personality. Did the interviewees know how others perceived them? Did they know, as he phrased it, the "dark sides" of their personalities? Were they honest in their self-appraisal?

Honest, accurate self-awareness is a quality we look for in our assessment practice. We use a variety of techniques to dig deep on the issue of self-awareness, but during the course of traditional one-on-one interviewing, we might frame our questions this way: "No one is perfect. Tell me one thing about yourself that you don't like."

We'll wait for an answer and then ask, "Are you trying to change it?"

Then: "Tell me something about yourself that you didn't like in the past and that you were able to improve. How did you do it?"

It is difficult for candidates to think on the spot about something they don't like, that they've acknowledged is wrong, and that they're working to fix. The ability to stay calm and articulate this during an interview, when the stakes are high, is a sign of high emotional intelligence. It shows that the person has taken time for personal reflection and through this reflection has been able to act. Of course, we want to be certain that the identified problem isn't too serious (it's one thing for a candidate to have a problem with patience; it's quite another if she is obsessed with theft, to cite an extreme example).

Knowing that some of these answers might be rehearsed, we also like to probe beneath the surface of the leader's résumé, which is often no more than a carefully crafted marketing brochure. We want to understand the nature and diversity of his or her experiences and what, if anything, the leader has learned.

"You have quite an impressive résumé, Sarah. What accomplishments are you most proud of?" we might ask. This gets the candidate focused on a positive experience. We then follow up with, "What did you learn from this?" Since the candidate offered a positive experience, it is likely to have been one in which she felt quite comfortable. She therefore likely wasn't afforded the opportunity to learn new things. We then quickly refocus the conversation toward a more difficult experience: "Tell me about a job in which it was difficult for you to get your footing. What were some of the roadblocks? What were some of the biggest surprises? How did you get comfortable?" Every great leader has had tough challenges along the way, and they all have learned from those experiences. We are therefore looking first for honesty: "Yes, I have had plenty of tough challenges and some failures along the way," is something we hear often from the best leadership candidates. But even these answers can be rehearsed, and further probing is often necessary.

One CEO candidate for a large technology company remarked during an interview:

> My toughest challenge was moving from a division that was in turnaround mode into another division that was more of a start-up. My initial impression was "great," this will be a walk in the park given how much diagnostic work I had had to do to fix the broken business, not to mention how low morale had been among my team in the turnaround situation.
>
> I couldn't have been more wrong. In the start-up, team members had much higher spirits, but they were craving more direction and rules because none existed. Well, there was no road map for me either. I wasn't used to the ambiguity, and frankly I struggled at first. But I found a great mentor, talked regularly with one of our board members who was also a CEO of a high-tech start-up, attended a leadership workshop at the University of Chicago, and found a great executive coach to help me think through the complexity and how to communicate an overall vision to the rest of the team. It wasn't easy, but looking back, it was the most pivotal learning experience of my career.

Rather than focus on the experience itself, we focus in our assessment role on the willingness and ability to learn from the experience and grow. How did he or she adjust? What proactive steps did the candidate take? What is he doing differently now? How has all of this turned him into a better leader? Is he equipped to tackle an increasingly complex and ambiguous challenge?

We also look for leaders who have a track record of taking charge of their own careers. This sounds counterintuitive. Most people think that they are at the mercy of their supervisors or HR departments. They sit back and wait for a new position to open up and then submit their résumés through an online human resource system within the company. Similarly, many people wait for a mentor to be assigned to them rather than seek one out.

The best leaders, by contrast, are much more proactive and passionate about career development. Not only do they seek out formal and informal mentors across the organization, they also seek out completely new challenges and jobs. They get to know leaders and influence makers. They are not shy about asking for help or the opportunity to share ideas.[25]

As part of the assessment process, we also want to know what others think about a candidate. If there is a lack of consistency between the candidate's view of himself and what others say, that's an immediate red flag. To accomplish this goal, we conduct specialized 360-degree interviews, 120 degrees at a time. What does this mean? As we explained earlier, 360-degree interviews provide an opportunity to speak with a candidate's current and former bosses, subordinates, or peers. The interviews offer a chance to check a person's background, probe more deeply into specific issues, and get a cross-section of input with respect to his or her leadership potential.

A traditional 360-degree interview is a one-on-one encounter. Whenever possible, we like to take this approach a step further, however, by conducting them in "slices." We invite a group of the candidate's peers, subordinates, or former bosses into the same meeting (or conference call, depending on logistics) and ask open-ended questions: "What is this candidate like to work with?" we might ask. "Tell us about a project that you worked on together." "What were his strengths?" "Where did he struggle?" "How did he recover from initial setbacks?" "How did he learn new things?" "Was he aware of areas in which he lacked understanding?" "How did he interact with the rest of the team?" "In general, does he know how he comes across to others?"

As you might expect, participants are usually slow to offer frank, insightful feedback during these 120-degree interviews. They don't want to throw one of their colleagues under the bus. Nor do they want to take the chance that any negative feedback might come back to bite them in the future, particularly knowing that the candidate is in line for a promotion. However, as the interview process progresses, usually after fifteen minutes or so, people begin to open up and share "war stories." This is encouraged by setting some clear guidelines up front. First and foremost, we frame the conversation as a "developmental conversation" to help one of the participants' colleagues succeed at the next level. We also emphasize confidentiality by assuring participants that we won't attribute specific comments to any particular individual. In other words, we are careful to explain that we will not tell the candidate who said what, but rather only that certain things were said. Given these parameters, peers are typically more eager to offer candid opinion and advice.

As the 120-degree meeting progresses, participants build off one another's comments. For example, as part of a CEO succession planning assignment for a high-profile media company, we conducted a live interview with a group of the CEO candidate's current and former subordinates. At first, these people were extremely reluctant to offer anything but positive stories about the candidate. About fifteen minutes into the meeting, however, one of the participants sparked a great conversation by saying, "Well, I sometimes feel that I have great ideas, but he [the CEO candidate] doesn't ask me what I think. I just want to see this company succeed and reach it's full potential." Without missing a beat, another person in the room jumped right in and said, "Yeah, he's a really smart guy, but he has strong, preconceived notions and can dig in his heels." This discussion thread developed and led to some valuable insight. We learned that the CEO candidate could at times be rigid, didn't cast a wide net when exploring options for tough business challenges, and didn't get advance buy-in from his team before reaching a critical decision.

More worrisome, when we interviewed the candidate himself, he seemed oblivious to these concerns. This lack of awareness constituted a big red flag in our assessment of his emotional intelligence.

We also conduct classic 360-degree interviews. As assessors, we like to go beyond the traditional practice of limiting these to subordinates, bosses, and peers, though. In particular, we try to speak with a cross-section of strategic partners, board members, and even customers if possible. Often these people provide a perspective that others do not see. For example, we were hired to assess a candidate who was in line to become executive vice president of a large online retailer. The CEO of the company thought the candidate was perfect for the job and emphasized the candidate's brilliant strategic thinking and sharp analytical mind. Through a series of customer interviews, however, we learned that the candidate could come off as arrogant, and even dismissive, of their needs. As you might imagine, this was valuable information for the company to have and quite a surprise given the CEO's stellar appraisal. Moreover, although this wasn't the end of the candidate's consideration for the new role, it was clearly a red flag and a developmental opportunity that he needed to be made aware of.

Based on these interviews, we can determine if there is consistency between the insights gained from references and that shared by candidates themselves. As assessors, this consistency not only helps us become more comfortable with the candidate's honesty but also demonstrates the degree to which she is self-aware. Does the candidate really understand how others view her, or is there a nagging disconnect? Is she aware of her bad habits? The best candidates are able to accurately zero in on how they come across to others and on their developmental needs.

Finally, the best assessment experts use more than one-on-one interviews and 360-degree referencing. They use case simulations and group exercises to get their fingers on the pulse of the leader's emotional intelligence. During this process, a real-life business scenario is provided to the leader. One approach we often use is to create a small case study concerning a tough business challenge that is occurring in a part of the organization with which the candidate is unfamiliar. For example, we may present a marketing executive in line for a big promotion with a complicated operations and manufacturing challenge. Or we may present a division head in Cincinnati with a challenge occurring in Beijing. The key is to ensure that the business challenge falls outside the candidate's comfort zone but feels and actually is "real" and "important." After presenting the case, we ask several questions about the leadership challenge. Then, when the candidate provides an initial answer, we throw new information into the mix. Our focus then becomes: Can the candidate process the new information and adjust her thinking? Can she revise her original stance if necessary?

The candidate with low emotional intelligence stubbornly clings to her original answer. She thinks any adjustment is a sign of weakness or waffling. She won't concede that she missed a key point, for example, even after we've offered a better alternative. The best leaders know to adjust course when the world around them has changed. They also know how to communicate why they have changed their thinking, and they do so in a convincing way.

We leave you with one last question as you consider the importance of emotional intelligence. If we were to talk to several of your peers, your boss, and maybe a few people who have worked for you, how accurately could you predict what they might say? What are your weak spots? Where do you need to grow and develop? Do you have a plan to reach and succeed at the next level?

Vision

Few rock stars have the staying power of three decades. Between fame and temptation, grueling tour schedules, and an ever-changing fan base, this is not an occupation that lends itself to a lengthy career. Far more typical are the one-hit wonders—the young meteorites who have their fifteen minutes and then quickly burn away.

Four decades after bursting onto the music scene, Bono is clearly one of the exceptions. Since forming U2 in the late 1970s, Bono and his fellow bandmates have as of 2010 released more than twenty albums, sold in excess of 150 million records, won twenty-two Grammy awards, and been inducted into the Rock and Roll Hall of Fame. They have performed in countries around the world and collaborated with everyone from Frank Sinatra to Luciano Pavarotti, Jay-Z to BB King.

As the band's front man, Bono has been particularly adept at settling into the role of living legend. Sure, his salt-and-pepper stubble and crow's feet attest to several dozen trips around the globe, and he is no longer the same boyish crooner whose shaggy locks graced the cover of *October*, one of his first albums. Yet despite the years, Bono remains timeless and indomitable. He wears the same trademark wraparound sunglasses, which partially shield the same penetrating eyes. He still photographs well, and his image is a fixture on billboards everywhere. It almost seems as though Bono was born to be a rocker—the rare breed who wakes up in the morning with a catchy treble beat flowing through his head.

All of which makes it even more striking to hear him say something like this: "I really believe that we can be the generation that ends extreme poverty. I really believe that. And by extreme poverty . . . I mean the sort of brutal, stupid poverty that has a child dying for lack of food in its belly in a world of plenty; that has a family lose their life because of a [lack of a] twenty cent immunization."[1] It isn't the kind of comment you'd normally expect from a man who wields guitars for a living.

Since the late 1990s, Bono has been moonlighting as the world's leading spokesperson for poverty reduction and economic development in Africa. Or maybe it's the other way around—maybe he's been moonlighting as a rock star between his frequent high-profile visits with policy wonks and heads of state. However you look at it, his work is paying off, because people are taking notice of Bono's clear, unwavering message: Africa offers a great opportunity. Investing there makes great business sense given Africa's vast, untapped and growing market. As millions of inhabitants rise from extreme poverty, they will demand more and more of the goods that are produced in Western countries—cell phones and soccer shoes, deodorant and TVs.

Several trends support Bono's optimism. For example, from 2000 to 2008, the continent's economic output increased by 4.2 percent per year, double the pace of the 1980s and 1990s, and foreign direct investment was significantly higher there than in India.[2] Multinational giants like Walmart, Procter & Gamble, and Unilever were investing heavily in the region,[3] and China's trade with Africa exceeded $106 billion in 2008.[4] Demographic shifts also point to a surge in consumer demand. A study published by McKinsey &

Company predicts that the working-age population in Africa will grow from the 2010 level of 500 million to 1.1 billion by 2040.[5]

Despite these clear advancements, progress in Africa is clouded by another set of figures and facts. In 2010, thousands still died daily across the continent for lack of food and basic health care, and malaria infection was rampant.[6] Africa's penchant for political calamities also tends to overshadow the emergence of any positive news. During the 2003–2009 civil war in Darfur, for example, 300,000 people were killed, and the United Nations estimates that at least 2.7 million others were displaced.[7] Alleged election fraud in Zimbabwe, as well as lawlessness and piracy in Somalia, reinforce the perception that the entire continent is too risky for investment, too backward, or incapable of repair.[8]

Earlier than most others, Bono started working to change that perception. Along with music producer Bob Geldof and several others, in 2002 he formed an advocacy organization called DATA (Debt, AIDS, Trade, Africa) to influence governments and policymakers.[9] Its goal was to educate and pressure government leaders about what they could do to improve life in Africa. Bono realized that in order for his vision to take hold, however, he'd need to enlist the help of millions of other people. So in 2004 he formed the ONE Campaign to raise grassroots support for the same issues, and in 2008 these organizations were merged into ONE, which became Bono's signature group.

The RED organization is another important piece in his efforts to raise money and social awareness. RED enlists companies to produce special consumer items such as red iPods, red Converse shoes, and the red Nike shoelaces that LeBron James wears. Every time consumers buy these goods, a small percentage of the purchase price goes to Bono's campaign. As Bono explained, these organizations are linked: ONE is the grassroots and public policy arm, and RED is the consumer arm.[10] Their joint goal is to reshape Africa.

David Lane, ONE's chief executive officer and former executive director at the Bill & Melinda Gates Foundation emphasized to us that the group's vision was to change fundamentally the way in which the developed world and developing world interact.[11] After coming on board in 2006, Lane worked closely with Bono to strengthen ONE's mission, and he drew on his record at the Gates Foundation, as well as a former stint working with the U.S. government, to raise ONE's stature within the Washington Beltway. For Lane, the experience of joining Bono's group also meant getting accustomed to the fanfare that accompanied his high-profile colleague. One of the interesting things about his job, he told us, was that he had the world's biggest rock star on his board.

ONE has benefited from Bono's exposure, too: since its inception in 2004, the organization has enlisted more than 2 million members.[12] Part of Lane's early work involved figuring out how to best leverage the power of that base. Along these lines, ONE, which initially focused mainly on poverty and disease, subsequently added climate change, corruption, governance, and other issues to its agenda. In 2010, Lane also devoted an enormous amount of time holding countries to account for progress on the Millennium Development Goals adopted ten years earlier. For Lane and Bono, this meant "working the G-8 circuit," influencing policymakers, touring Africa to monitor progress, and simultaneously making sure that grassroots supporters back home continued to stay attuned.

In order to accomplish this, Bono and Lane constantly honed their message, or what they referred to as the "melody line." In musical terms, a melody line is simply a line of rising or falling notes that gives a song its recognizable theme. It is the part of the song that a listener remembers, the notes that stand out above the rest. Bono and Lane turned this into a metaphor for giving voice to their organization's big ideas. The melody line was how they communicated their vision to the masses to inspire and unite them.

Back in the early days of Jubilee 2000, when the focus was on erasing Africa's crippling debt, the melody line was, simply enough,

"Drop the Debt." (Jubilee 2000 was an international coalition of activists that successfully petitioned more than forty governments to forgive crippling debt in the world's poorest countries.) Bono was a leading voice during the campaign.[13] He spoke in front of the United Nations and the U.S. Congress and met with such key figures as Bill Clinton and Pope John Paul II.[14] His persistent efforts paid off, and people welcomed his inspirational contribution. In fact, after signing legislation authorizing $435 in American relief, Clinton praised Bono: "When we get the Pope and the pop stars all singing on the same sheet of music, our voices do carry to the heavens," the president said.[15]

In 2004, the melody line was tailored to focus attention more closely on AIDS. Lane explained that in order to advance common understanding of how easy it was to make a difference in the fight against the disease they've adopted the phrase, 'Two Pills a Day.' Bono repeated this slogan over and over. Doing so raised awareness that just two pills costing forty cents could keep HIV-infected children alive.[16]

The key was to make sure the melody line connected with people and tapped into their deepest values and aspirations. That's why Bono frequently referred to the American dream when speaking to an American audience or about how it made good business sense to invest in Africa. Lane and Bono didn't use the word "charity" because they wanted the focus of their work to be about "investment." Their message was an attempt to tap into the human ideal of self-empowerment, of giving people the opportunity to pick themselves up, work hard, and achieve.

As a musician, Bono must have understood this from the start. After all, music itself is a form of inspiration that reaches across time and culture to bring people together. With each hit song, Bono and U2 created and participated in a dialogue. With "Sunday Bloody Sunday" and "Where the Streets Have No Name,"Bono put charged ideas into melodies that call out for social change.

It is more than just Bono's words that move, however. At a live concert, U2 fans are treated to a variety of imagery. Giant video screens flash political and consumerist messages. During the 2009 tour, U2 paid tribute to the imprisoned Burmese president, Aung San Suu Kyi, and spectators were encouraged to join in a mask-wearing protest to focus attention on her plight (she was released from house arrest in 2010).[17] Similarly, Archbishop Desmond Tutu appeared in prerecorded videos for the ONE Campaign, and Bono himself often asked concertgoers to dial a number onto their cell phones to offer support. During a 2006 tour, 600,000 new contacts were added this way.

Now far more than a celebrity showman, Bono has become a respected expert and regular speaker at G-8 summits, the World Economic Forum, and other high-profile global events. At these meetings, he sits with heads of state to give voice to the ONE agenda. In 2003, he played an instrumental role in convincing President George W. Bush to sign an unprecedented $15 billion budget increase for AIDS relief in Africa. He also pushed world leaders to agree to sizable aid and relief commitments at the 2005 Gleneagles G8 Summit and has been using ONE to keep the pressure on countries that subsequently let their commitments slip. During 2010 he met with Russian president Dmitry Medvedev to petition the Kremlin leader on AIDS and governance issues in that country.[18] For his efforts, Bono has even been named a candidate for the Nobel Peace Prize.[19]

"Bono inspires," said former British prime minister Gordon Brown. "He changes people's opinions about what's possible. I think he has had a huge impact on public opinion right across the world."[20]

THE IMPORTANCE OF VISION

Like the concept of leadership itself, the term *vision* is frequently abused. Undisciplined commentators treat it as a kind of catchall for everything that they can't easily explain. This is unfortunate because few aspects of leadership are more important than vision, and no serious treatment of the subject could ignore the critical role that it plays. "To grasp and hold a vision," Ronald Reagan once stated, "that is the very essence of successful leadership," and Frederick Smith, CEO of Federal Express, said that "the primary task of leadership is to communicate the vision and values of an organization."[21]

Perhaps more than anyone else, leadership guru Warren Bennis has studied the difference between organizational failure and success. "All leaders have the capacity to create a compelling vision, one that takes people to a new place," he wrote.[22] Bennis looked at scores of leaders, and he determined that none of them possesses all of the characteristics of great leadership. But every good leader, he found, has vision.

Why is vision so important? For starters, how could anyone persuade a group of people to follow without knowing where they were going? How could he or she convince them to sacrifice significant time and energy without also highlighting the benefits of the journey? Imagine Columbus trying to solicit funds from the Spanish Crown or months of dedicated labor from his sailors without a compelling vision of the New World and all its glory and riches. Picture President Kennedy trying to rally the country toward an ambitious lunar program without also tying it to a larger theme of American freedom, progress, and strength.

The truth is that we all want leaders who possess a sense of where to go. We need direction. This is true for individuals and for organizations. Otherwise we get bogged down in our daily lives with no sense of purpose or overall mission.

Leaders Imagine a Better Future

Winston Churchill once said that it is always wise to look ahead but difficult to look farther than you can see. What he likely meant to underscore is that shortsightedness often plagues our everyday lives. Most people, most of the time, are not able to see beyond a very limited horizon. However wide-eyed we may have started out as children, by the time we reach adulthood, we are creatures of habit. Conditioned to the rules, norms, and expectations of our immediate surroundings, we fall victim to cynicism. We lose the ability to think big, to dream big, to embrace the mystery of the not yet started.

Visionary leaders, however, are unusually forward minded and imaginative, and they can look out into the horizon with a sense of possibility and wonder. While the majority of us are focused on next week, or the next quarterly report, or the next election, visionary leaders see beyond immediate distractions to seize hold of big ideas.

John Maeda, president of Rhode Island School of Design (RISD), told us that part of vision consists of "having sort of an unnatural optimism." As head of RISD, Maeda has gotten to know scores of extraordinarily creative leaders. "Their minds are wandering," Maeda said. "They are looking for something else. But in doing so, they stumble across new ideas and put them together in a way that others wouldn't have dreamed of."[23]

Amazon CEO Jeff Bezos is known for pushing others in large, imaginative ways. He is credited with creating the blueprint for a global online bookstore before most people had even heard of the World Wide Web. Back in 1994, he quit his job in New York and drove from Texas to Seattle with his wife as he mapped out final preparations for the new company. Not many investors were convinced that his business plan could work—until they met and heard Bezos in person.

Known for moving others in large, imaginative ways, Bezos told us the story of Akio Morita, the cofounder of Sony, and his own professional inspiration. "After World War II Morita set a mission for Sony to make Japan known for quality. Not just the company, but the entire country," he told us. "This was when Japan had a reputation for inexpensive, low-quality products. Vision is bigger than the company. Morita was, and still is, a role model for me and for Amazon. I want to set a standard that transcends our corporate boundaries."[24] For Bezos, that has meant consistently pushing the limits of how we shop and read. His original conception of an online bookstore grew to include a wide variety of consumer goods, including electronics, toys, housewares, and other items, sold and delivered across the world, and his Kindle device has revolutionized the concept of e-reading.

When we spoke with him, Bezos also emphasized that holding a long-term perspective is an essential feature of having a good vision. "For me, I would not know how to hold on to a vision if I couldn't couple it with long-term thinking," he said. "You can't have vision if you're trying to do it in the next three or even twelve months. Interesting things take a lot of time."

Another leader who has earned a reputation for vision is Steve Wynn, founder and CEO of Wynn Resorts. Since the 1990s, he has been a trailblazer in the hotel and gaming industry, erecting such Las Vegas landmarks as Treasure Island, Golden Nugget, Mirage, Bellagio, Wynn Las Vegas Resort, and Encore. With each venture, he focuses on taking the customer experience to a higher level, with an imaginative flair that somehow manages to be colossal, luxurious, and surprising, without being kitsch. When he opened the Bellagio, for example, he hung masterpieces by Picasso, Rubens, Degas, Monet, Gauguin, Van Gogh, and Andy Warhol on the walls. In effect, Wynn's talent is creating giant playgrounds for adults. Visitors can forget about their lives for a few days and delight in Wynn's sense of grandeur and magic.

Wynn's vision is credited with creating a spree of other mega-resorts in Las Vegas, such as the Venetian and Mandalay Bay. Developments in Dubai and Macau also bear the imprint of his original thinking. *Time* magazine described him as "not only a great salesman of insane ideas and a clever real estate player, but also the gaming industry's most brilliant designer."[25] Former Nevada governor Bob Miller remarked, "I think that without question he has been the greatest visionary in the history of Las Vegas."[26]

Leaders don't just imagine a future out of thin air, however. Their ideas, while filled with possibility, are also grounded in reality. This key aspect of vision can sometimes get lost. Part of what makes a good vision is the ability to connect it to current or past events. Visionary leaders see past, present, and future as different fibers of a single, continuous thread.

Omar A. El Sawy of the University of Southern California determined that the most forward-minded leaders are those who maintain a strong sense of the past. He divided thirty-four CEOs into two equal groups in order to test their time orientation. Each group was asked in one part of the test to look ahead into their personal future and in another part to look into their personal past. The group that focused on their past first had a significantly longer future time horizon than did the CEOs who listed future events first. El Sawy's explanation is that we make sense of our world retro- spectively: "We construct the future by some kind of extrapolation, in which the past is prologue, and the approach to the future is backward-looking."[27]

His findings put an academic veneer on something that Churchill said many decades ago. Churchill felt that people can see only as far into the future as they can see behind. For this reason, he believed strongly that leaders should read and understand history. Whatever the context—politics, business, military—he held that the leaders best equipped to articulate a vision were those who could connect an approaching horizon with the lessons of the past.

Leaders armed with this visionary mind-set are in a position to act strategically. They recognize how larger forces can be harnessed or nudged in order to reach desired ends. For example, and despite his many flaws, Richard Nixon was at least twenty years ahead of his time when it came to recognizing the long-term strategic importance of China.[28] Until the late 1960s, Sino-American relations had been locked in a deep freeze, and China was joined at the hip with the Soviet Union in its hostility toward the United States.[29] But when a rift opened between China and the Soviet Union, Nixon saw an opportunity. He predicted that the balance of world power would shift to the West if the two Communist countries could be wholly untied. As a result, he encouraged a thawing of relations between Beijing and the United States, and in 1972 he was the first U.S. president to visit China. It was a bold move, and not without controversy.[30] Some advisors thought that the trip was a big mistake. But Nixon saw the bigger picture, and for eight days television cameras sent back the first images of China that Americans had seen in more than twenty years. It was a big diplomatic victory, and after a week there, the president was able to set the relationship between China and the United States on a different trajectory. He achieved détente with both China and Russia, which set the stage for a peaceful end to the cold war. Historians frequently look back on the 1972 trip as Nixon's biggest foreign policy success.[31]

In the business world, we often associate vision with daring individuals like Paul Allen, the cofounder of Microsoft; Richard Branson, the brash founder and CEO of the Virgin Group; and Sergey Brin, the Stanford student-turned-entrepreneur who cofounded Google. As of 2010, their collective net worth was in excess of $50 billion, largely because they were the first ones to see and capitalize on important new trends in personal computers, music and global travel, and the Internet, respectively. Less talked about is the fact that since as far back as 2000, these men have had their eyes set on a new target. While the rest of us still marvel at the thrill and convenience of online search tools and electronic shopping, they are focused on what they say is the next big thing: space.

When Yuri Gagarin of the Soviet Union was the first to reach outer orbit in 1961, he set off a space race that eventually landed Neil Armstrong, Buzz Aldrin, and others on the surface of the moon. In the ensuing years, NASA spent billions on satellites, planetary probes, and the ambitious International Space Station. But manned missions are no longer a top priority. They are too expensive for budget-strapped public spending, and rocket propulsion technology hasn't improved much under the government's fifty-year watch. In fact, in 2010 the Obama administration scuttled plans for a return trip to the moon, and the U.S. government announced that it will consider outsourcing "taxi" rides to the International Space Station, which is where the visionaries might come in.[32]

Allen was one of the first people to envision space travel as an area ripe for private commercialization. In the early 2000s, he invested millions of dollars in a jet-fueled carrier aircraft called *White Knight One* and an experimental space plane called *SpaceShipOne*. In 2004, *SpaceShipOne* received the $10 million Ansari X Prize for being the first privately funded spacecraft to carry humans into space twice within two weeks.

In the ensuing decade, over $1 billion was invested in the private space flight industry. One of the most bullish investors is Sir Richard Branson, whose Virgin Galactic Group picked up where Allen left off by rolling out *White Knight Two*, a special aircraft due for commercial flight in 2011. *White Knight Two* carries a six-passenger rocket plane, *SpaceShipTwo*, between its two fuselages, and then releases the payload at an altitude of fifty thousand feet. From there, *SpaceShipTwo* rockets itself to sixty-two miles above Earth, the edge of space. Passengers experience five minutes of weightlessness, and the entire trip lasts three hours. Virgin Galactic expects one flight per week at a cost of $200,000. As of late 2010, over three hundred eager passengers had already purchased tickets, and 80,000 had placed their names on a waiting list for seats.[33] Branson expects several thousand passengers per year as early as 2015.

At a speech to commemorate the opening of the world's first spaceport in the New Mexico desert in October 2010, Branson said: "For me and for the thousands of astronauts who will follow, our journey to Spaceport America will likely be one of our most important moments in our lives. We will learn more, we'll experience more, and we'll open up more opportunities, that we cannot even conceive of today. This is history. We're making it right here."[34]

While cofounding Google might seem to be enough for any visionary, Sergey Brin also has his sights set high, literally. In 2008 he became the founding member of the Orbital Mission Explorers Circle by putting down a $5 million deposit for a future space flight with Space Adventures, a company based in Virginia. Space Adventures had already launched several clients on visits to the International Space Station by 2010. Its future plans included additional visits to the space station, space walks, and a mission lasting eight or nine days to circumnavigate the moon at a cost of $100 million per person. (Note that this last feat would not qualify for the Google Lunar X Prize, a $30 million competition sponsored by Brin's company to award the first privately funded group to land a robot on the moon and transmit images back to Earth.)

Will private space travel flourish the way Branson, Brin, and others think it will? Only time will tell, and their plans are not without skeptics. Some experts wonder about the extent to which space agencies will accept a secondary role, and questions also exist about possible regulatory impediments to mass space tourism.[35] There are a lot of ways that these ventures could fail. But not too long ago, the same could have been said about a simple-to-use operating system for home computers. Or an innovative airline based out of London. Or a couple of Ph.D. students who set out to create a company that would quickly rival Bill Gates's Microsoft.

Inspiring a Common Vision with Storytelling

Visionary leaders are more than just forward thinking and full of imagination, and their sense for the unfolding of history is not the only factor driving their successes. Visionary leaders also inspire. They have the ability to move our spirits and awaken our ideals.

Sometimes they communicate this vision with written words or great speeches: Lincoln at Gettysburg and Martin Luther King Jr. at the Washington Mall, for example. When John F. Kennedy uttered the following lines in his inaugural address—"My fellow Americans: ask not what your country can do for you—ask what you can do for your country. My fellow citizens of the world: ask not what America will do for you but what together we can do for the freedom of man"—he inspired others with this call to a common vision.

Leaders also use symbolism to make their goals more compelling. For example, when employees and visitors enter the corporate headquarters of Sherwin-Williams, the Cleveland-based Fortune 500 company that patented ready-to-use paint, the first thing they see is a Wall of Innovation. "We have window boxes in the front lobby," CEO Chris Connor told us.[36] "Each box contains a major innovation in our company's history, along with the name of the person who created it." Near the front door, employees see the first resealable can of paint patented by Henry Sherwin in 1877; then the first latex paint, from the 1940s; then the first roller cover; the first polymer; and so on. It's a striking display of the company's many achievements. "But the last window is empty," Connor says. "Except for a small sign that reads: 'To Be Filled by the Next Great Innovator at Sherwin-Williams.'" Sherwin-Williams stands for past and future innovation and makes clear to every employee that he or she is a participant in that ongoing creed.

Whatever the strategy for delivering the message, it is critical for a leader's vision to touch people's inner aspirations. It must speak to their values and needs, and it must clearly explain the benefits of participating in a common journey. In this sense, communicating the leader's vision becomes a form of storytelling that frames something essential about followers' lives.

Harvard scholar Howard Gardner wrote, "Leaders achieve their effectiveness through the stories they relate. As a rule of thumb, creative artists, scientists and experts in various disciplines lead indirectly, through their works; effective leaders of institutions and nations lead directly, through the stories and acts they address to an audience."[37] Gardner went on to say that the most basic story is about the identity of the group: who they are, why they are special, how they can be distinguished from other groups. It is a narrative that brings people together.

Seen in this light, the source of inspirational power for great leaders becomes clearer. David Gergen served as advisor to four presidents (Nixon, Ford, Reagan, and Clinton), but none impressed him as much as did Ronald Reagan.[38] According to Gergen, it was Reagan's ability to inspire through stories that made the fortieth president so special. "Reagan was weaving a large tapestry for his listening public, one that told them who they were and what they could become. Each of his stories—about Jimmy Doolittle or Davy Crockett or General Custer—was a thread." Together, Gergen says, these stories framed a heroic past, stretching back to the earliest days of the American Republic and forward to Vietnam. Reagan's stories were different—some were uplifting, some amusing, others tragic—but they were all connected. The point was to remind all Americans that they were, and continue to be, part of a brave and important journey. "Surely, he was suggesting, we must have the gumption to stay on that same road in our own generation so our grandchildren will enjoy even more freedom and well-being. . . . Far more than a pleasant diversion, his stories were a form of moral instruction."[39] Reagan inspired because he was able to tap into the larger public consciousness. His words reinforced a fundamental narrative that listeners carried with them—a narrative about their country, its history, its values, and the kind of society they wanted to shape.

In the corporate sector, we have spoken with many leaders whose focus on vision follows a similar pattern. Philip Francis is the executive chairman of PetSmart, America's largest pet supply chain with over eleven hundred retail outlets. At PetSmart, as at a lot of other large organizations, one of the mantras is that diversity is important. Management also likes to think of the company as being in the "family care" business as opposed to the "pet care" business, the idea being that taking care of pets means making for better families. Indeed, the company's Web site states: "Our vision is to provide Total Lifetime Care, to every pet, every parent, all the time." According to Francis, however, just having a policy is not enough. People have to feel it. They have to believe it and internalize it. Otherwise it's not a vision. And at a town hall meeting in Phoenix in October 2009, Francis had an opportunity to demonstrate what he means.[40] "We give out awards at these meetings," he said. "The last recipient was too embarrassed to come, but we honored him anyway. He's from Sudan. He's got a great story. Really, it's a story that represents a lot of what we are trying to build at PetSmart."

The absent honoree, Panek, is one of four thousand Sudanese who escaped to the United States during the Sudanese civil war. Sixty of them settled in Phoenix, where PetSmart's headquarters is located, and several work for the company. "We are the largest employer in Phoenix of the 'Lost Boys of Sudan,'" Francis said.

Initially the company hired Panek as an order taker. He put crates on pallets and loaded them onto trucks. At night, he went to nearby Glendale Community College to get an associate degree, and five years later, with the help of PetSmart's tuition reimbursement program, Panek completed his bachelor's degree. In 2009, he was promoted to supervisor, an important job at PetSmart, and the company decided to honor him at its town hall meeting. Francis stood up and told everyone there about Panek's trip home.

A couple of years earlier, in 2007, PetSmart had given Panek four weeks' leave to return to Sudan. When he arrived there, the people in his village were shocked. They all thought he had died. In fact, after walking thirty miles back to his village, he found his own gravestone. The village had no e-mail or electricity, and no correspondence had taken place since his escape. People just assumed that he had disappeared, like so many others of his age.

"Everyone at the town hall meeting was in tears," Francis told us. The audience was overwhelmed by the thought of how relieved and proud Panek's fellow villagers must have been. Not only was he still alive, and safe, but he had transformed his life. He had also managed to save quite a bit of money, which he used to help transform the lives of the people of his village too.

As Francis ended his words, he reframed the story about Panek into a larger story about PetSmart. His message was that the entire company played a part in getting Panek back home. "Now, does the company value diversity?" Francis asked us rhetorically as he reflected on that town hall meeting. "Here's a story that marries our commitment to diversity and family improvement for all our employees to see. Everyone feels a real connection to our vision." By linking PetSmart's corporate vision with something deeper, a compelling personal story, Francis made it real.

SPOTTING LEADERS WITH VISION

Vision is one of the most difficult attributes to recognize in a leader. Often people confuse it with charisma. They mistake confident speech about big change as being the same as having a vision. It isn't. In fact, a good vision is much more sophisticated than that.

It all starts with imagination and an inquisitive mind. During an interview, we look for a candidate's ability to ask big, unusual questions, to demonstrate the kind of imagination that leads to "what if?" For example, we once interviewed an executive at a computer supply company. He was an engineer who had quickly moved up the ranks. Unlike most other engineers, though, his career path spanned multiple functions, including operations, marketing, and finance. He told us a story about how he convinced the company's chief marketing officer to use an engineering technology that the company had developed to move into a new market. This wouldn't have been a big deal, but for the fact that the new market was in the health care field—and his company had never ventured outside computer supply. Eventually the project was given the green light, and within eighteen months, this new market constituted 20 percent of the company's sales. Were it not for that engineer's imagination and vision, the new project never would have happened.

With this in mind, we probe during the interview process for concrete examples of a time when the candidate was able to imagine a solution to a problem when others on his or her team had reached a dead end. Typically candidates stumble around for a while when we ask this. If they do arrive at an answer, we follow up with an even tougher question, such as, "Tell me about how this solution became obvious to you when others on your team were unable to arrive at a viable solution. What went on in that brain of yours?"

We also look for candidates who are skilled at articulating a theme, whether in their backgrounds, industries, career goals, or more generally in the way they see the world. Visionary leaders are good storytellers who are capable of weaving together interesting connections. They draw inspiration from a wide variety of sources and notice ideas in novels, plays, advertising campaigns, even sports, politics, or cooking, and they tie these ideas together in creative, practical ways. During the assessment process, we focus on the manner in which candidates connect and express their experiences and ambitions. If they use powerful language and demonstrate how their career arc is part of an overall theme, this is indicative of someone who possesses vision. Likewise, if they are adept at articulating how others (colleagues, potential partners, customers) fit into their overall mission, we are more likely to conclude that they will carry a compelling voice with them in a new position.

Visionaries also use history as a resource for inspiring others about future possibilities. For example, when a candidate with vision is asked to talk about some of his most ambitious ideas, he often cites parallel historical challenges as a way of preempting expected skepticism. He might refer to the Wright Brothers, or the *Apollo* mission, or even Moses in order to make his case. After all, humans respond to stories. We are moved by legends, folk heroes, and myths, and we are more likely to get excited about an issue if someone relates it to what's happening on our own streets. By contrast, even the most carefully formatted PowerPoint presentation never attracts a crowd. Nor is mention of a research project or financial investment likely to move a group's collective spirit.

Along these lines, an essential part of good storytelling is the ability to frame a story within the context of the followers' values and needs. Visionary leaders aren't spinning yarns for entertainment purposes. They know that serious commitment attaches itself only to ideas that confer a long-term benefit. Like Bono's references to the attractive human ideal of self-empowerment, leaders with vision know how to get an audience emotionally connected.

The cleverest marketing pitches are simple demonstrations of this. A florist who advertises selling "beauty" rather than flowers is an example of an appeal to the customer's deeper needs. Similarly, Kodak sells "memories," not cameras (and before that, film). We once met a guy who offered classes in business English to executives at foreign companies. When the companies asked him why he was qualified to teach English, he answered, "I'm not just teaching you English. Anybody can teach you English. What I am going to teach you is how to *sell*." While these are very basic examples, the ability to tell a story compellingly and persuasively is indicative of someone who knows how to inspire.

VISION AND INNOVATION

Whenever we are called on to assist an organization in identifying its top talent, one leadership competency seems to pop up again and again: innovative thinking. Especially in a tough economy, this quality is always high on any group's wish list. Innovative ability might also be the single aspect of leadership that organizations tell us is most difficult to find. "Is the next Steve Jobs already working for us? Can you help us figure out who that person is?" they often ask. Innovative thinking is closely related to vision (one cannot be innovative without having vision), but what exactly does it mean, and how do we identify this quality in high-potential leaders?

Good innovators have the rare ability to bring their visions to life. Doing so requires a special combination of many leadership attributes and skills: empathy, courage, emotional intelligence, communication skills, passion, varied experience, and plenty of imagination. The imagination piece is what great innovators derive from vision.

John Maeda from RISD described innovative thinkers as possessing "wandering" minds and being comfortable talking to others about big ideas.[41] But that is not all they do. Our mention of "others" is important because, contrary to popular opinion, top innovators do not work alone. They do not conjure up new products or business models out of thin air. Rather, innovative minds are great recyclers of existing ideas. They are able to recombine available resources—objects, plans, frameworks, technologies—to create something new. And in order to do this, they must be good at interacting with and influencing other people.

As we explained in Chapter Two, empathy is one of the key drivers of successful social relations. It keeps leaders attuned to the shifting needs and temperament of others. Combined with vision, it is also the primary component underlying strong communication skills. Armed with a visionary sense for storytelling, as well as the capacity to understand and share the emotional pulse of other people, leaders are in a position to articulate themselves in a way that resonates. They are persuasive and get much-needed buy-in. They are likely to impress others with their clarity, poignancy, and determination of will—important because innovators must constantly build networks. They rely on experimentation and connecting different people across the organization. Getting others to believe in the value of their work is a big part of what great innovators do. Having the confidence to fight for their projects—a healthy dose of courage—is also necessary for them to succeed.

Finally, the best innovators tend to have a variety of experiences. Like the engineer we mentioned, their professional backgrounds often include exposure to different organizational functions, if not fields. Other times they have varied academic backgrounds, such as course work in business administration and classical studies, or perhaps even an eclectic outside interest or two such as photography and architecture. This history of combining disparate disciplines prepares them well for the work of innovation.

In addition to assessing for these attributes, we pay particular attention during our interviews to the candidate's ability to create win-win situations even when it seems hopeless. We look for a healthy blend of realism and optimism. We also look for candidates who have a track record of getting others to accept change. Are you a visionary leader with the ability to drive innovation?[42] To find out, ask yourself these questions:

- Do you create order out of the highly complex, ambiguous, even chaotic, situations?
- Can you see how an idea or resource in one part of your organization can be applied in a totally different part of the organization?
- Can you handle ambiguity? Even without a road map, are you comfortable embarking on a new journey?
- Do you feel comfortable relying on your own good judgment to make sense out of situations with no clear rules?
- Do you see the world as static and well defined, or dynamic and in constant flux?
- Do you sometimes feel you are a cog in a big, complex, rigid machine? Or do you think you can make a difference and drive change?

- Do you fully understand when you should push forward despite heavy opposition and when it makes sense to adjust course? (This can be a tricky balance. Going down a particular path is usually self-reinforcing).
- Do you understand when your set of past experiences serves as a guide for future challenges? When they don't, do you seek input from others?
- Are you open-minded enough to solicit input from others across the organization, and smart enough to recognize the good ideas while quickly discarding the rest?
- Do you feel a sense of pride when creating new solutions?
- Do you have a deep knowledge in at least one discipline and a curiosity across many others?
- Do you possess the discipline to achieve results within a tight time frame? (Visionary leaders realize that they can create a logjam in the overall system if they meander. As a result, they don't insist on a "perfect" answer and are capable of making trade-offs.)
- Do you sometimes feel like an ethnographer—someone with a keen observational sense (and respect for history)? When asked to describe prior experiences, do you bring to light important observations that others missed?
- Do you ask broad, open-ended questions, unsure where the answer will lead while staying attuned to important details?
- Do you have the ability to help others understand potential benefits of new approaches and solutions?
- Are you always envisioning a better future?
- Are you eager to stretch beyond your natural comfort zone?
- Do you love to tinker and explore? Do you need to devise a perfect plan before moving forward, or can you create prototypes when you are 80 percent there and then see how others respond?
- Do you have the ability and desire to communicate your vision to others in a simple but meaningful way?

Naturally organizations are curious to know if the future Steve Jobs is working for them. And who among us wouldn't want to grow into the next great innovator? Unfortunately, these people are few and far between, and they must possess a large set of specific attributes and skills. Just having imagination alone, strong judgment, good communication skills, or a high degree of empathy, is not enough. Great innovators have all of these, and then some.

This does not mean that innovators are preternaturally gifted. Instead, these leaders work hard at developing their skills and experiences, and they don't let up. Innovative thinking is something that a person can learn and improve.

In fact, in our assessment practice, we have found greater numbers of potential innovators in organizations that both assess rising stars early and focus on their continuous development. Doing so ensures that these people get a diverse range of experiences, access to different products and technologies, solid interaction with influence makers across the organization, practice at taking calculated risks, and experience articulating a theme, or "melody line," that resonates with others. Linking the assessment and leadership development process in a robust way, with careful attention to the qualities explained in this chapter, is a good strategy for fostering more innovative leadership in your company or your career.

In Chapter Eight, we discuss in detail how an organization can achieve this goal and develop better innovators as well as better overall leaders. Before we get there, however, it is important to explain the remaining essential attributes of effective leadership, including good judgment, which is the subject of the next chapter.

5

Judgment

Siemens, the German engineering giant, is one of the oldest, largest, and most prestigious companies in the world. With more than 400,000 employees in 190 countries and revenues in excess of $100 billion per year, the breadth and depth of its operations are impressive by any standard.[1] A global leader in most of its businesses, Siemens makes a wide range of industrial, infrastructure, and consumer products: turbines, energy grids, subway trams, kitchen appliances. Many experts have referred to it as the European counterpart to U.S. powerhouse General Electric.

But in 2007, Siemens was not basking in praise. On the contrary, a series of scandals and uncertain growth metrics had left insiders reeling. Moreover, the international business community wondered if the Munich-based conglomerate had lost its competitive edge. First to emerge were revelations that Siemens had paid hundreds of millions of dollars in illegal bribes and kickbacks to foreign officials. In order to win company contracts, employees and middlemen carried suitcases full of cash to places such as Argentina, Libya, Venezuela, and Bangladesh.[2] Altogether, nine board members were implicated in the corruption, and the company's two most senior officers resigned amid concerns that Siemens had institution-alized this kind of behavior.

The company's operational condition was also a source of con-cern. Although cost-cutting and restructuring efforts had yielded revenue growth that compared favorably with GE, particularly in high-growth markets such as India, profit margins were not as good. GE's profit margins were a full three times higher than Siemens—3.5 percent compared with 12.6 percent.[3] Worse, there was concern that the company's widespread bribery practices masked an underlying inability to compete fairly in several business lines. With fallout from the scandals imminent, including nearly $2 billion in penalty fees, no one knew exactly what kind of company Siemens would become.

Amid this climate of uncertainty and despair, the company turned to the outside for the first time in its 160-year history in order to find a new CEO: Peter Löscher. Löscher came to Siemens with global experience, having worked in Europe, Asia, and the United States. His two prior posts were at General Electric (Siemens's big-gest competitor) and Merck. In the former, he was president and CEO of GE Healthcare and a member of the company's Corporate Executive Board, and at Merck he served as president of a global division.

With this strong, tactical background, Löscher had many ideas for how to transform the company and reestablish its once-stellar reputation. "It was a big challenge," he told us, "but also a great opportunity. As an outsider, I had the chance to do some dramatic things, to shake up the company and get us back on track."[4]

Needing to rehabilitate the company's image, he focused on creating a new culture of transparency. He also emphasized a shift in company resources to emerging markets, green technology, and the way that the leadership team in Germany interacted with local markets. In the past, Siemens had been a relatively insular com-pany. Global businesses units, regardless of their territory, were based solely in Germany, and the CEO of a major market such as China would have been a German sent into China from the outside. Löscher admitted, "Siemens was too German, too white, and too male." This homogeneous culture bred inefficiency and insular thinking, which led to some of the problems associated with the compliance scandal.

In order to change all that, Löscher ordered a large restructuring. He consolidated the business from ten operating groups into three sectors and the regional structure into 17 geographical clusters. He wanted regions to become more entrepreneurial and responsive to local customization needs. He also changed profit and loss responsibility and the way leadership decisions were made. Before, the CEO and chief financial officer of every business division and subdivision had to agree in order for a decision to move forward. It was called the "four eyes principle." Löscher did away with that. "People didn't know how to respond to the change at first, but when they asked, I told them 'the four eyes principle is dead,'" he said. He believed it led to lack of accountability, delay, and an inefficient use of valuable human resources. Finally, he retooled the company's strategy to focus on the four twenty-first-century megatrends that he predicted would provide Siemens with an opportunity for significant growth: shifting demographics, urbanization, globalization, and climate change. This last category, in particular, is something that Löscher has emphasized. "Siemens will be the pioneer in green infrastructure," he said.

It all looked good on paper, but Löscher saw that one critical piece was still missing: the right people. How would Siemens become more transparent, more entrepreneurial, and less insular with the same people in place? How was the company going to change the relationship between local markets and global leadership—not just on paper but in practice? And how could he ensure that Siemens had the right personnel to meet the unpredictable strategic challenges that would inevitably surface?

The answer, he decided, didn't involve baby steps. Rather, he quickly and decisively ordered a massive change in the company's top-level leadership. "I changed 90 percent of the managing board," he told us, "70 percent of the senior leadership below that, and 50 percent on the level below that. It was probably the biggest leadership transformation in the shortest period of time among any multinational that is globally operated."

As part of this process, Löscher and his team identified the company's top positions and performed five hundred leadership assessments at the senior management level. This initiative included both internal and external candidates, who were evaluated across seven leadership dimensions and benchmarked against best-in-class executives from around the world. "As you can imagine, for the older leaders it was probably perceived as a threat. All of a sudden after thirty years of experience with the company, they think, 'I have to go through an assessment.' For the younger people, it was perceived as an incredible opportunity." This new leadership framework constituted a critical dimension of Löscher's strategy for Siemens. In order to make the company's repositioning work, he needed to know what kind of talent he had and where to place these people so they could effectively lead.

Moving forward, Siemens extended its assessment and placement framework across the organization so that thousands of its top leaders could be evaluated side-by-side. The company also revamped its annual management review process. Review meetings took place once a year at different locations over about ten to fourteen days. In attendance were Löscher and Siemens's head of executive development, Nicolas von Rosty, as well as the managing board.

In the review process, the entire group looked at any new strategic or organizational challenges that Siemens was facing, or was likely to face, in the coming year. They also determined the management implications of these challenges. For example, if a new market in India showed explosive growth, the company might decide to spin it off into an entirely new business unit. This had managerial implications because senior management had to find the right person to lead it. Using Siemens's leadership database (and up-to-date performance management system), senior management could compare leaders throughout the organization and get accurate feedback on the availability of "ready-now" talent.

"For that particular example, we'd need someone with especially strong change management skills in order to effectively create a new spin-off entity," von Rosty told us during a visit to the company's headquarters in Munich.[5] "We can look at who has that profile, across the organization, and find the right person for the job. That never would have been possible before. We'd probably just have sent someone from Germany down there to try and lead it." Similarly, during the management review process, the board looked at succession plans for every key position in the organization. This might have been critical if the CEO of a division was due to retire, for example, or if her number two was likely to get sent to another place in the company. Von Rosty could see at a glance the entire talent landscape and chessboard, and moving one leader across the organization had a ripple effect on several other positions.

The management review sessions also gave rising stars in the organization a chance to interact with the board. "We invite up to about ten people max, from each division," explained von Rosty. "These are people who have been plucked from the masses, but are not yet on any formal radar screen for senior leadership." Those selected were asked to give a fifteen-minute presentation to the board, followed by fifteen minutes of direct question-and-answer. After the presentations, they all met for dinner where board members could get to know rising stars on a more personal level.

"The rising stars eat at rotating tables, with two Siemens executives at each table," von Rosty explained. "After each course, the executives change places and sit with other high potentials. These are really fun, informative dinners. Last time we were in China and

Mexico. And the food is great. But with all the dishes, it's easy to get fat." Aside from the food and fun, the presentations and dinners also gave rising stars valuable exposure to senior leadership. Similarly, Löscher and the board were able to keep abreast of circumstances developing out in the field.

When we talked with Löscher and von Rosty in November 2010, the new leadership framework had been in place for only three years, but already several indicators of success were apparent. "In the beginning, only about half of the board came to the management review process," said von Rosty. "Now they all come. They say it's a highlight of their year." Löscher confirmed this sense of buy-in: "The whole board is owning it. It is one of *the* core processes of the company."[6]

Getting senior leadership to embrace this change, Löscher said, was a critical part of turning Siemens into a company with a more transparent culture. Everyone was benchmarked along the same dimensions, the system was fair, and there was awareness across the organization of the strengths and weaknesses that might exist in any given place.

Along the same lines, the management review process was also a catalyst for making advances in the emerging market countries and green technology segment that Löscher had pinpointed in his vision. For example, in 2010 a Chinese leader was selected as CEO of Siemens China for the first time ever. Mei-Wei Cheng assumed full responsibility for all activities in mainland China, Hong Kong, Taiwan, Korea, and Mongolia. Local to the market he was serving, Cheng was well positioned to forge regional partnerships and realize synergies that were central to the company's growing business in that market. In the past, Löscher said, this individual's strong leadership skills would not have been noticed from Germany. By becoming less insular at the leadership level, the company has been better able to engage in the cross-fertilization efforts necessary to leverage its global expertise with the changing dynamics of newer markets.

Löscher's decision making helped turn the company around. Within three years, the scandals were behind Siemens, and financial results showed that the company was in a decidedly better position than key competitors. For example, it increased its 2010 dividend by 70 percent over the prior three years and was extremely bullish about future growth, particularly in emerging markets. Indeed, emerging markets counted for 30 percent of revenues compared to just 19 percent five years earlier.[7] "Siemens's growth spurt has even placed it ahead of its archrival, General Electric," wrote the *Economist*. "In areas of more or less direct overlap . . . Siemens's sales are 50% greater than GE's."[8] By wisely integrating a new leadership assessment, placement, and succession planning framework with the company's strategy, Löscher gave a boost to Siemens's overall competitive position.

THE IMPORTANCE OF JUDGMENT

Good judgment is essential for effective leadership. Whether in the executive suite, on the battlefield, or even on the set of a Hollywood movie, an ability to make sound decisions is something that every great leader needs.

In the previous chapter, we explored the importance of vision. Vision gives followers an overall purpose—a mission; it inspires them with a compelling image of the future. That's the end point. Good judgment, by contrast, is what everyone relies on to get there. Judgment enables a leader to steer the group from point A to point B.

The quality of a leader's judgment doesn't fit neatly into a headline the way integrity might. Moments of bad judgment do not necessarily scream out "villain" or "scandal." Nor does good judgment lend itself to the fiery adjectives that we often reserve for individuals who possess great passion. Judgment is more nuanced, more process oriented, more ongoing. Many years can pass before the effects of a leader's judgment are made clear.

This is not to suggest that judgment is any less important than the other attributes. On the contrary, although sometimes the results are less immediate, the impact of a leader's judgment is usually quite profound. It can equal the difference between war and peace, prosperity and decline, or corporate success and failure, especially when the stakes are high. At these moments, the impact of a good or bad decision is much clearer. During a time of crisis, judgment has a way of eclipsing all other leadership traits.

WHAT IS GOOD JUDGMENT?

Good judgment essentially means good decision making. This sounds simple enough, but the origins of how and why people make the decisions they do are actually quite complex.

It is tempting to believe that most choices we make are the product of rational thinking. In reality, emotion, bias, social preference, trust, stress, and instinct all have a way of creeping in. For example, many people vote for a political candidate based on "gut" or because they consider the candidate "likable." Similarly, all of us have made impulse purchases at one time or another. Remember that new watch or pair of shoes that you just had to have? What about those trendy sunglasses? Or consider what we eat. Given that the average waist size in much of the developed world has increased significantly during the past thirty years while quick-fix diet books remain perennial best-sellers, it is obvious that our dietary choices do not conform to any rational path.

Another important determinant of judgment is experience. How important is experience for making good decisions? Some people believe it is everything. Georges Clemenceau famously remarked, "All that I know I learned after thirty." Others believe good judgment can emerge at a relatively young age. Where you draw the line in this argument probably depends on what kind of activity you have in mind. For example, most people can drive a car reasonably well after only a modest amount of practice. They can comfortably judge the speed at which to merge onto an interstate highway after maybe a dozen tries. But true wisdom, the kind of measured decision making that is impervious to emotion and ego, probably takes closer to a full lifetime to obtain.

When it comes to effective leadership judgment, the balance lies somewhere in between. Leaders require a certain amount of experience in order to succeed. They need to make mistakes and learn from them. They need to reflect and grow. A steep learning curve exists in the early years of a leader's career. At some point, however, the learning curve flattens out, and leaders have enough experience to make tough decisions. This is not to say that experience ceases to matter or that judgment doesn't continue to improve. On the contrary, the best leaders always want to find ways to learn more. The point is that once a person reaches a certain threshold, his lack of experience no longer constitutes a disqualifying factor.

The founding fathers recognized this dynamic and placed a minimum age requirement in the Constitution for holders of public office. In order to be a member of the U.S. Senate, for example, a person must be thirty years old. The presidency, a much more challenging leadership position, has a minimum age requirement of thirty-five years (and life expectancy was much lower in 1787).[9] Similarly, most CEOs and other senior corporate leaders do not hit their stride until they are well into their forties or fifties. Before then, they lack the experience and wisdom required to make complex executive decisions.

Eric Wiseman, CEO of VF Corporation, explained, "When I see someone that I think is a high-potential leader, I want to make sure he or she gets the exposure needed to keep moving ahead." VF Corporation is a global apparel company, with brands such as Wrangler, Lee, North Face, Eastpak, Reef, Nautica, and Vans. Leading a business with so many disparate brands requires knowing how all of the pieces fit together, including when it is appropriate to draw headquarters into centralized decision making and when action is better delegated to the field.

When we spoke with Wiseman, he was preparing to offer to move a rising star to Shanghai. "This is someone who I think can be a business unit president and beyond," Wiseman explained. "We're actually creating a new position to give this guy some experience. I don't know if he'll take it. He has a family, and having been an ex-pat myself, I know that's tough. But he's relatively young, and I think having him go to China for three or four years would be a transformational professional opportunity."[10]

An understanding of how the brain works provides additional clues about why experience matters. Clinical neurologist Elkhonon Goldberg, author of *The New Executive Brain: Frontal Lobes in a Complex World*, uses an analogy of a computer search engine to describe how the brain handles novel situations. Goldberg's search engine, the region occupying the frontal lobes, acts as a central coordinating mechanism. It is responsible for retrieving stored information (past experiences) as well as analyzing and making sense of new information. When encountering a problem, the brain automatically checks its inventory of past lessons learned. At the same time, it processes and stores new data in the form of knowledge. Over time, this database grows, and the brain is able to process increasingly complex data.

Goldberg's analogy is strikingly similar to the one that Sprint CEO Dan Hesse used when he told us how he evaluates leadership readiness. For Hesse, it is imperative that a candidate have sufficient experience and understand the business. "That's key," Hesse said. "A lot of times people have the brain power, have a good processor, but just don't have much of a database. You need to have lots of live experience, or you just don't know how a decision will impact the business."[11]

In other words, no matter how smart a person might be (or how fast her processor), there is no substitute for a minimum amount of experience.

In truth, all this talk about processors and experience is a bit of an esoteric mess. (Psychologists and economists have been arguing for years about everything that goes into making even a straightforward decision.) But the good news is that the why or how of good judgment doesn't really matter. More important is the what of judgment. What do effective leaders demonstrate that shows they have good judgment? What problem-solving skills do they possess? And what do you look for to determine if an aspiring leader meets the test?

The answer comes down to the following three abilities that effective leaders share:

1. Zeroing in on what's important
2. Seeing the whole chessboard
3. Taking decisive action

These three abilities together form the essence of good leadership judgment.

Zeroing In on What's Important

On his blackboard at Princeton, Albert Einstein would write, "Not everything that counts can be counted, and not everything that can be counted counts."[12] Leaders are constantly bombarded with information in the digital age. A staggering amount of data— research reports, intelligence briefings, cost-benefit studies, inter-office memoranda—is exchanging hands, and leaders must process more than ever before.

Similarly, countless human voices are clamoring for attention: employees, customers, the media, analysts, unions, charities, each of them claiming to possess a matter of utmost concern. Many senior executives receive more than two hundred e-mails every day. Structural changes are also occurring at unprecedented speed. Technological advances and globalization mean new markets, new competitors, new methods of communication and distribution. Trying to keep track of it all can be dizzying.

Leaders need to know how to cut through this morass. They must be able to zero in on what's important, and this requires an ability to frame the central issue of a situation. It means being able to put their fingers on the context in which organizational challenges are taking place. Is this a crisis situation? In what cycle is the market? Are we faced with a human resource problem? Is it a problem with execution? Do we have enough production capacity? Is it a matter of public relations? Does it require my attention, or should it be delegated? A good leader can quickly identify the most salient facts.

Leaders know when and how to ask the right questions. Frequently the kind of information they need is exactly the kind that no one else has sought before. Without an ability to make intelligent queries, the leader will not be equipped to accurately diagnose the situation.

A great example comes from Pacific Gas & Electric (PG&E). When many of us think of a 150-year-old California utility, we probably visualize leisurely paced servicemen and humming gray meters attached to the backs of garages. But the old energy paradigm of heavy regulation and slow technological change is quickly becoming obsolete. The sector's new focus is on innovation, with impressive breakthroughs in hydro, nuclear, bio, and natural gas. "We want leaders who can evolve from managing stability and predictability to those who can boldly navigate through highly unchartered terrain," PG&E CEO Peter Darbee told us.[13] To do so requires asking the right questions in order to uncover hidden opportunities, and few companies do it as well as PG&E.

In 2010, *Fast Company* ranked PG&E as one of the top ten most innovative companies in the United States for precisely this reason.[14] "Making good decisions in this kind of environment," Darbee said, "requires our leaders to quickly and accurately cut through the clutter, to focus on what really matters, and to come up with simple but effective solutions."

There is an old joke in academia about a man who goes out searching under a lamppost late at night. A stranger comes upon him and asks, "What are you doing down there on your hands and knees?" The first man answers, "I lost my watch in the park, and I'm looking for it." The stranger replies, "Well, if you've lost your watch in the park, why are you looking for it here?" The first man answers, "Because this is where the light is."

Good leaders understand that sometimes you have to reevaluate the context in which challenges are addressed. In other words, it is impossible to move forward without an ability to identify and understand the nature of the fundamental problem at hand.

In the case of Siemens, Löscher clearly understood that his situation required much more than a slight adjustment in strategy. When he assumed the role of CEO in 2007, the company was reeling from ethics scandals, and management was shaken. Many structural problems on the inside, including the company's insularity and a lack of synergy between global leadership and regional markets, needed fixing. Because these were massive demands, a piecemeal approach wouldn't work. "The context of my coming in to Siemens provided a great opportunity," Löscher said. "It was a crisis, but a crisis we could change. And being an outsider was absolutely critical. I had the opportunity to reposition the company in a way that wouldn't have been possible in a different environment." Löscher's ability to frame the overall situation was an important first step in getting Siemens moving in the right direction.

Another leader who demonstrated a keen sense of judgment was Nicholas Chabraja, who served as CEO of General Dynamics Corporation (GD) from 1997 to 2009. Based in Falls Church, Virginia, GD was the fifth largest defense contractor in the world as of 2010.[15] A supplier of a variety of military goods and services, including M-1 Abrams tanks and other armored vehicles, navy ships, and high-tech information systems, the company also manufactures Gulfstream business jets and provides business aviation services. GD competes against Lockheed Martin, Northrop Grumman, Boeing, and Raytheon.

During Chabraja's tenure as CEO, GD enjoyed a period of dramatic growth and significantly outperformed most of its competitors. When Chabraja took office, its annual revenues were approximately $4 billion. When he stepped down twelve years later, annual revenues had grown to more than $32 billion.[16] As CEO, Chabraja was known for consistently hitting or exceeding analysts' numbers. In fact, when he retired, one investment analyst referred to him as the "Jack Welch" of defense contractors for his long record of unusually strong performance.[17]

When we asked Chabraja to explain how he steered the company so successfully, one of the first factors he pointed to was the importance of understanding the context. "You need to be able to understand your market, and its movement," he told us.[18] "Where is it precisely in cyclical terms? Are you in an upmarket, steady market, market that's degrading modestly, or one that's in a severe cyclical decline or maybe even structural change?" Understanding the context, he also said, means recognizing the condition of the company's balance sheet in relation to that of its competitors, as well as the company's relative weaknesses and strengths. It means having a grip on the regulatory environment and other external factors that may or may not be about to change. If a CEO isn't able to grasp that, Chabraja said, "he's not going to be an effective leader."

For Chabraja and others in the defense industry, the end of the Cold War posed a unique set of circumstances. In the early 1990s, a decline in defense spending led many companies to believe that the industry was experiencing a severe structural change. As a result, many players exited the market or scurried to make deals. But Chabraja felt that much of the consolidation that took place was premature. "I believed starting in 1994 or 1995 that we were in a market that had not undergone structural change," Chabraja told us. "I believed that defense spending was going to turn around because I watched the first Clinton administration being embarrassed by deployment that didn't quite work out. So President Clinton, true to my belief, began to spend money on defense again during the rest of his administration." By that time, Chabraja said, other companies had been so busy consolidating that they put themselves in a poor balance sheet position with not much cash on hand. GD, because it had accurately perceived the market and stayed patient, was sitting with—as Chabraja stated—"a pile of money."

Based on this understanding of the business and political context, Chabraja and the rest of his executive team were then able to make several strategic acquisitions just as defense spending started to rise. For example, GD purchased Gulfspace Aerostream, General Motors's defense business, and Motorola's integrated information systems, among many others. These acquisitions provided GD with a healthy profit stream and shareholder returns during a period when overall growth in the industry was relatively modest. Without his recognition of fundamental market trends, Chabraja would not have been able to make this happen.

Contextual thinking is critical across all domains. Leaders at top international law firms, for example, have begun to rethink whether traditional legal training equips them with the skills that they need to manage a global practice. They recognize that the profession is moving from one that was traditionally localized and static toward a new model that is borderless and constantly changing. Indeed, many of the largest firms have offices around the world; sophisticated internal marketing, finance, technology, and human resource functions; and multinational clients who expect increasingly sophisticated advice. For them, the practice of law truly is a dynamic, complex, international business.

Leading in this environment requires people who possess a variety of important skills. In 2010 we spoke in London with the managing partners of the city's top ten law firms to see what they were doing to meet this challenge. At Freshfields Bruckhaus Deringer LLP, senior management had created a leadership summit to focus on developing nontechnical skills such as team building and relationships, as well as self-awareness. At Simmons & Simmons, a new internally run leadership development program had become part of required training for all incoming associates. The firm had also performed follow-up coaching for over 70 percent of its lawyers.

The idea behind these ongoing initiatives is that lawyers need to understand both the legal side of problems as well as the client's basic business needs if they are going to lead the firm forward. "It's like pouring fuel in the bottom of the rocket," said Nigel Spencer, head of learning and development at Simmons & Simmons LLP. "By implementing an internal 'MBA' program and also using coaching as a core tool, we are accelerating lawyers' awareness of commercial and leadership issues at all levels."[19]

For him and others at the firm, getting a better understanding of the context in which clients make business decisions has enabled lawyers to offer better service. It has also advanced internal changes and permitted Simmons & Simmons to uncover new opportunities, such as new capital financing work in Qatar and the use of online services and collaborative technologies to strengthen client relationships. "Management language around here has changed. The whole attitude has changed," Spencer told us. Without this ability to recognize shifting market dynamics, law firm leaders will not keep pace with their competitors. They will not be able to make the critical decisions necessary to stay ahead in a global game.

Seeing the Whole Chessboard

Leadership judgment is not confined to a single, discrete moment or event. Instead it involves a continuous flow. A decision to grow the business isn't really a decision at all. The more pertinent question is how to get it done. Should we expand by acquiring another company? If so, which one? Will it be a friendly takeover? Are there any major hurdles? What steps are needed to carry it through? Or should we take an entirely different tack and pursue an internal growth strategy? Each of these decision points will affect the rest.

As a result, the ability to think strategically is a critical part of good judgment. We call this "seeing the whole chessboard." In other words, a leader must be able to anticipate, three or four or five steps in advance, the possible consequences of each decision he or she makes. This includes how to adjust course if things do not turn out well and seeing how all of the pieces fit together.

At Siemens, Löscher clearly recognized the direct link between getting the right people in place and executing a new repositioning strategy. Without the former, the latter could not have happened. Trying to rebound from Siemens's bribery scandal and a history of insular leadership required, from Löscher's perspective, an inflow of new people at the top. It also required a better picture of the strengths and weaknesses of these people in order to place them where they could effectively lead.

This was a big chessboard to oversee at Siemens, making it all the more an important part of the change process. Löscher's decision to implement an overall talent management system was a shrewd move because it permitted him to see and monitor data. He could seamlessly shift people and respond to vacancies on an ongoing basis. Finally, benchmarking all of the company's top leaders, and creating a system in which the board could respond to unanticipated organizational needs, helped to advance his vision. Löscher knew that in order to execute his plan, every one of these steps had to be hit.

Perhaps not surprisingly, the same leadership attributes that Löscher used to great effect at Siemens are found in the entertainment business. In particular, the job of a Hollywood director requires a similar ability to think strategically, although this fact is not always obvious to outsiders. Indeed, when many people think of a director, the first word that comes to mind is *vision*. They think of people like James Cameron, Christopher Nolan, or Peter Jackson, and the brand of original imagery and imaginative storytelling that these three talented directors create.

Vision is, without a doubt, an important element of a successful film. But every bit as important is judgment. After all, what use is great vision without an ability to translate that vision to the big screen? The truth is, most of what makes a film director's job difficult is decision making. Directors must deal with a barrage of tough choices throughout the filmmaking process, from initial casting all the way to the final editing.

In order to learn more about leading on a Hollywood set, we met with Ruben Fleischer, director of the 2009 hit *Zombieland*, staring Jesse Eisenberg and Woody Harrelson.[20] *Zombieland*, a bit of an underground favorite, was an unqualified success. Although its budget was a relatively low $25 million, it earned more than $100 million at the box office, and several critics awarded the film high praise. *Rolling Stone*'s Peter Travers called it a "scary-fun-house blast."[21]

More interesting to us is the fact that *Zombieland* was Fleischer's first movie. Despite a long record of impressive experience directing videos and television commercials, he had no prior feature film credits to his name. As a result, he couldn't rely on an established network of studio buddies, inflated budgets, or superstar cachet to make the project a success. Instead, he had to direct the movie the old-fashioned way, by rolling up his sleeves.

This meant making lots of tough decisions himself. Fleischer faced the usual hurdles: budget and timing constraints, getting the right personnel in line, location concerns, and other logistics. Once shooting began, the problems started popping up every day. "Unless I stepped in to make key decisions, anything that could have gone wrong did," Fleischer told us.

He faced his biggest crisis when a coveted actor backed out of a key cameo role at the last minute. At that point, he had to consider every option. Perhaps the scene could be scrapped, or a lesser-known actor could take the role. Alternatively, perhaps the whole script could be reworked. Maybe they should stop shooting in order to give the issue full attention. What would the studio say? How might that affect the budget?

The more Fleischer considered it, the more he knew that a big cameo role had to stay because it was an integral part of the script. Moreover, for many reviewers, this extra hook would constitute the kind of payoff moment necessary to garner critical success.

Fleischer made phone calls to contacts and friends to see if he could find a replacement. But who? Each potential replacement had to be considered in a bigger context. Each would change the complexion of the film, and Fleischer had to find the right fit.

In the end, he took a risk and approached Bill Murray. The famously eccentric star agreed to do the cameo, although Murray's willingness to actually show up on set was a matter of concern right up until the day of shooting. Luckily, he did show up, and his scene became an audience favorite. (Roger Ebert called Murray's cameo "the single biggest laugh I've heard this year.") Clearly Fleischer had found the right man.

Another example of good strategic decision making is illustrated by the approach to innovation taken at SunGard, a Fortune 500 company located outside Philadelphia. SunGard provides software and IT services to a variety of customers in the education, financial services, and nonprofit sectors.

In terms of driving innovation, CEO Cris Conde told us that SunGard relies on a two-pronged strategy: organic growth coupled with targeted acquisitions.[22] When we spoke with Conde, the company had made over 170 acquisitions in recent years, and within its ranks were over ten thousand programmers. With these numbers, the key to sustaining organic innovation lay in knowing how to find value-added opportunities within the organization without getting overwhelmed by the mass of people and data. As Conde told us, "My role for the last few years has been to determine what it is that's going to make innovation something we can count on. We wouldn't want a situation in which we had to hope for a string of random hits, like top 40 hits, that had no connection to each other. Then we wouldn't have any differentiation with competitors that are perhaps smaller and more nimble, and we wouldn't be using our size advantage."

Moreover, with ten thousand programmers at SunGard, it was likely that several of them were working on the same thing. But how could management keep track of it all? How would people know when there were important synergies to be gained?

To answer this challenge, SunGard started using technologies that had helped foster collaboration in the open source movement. "We were fascinated by the open source movement technology," Conde said. "Here are people who have never met, people who work in different companies and don't have the same boss, who choose to work together and improve on each other's work. . . . So there's an example of extreme collaboration without any management intervention."

The key, Conde said, was making it fun while tapping into a natural desire for peer recognition. Using this approach, SunGard constructed a vast peer-sharing network that enabled programmers to improve on each other's work and recombine components that others had built. They commented on posted work and tried to figure out ways to collaborate and gain more widespread attention. The good ideas got funneled up; others stayed unnoticed. From a product development standpoint, the result was incredible. "It's not just faster and cheaper to build, it's also better for clients because they end up with five products instead of one," Conde enthused.

From a senior management perspective, this system freed time for leaders to focus on key acquisitions, marketing launches, or big strategic ideas. Less time was wasted trying to monitor activity or start product development initiatives from scratch. In the traditional model, a product manager would have come up with an idea for a new product and then would have told programmers to go out and assemble it. Using SunGard's approach, by the time a product manager got involved, 90 percent of the code was already written. Multiple components were recycled based on the efforts of people who had never met face to face. By adroitly thinking two and three steps ahead and putting together the pieces, Conde and his executive team created a culture of rapid innovation.

Taking Decisive Action

The first two components of judgment—zeroing in on what's important and seeing the chessboard—are cognitive activities. This third element, taking decisive action, is emotional. It requires putting one's credibility and reputation on the line. If something goes wrong, leaders have little safety net other than their own confidence and courage on which to rely. For many people, this pressure is too much. They would rather pass the responsibility on to someone else. Others are paralyzed when faced with having to make a tough choice, and nothing happens.

"In almost every instance, a wrong decision is better than no decision at all," says Chip Bergh, group president of Global Male Grooming, Beauty and Grooming at Procter & Gamble.[23] Among other responsibilities, Bergh oversees the Gillette and Old Spice brands at P&G. "The reason I say in most instances it's better to make a wrong decision than no decision—no decision paralyzes an organization. Especially if people are waiting for a decision from you. Everyone goes into paralysis, trying to generate more data to try to get to a decision. Unless the risk is really, really high, even if you make a mistake, you're going to learn from it and with that knowledge you're going to be able to move forward. We can paralyze an organization for six to twelve months waiting for more data, and in that amount of time, you could have been out in the market learning, or at least starting to learn," Bergh told us.

A Polish children's story tells of a hungry horse deliberating between eating oats or hay for dinner. The horse has plenty of both, but as he weighs his options, he cannot decide. Oats are delicious, but he might regret not eating the hay. On the other hand, he might feel a pang of disappointment if he chooses the hay. In the end, the horse cannot make up his mind and dies of starvation.

The moral of that story for leaders is that indecision can be fatal. If a competitor is investing in new products and technology, your company better be investing as well if you hope to survive. If an enemy force is preparing to attack, the status quo likely won't be enough to save you. If your country is running up record deficits year after year, pretending that the problem doesn't exist won't make it go away. Good leaders know this, and they do not waffle or fall into the trap of endless delay. They understand that even without perfect information, it is imperative to act.

This point applies even when economic times are tough. In fact, during these periods, the temptation to do nothing can be particularly fierce. But good leaders know that sometimes opportunity appears precisely because others are incapable or wary of taking bold action.

This is the situation that Western & Southern Financial Group CEO John Barrett faced in 2008. When the global banking crisis engulfed legendary firms like Lehman Brothers and Bear Stearns, most surviving financial institutions predictably buckled down. Budgets were slashed, panic set in, and a willingness to take risk all but disappeared.

Although Western & Southern, a Fortune 500 financial services and insurance conglomerate based in Cincinnati, Ohio, weathered the storm much better than most others, senior management still remained mindful of the potential for difficult times ahead.[24] Indeed, even after President Obama signed a bailout package into law in early 2009, the possibility for industry-wide collapse remained very real. Moreover, as the crisis unfolded, most experts agreed that the world was entering the worst economic cycle since the Great Depression. Credit froze, asset values plummeted, and consumer spending came to a standstill. No one at Western & Southern, or anywhere else, was quite sure how deep or how far the damage might spread.

Even before this grim economic outlook, Western & Southern carried a conservative business philosophy. The company wasn't known for taking significant uncalculated risks. This cautious approach helped to protect it when declining asset values struck a severe blow to less prudent, firms. "It is safe to say that we typically carry about twice the capital the average large life insurer would, and that really helps when the value of your capital is evaporating fast," Barrett said.[25] With this tradition and the looming economic crisis, Western & Southern wasn't exactly eager to make any sudden, unanticipated moves in 2008.

It was against this backdrop that Jill McGruder, CEO of IFS Financial Services, a large Western & Southern subsidiary that includes the Touchstone mutual fund family, marched into Barrett's office with a bold idea: rapidly expand the fund division's product offering through start-ups and strategic partnerships with top-notch firms that would not have considered partnering before the crisis. For a long time, the company's plan had been to provide its customers with more choices. This was part of Western & Southern's long-term vision. But McGruder saw an immediate opportunity, and she argued that everything had to be accelerated. With the asset levels and investment performance of competitor fund groups decimated, Western & Southern could jump in and use its capital to start new funds managed by the best investment management firms available (many of which were eager for new revenue in light of the crisis). "She [McGruder] made her case," Barrett told us. "And it made sense. So we did it."[26]

McGruder's team introduced ten new Touchstone fund in October 2009, long before many other financial services firms began to emerge from the 2008 Great Recession. She correctly anticipated that these funds would allow clients to meet their own complex, evolving investment strategies. Internally, McGruder leveraged the existing IFC sales force to distribute the new products, which boosted overall efficiency and provided a net increase in return on invested capital. Barrett told us that "he couldn't have been more pleased in the outcome" and then further confided, "and so was our board of directors."

In retrospect, all of this might sound obvious, but at the time there were compelling reasons for Barrett to have responded differently. Postponing any additional investment would have been the safer course, and few people would have argued with that decision. Of course, if Barrett had waited until the markets rebounded, the window of opportunity for Western & Southern to beat out its peers might have closed as prices climbed. Taking advantage of the company's healthy balance sheet while competitors were suffering was a smart gamble.

"It's important to take calculated risks and act with conviction, even in really tough economic times," Barrett said. "But it always must be balanced with the right risk-control procedures." In this case, his shrewd decision making met that test.

An important aspect of being able to pull the trigger and make judgment calls is the ability to believe in one's team. Some leaders waver or express doubt when their people's talents are most needed, and that can have a demoralizing effect. But good leaders like Barrett know that when they offer responsibility to key people, this confidence extends to good times and bad.

Altogether, this willingness to make tough decisions is a key aspect of leadership judgment and one of the reasons why that has enjoyed so much success at Western & Southern. During his seventeen-year tenure as CEO through 2010, the company continued on a path of strategic diversification and profit growth. Not a single person was laid off during the 2008–2009 recession, and the company's life insurance division had an AA+ rating from Standard and Poor's for the fifth consecutive year (as of 2010 only seven other insurers worldwide held a AA+ rating or better with S&P).[27]

• • • • • • • • •

As CEO of United Parcel Service (UPS), the world's top package delivery company, Scott Davis is no stranger to thorny budget and human resource issues. As a matter of fact, how to consistently deliver strong financial results and simultaneously maintain a loyal, hard-working employee culture is a challenge to which he devotes much of his time.

When we talked with Davis, he had just implemented a particularly difficult decision.[28] He had been troubled by the management of a union-run pension plan for forty-five thousand Teamster employees at UPS and thought the plan was putting employee retirement funds at risk. With that many workers, the amount in question was not a small sum, and Davis wasn't sure exactly how to calibrate the risk. He thought the plan *might* turn out all right. Even if it didn't, Davis felt that the employees wouldn't be negatively affected for at least twenty years. If and when any shortfall occurred, it would be long after Davis's tenure had ended.

Thus, he had a decision to make: buy the employees out of the union-run fund and put them into an internally managed portfolio, at a cost of $6 billion ($4 billion of it borrowed), or do nothing. Incurring the debt would fully protect employees' accounts, but the company's short-term financial results would suffer.

Davis chose to act. "This was a huge hit that I had to explain to Wall Street," he told us. "Our credit rating got flagged, too, when the recession came." Davis called the decision "difficult," but he "felt that sustaining our long-term culture was more important than avoiding the short-term pain."

The buyout wasn't his only option. Davis might have waited. Twenty years can seem like a long time, after all. For many leaders, shelving the issue, sending it off for committee review, or simply letting the next CEO deal with it would all have been tempting choices. But Davis knew that danger lay in delay. Postponing the decision might have made it a more difficult one at a later date, especially if UPS were in less robust financial condition. Waiting would have further occupied Davis and his executive team, and perhaps kept their attention distracted from other pressing matters. Finally, Davis knew in his gut that taking care of the pension funds was the right thing to do.

In the next chapter, we discuss the importance of courage for effective leadership. Courage and judgment go hand in hand. Decision making isn't just about analyzing the facts. It is not limited to strategic thinking. It also means being able to make the tough calls, to put the fate of yourself and others on the line, just as Davis did.

ASSESSING JUDGMENT

In our assessment work with executives and high-potential leaders, we focus heavily on the candidate's capacity to exercise good judgment. We want to know if he or she will make good decisions under pressure. We are eager to see how the candidate approaches complex problems without the benefit of plenty of time, resources, or support staff. Typically we meet with only candidates who have already demonstrated an ability to get results. Being selected as a high-potential leader in the first place requires compiling a clear record of success. With this in mind, when we initially sit down with an aspiring leader, we try to get a better understanding of the expertise and wisdom this person has gained during the course of his or her career.

In particular, we are interested in a candidate's diversity of experience and what he or she has learned. This is a key indicator that the individual will be able to draw on lessons learned from a variety of past events when faced with a fundamentally new challenge. Age itself is not necessarily an accurate indication of good experience. Some of the best candidates we interview are relatively young, but with younger, less tested candidates, assessing judgment is all the more critical.

A central tenet of leadership development is getting exposure to new challenges, such as assignments overseas or in an entirely new product category. These are rich learning opportunities. During the assessment process, we probe the candidate to determine how such experiences have enhanced his or her decision-making capacity.

Although past behavior and performance provides clues as to a leader's capacity for good judgment, it tells only part of the story. The past is an effective predictor of future performance to the extent that the new position remains on par with the last, but a bigger leadership role will bring more complexity and ambiguity.

As a result, another approach for assessing leadership judgment is to have a candidate demonstrate problem-solving ability with hypothetical case studies that present the candidate with new situations and a lot of data, similar to the scenarios we present throughout this book. Consulting firms such as McKinsey, Boston Consulting Group, Bain, and others have been using this approach for decades.

In addition to this case-based approach, several academics have written about techniques for testing a person's analytical strengths. Roger Martin, dean of the Rotman School of Management at the University of Toronto, wrote in his book, *The Opposable Mind: Winning Through Integrative Thinking*, how certain scenarios reveal a person's ability to engage in integrative thinking. The example Martin uses to illustrate his research is a vacation decision. Presented with three vacation ideas that sound equally compelling (in Martin's case, a trip to Tuscany, Cambodia, or Hawaii), a person might decide where to go by asking and then answering a wide range of questions—for example:

- How much will each trip cost?
- What kinds of accommodations are available?
- What sorts of tours are offered? Can we find knowledgeable guides?

- Which destination is the most exotic and likely to offer the most unusual experiences?
- Will we learn something new on the trip?
- How safe is each alternative likely to be?
- How much time will we spend in transit compared to the time we'll spend at our destination?[29]

These questions reveal which factors the person believes are most relevant or salient. What she leaves out tells you just as much as what she keeps in. Note also that if pressed, a person could be made to reveal what causal relationship she sees, if any, between one or more of these factors (for example, is a more exotic vacation less safe?). Finally, this decision involves a lot of moving parts. If a person focuses on one of the factors listed above, she is likely to foreclose the possibility of giving another factor subsequent attention. For instance, if she worries about cost first and foremost, she might not give safety much thought (something that she might later regret).

By asking a candidate to work through this kind of scenario aloud, from the beginning to the final decision, an outside observer can learn a lot about the kind of rigor and process that this person brings to an analytical situation.

The key to a leadership judgment scenario is to tailor the kind of general approach used by McKinsey or Roger Martin to a real leadership decision. Martin's illustration is obviously geared toward a wide audience, and the case interviews that McKinsey and other consulting firms use are typically aimed at recent M.B.A. graduates and people with a managerial bent.

In our work, we have found that a more effective approach for assessing leadership potential is to create a series of custom-tailored cases that reflect real issues in the candidate's organization.[30] In discussing these cases with the candidate, we ask probing questions to see how she thinks about the issue. The key is striking the right balance to make sure the case feels real to the candidate while stretching her beyond her natural comfort zone. We might, for example, use a case study about a new product launch in the Chinese market or a potential strategic alliance to capture a promising new technology with which the candidate has no prior experience. We work with senior executives (or board members, if it's a CEO succession project) ahead of time to craft the right approach and ensure that the case is sufficiently challenging. This step also allows us to confirm that the candidate has had no prior experience dealing with the central issue.

We then begin a highly interactive dialogue to learn how the candidate thinks on her feet. What kind of analytical thinking does she possess? How does she frame the central issue? Does she get to the heart of the issue or focus on less important, ancillary concerns? Can she recognize the pros and cons of different solutions? What mental process does she go through to arrive at a conclusion? Does she demonstrate an ability to attack an unfamiliar problem, or does she get bogged down or even paralyzed by unexpected facts? Does she exhibit common sense? What does she do when she's asked to solve a problem in real time? The precise answer that a candidate gives is not as important as the process that she demonstrates in arriving at the answer. We are trying to gauge whether she can place this issue in the proper context. Can she identify the real problem? If so, does she recognize that getting buy-in from others across the organization will be important? Does she recognize the hidden agendas of her constituents as she tries to get them onboard? Is she able to think two or three steps ahead and recognize what the likely consequences of her actions might be? Does she see the pros and cons of each alternative? In other words, does she see the whole chessboard when making individual moves? Also, does she have the courage to make tough choices? Can she work her way through this hypothetical situation and then, after analyzing it, confidently come to a decision? If the answers to all of these questions are yes, this is a strong indication that the candidate possesses leadership judgment.

6

Courage

Leadership is not for the faint of heart.

Human relations involve conflict. Whenever two or more people get together, separate interests jockey for position. In some cases, these conflicts are subtle. They might occur at home or in the work-place and involve differences in taste, mood, goals, or beliefs. When an employee has to choose whether to assist a colleague, finish a group project, or leave the office early to watch his daughter's school performance, for example, several divergent interests are in play. Much of the time, human conflicts lay just below the surface of conversation. We hardly mention them. We consider them routine matters of give-and-take. But when the ante is raised and opposing interests are expressed, strategic posturing ensues, and heated discussions can take place. When conflicts are particularly severe, intense competition, and even violence, can set in. This result most often occurs when conflicting interests in territory, money, religious beliefs, or political preference are at stake.

Leadership means being on the front line of these conflicts. It means facing conflicts, mediating and shaping them, sometimes at the risk of great personal cost or freedom. James MacGregor Burns wrote, "Leaders, whatever their professions of harmony, do not shun

from conflict; they confront it, exploit it, ultimately embody it."[1]
A person who wants to lead must be willing and able to accept these
conditions as part of his or her trade.

· · · · · · · · ·

Judith Mackay is arguably the world's most prominent champion
of tobacco control. A British-born medical doctor, she is the recipient of the U.S. Surgeon General's Medallion, an OBE award from
Queen Elizabeth, a World Health Organization (WHO) medal, and
the *British Medical Journal Group*'s first Lifetime Achievement
Award for her "tireless and courageous campaigning on behalf of
patients and public health care." In 2006 *Time* magazine selected
her as one of its "60 Asian Heroes," and a year later she was named
to the Time 100, a designation reserved for the one hundred most
influential people in the world.

When we spoke with her in 2010, more than twenty-five years
after she began her full-time campaign in Asia against big tobacco
companies, she was serving as senior policy advisor to the WHO
and as the senior advisor for World Lung Foundation's tobacco
control program, which received a large grant from the Bloomberg
Initiative, a foundation established by New York City mayor Michael
Bloomberg.

Reflecting back on her early choices, Mackay initially set out
on a very different career path. A native of Yorkshire, England, she
attended medical school at the University of Edinburgh, and upon
graduating in 1966 her dream was to join the ranks of the medical
profession—to have what she thought would be a fun job and cure
the ill. "I thought I'd make a career in hospital medicine and save lives.
Oh, and I was definitely going to stay in Edinburgh," she told us with
a chuckle, recalling the innocence and idealism of those early days.[2]

After completing an internship in Edinburgh, she moved to
Hong Kong in 1967 and started clinical practice. But after years of

treating patients with smoking-related problems, she realized that the medical system she was serving wasn't working. She was treating symptoms and consequences of bad health, not the underlying cause.

"We used to joke that in the male medical wards we never admitted a nonsmoker. Everyone was coming in with cancer, emphysema, heart disease or bleeding duodenal ulcers," Mackay explained. "If I wanted to help these people, I realized that I had to move upstream."

Moving upstream meant taking on a formidable opponent: the tobacco industry. It also meant moving through uncharted waters. In the 1980s, a few voices in the United States and other developed countries were starting to speak out against the behavior of cigarette companies.[3] Some legislation against advertising and distribution existed too. But in Asia, efforts to fight big tobacco were almost unheard of. Public safety education was equally scarce, and there was virtually no legislation banning advertising or even requiring health warnings on packages.[4] Moreover, as cigarette companies started to get squeezed out by litigation in America and other Western markets, they began to shift their focus elsewhere.[5] "They were looking at Asia as their utopia," Mackay explained. "If they could persuade Asian men to change to international brand cigarettes and persuade Asian women to smoke, everybody in North America could give up [smoking] tomorrow and it wouldn't make any difference." The simultaneous fall of communism also created enormous incentives for cigarette companies to expand in the East. "I think they sort of reckoned that they could ride the Marlboro cowboy into Asia, and it would be theirs for the taking."

In 1984, when Mackay started fighting against the tobacco industry in Asia, she was on her own, waging a one-woman battle. She began writing a column on women's health issues for the *South China Morning Post,* and in 1989 she single-handedly formed and operated the Asian Consultancy on Tobacco Control. In this latter role, she appeared at conferences and often met with government leaders to campaign for tighter regulation.

It wasn't easy. Her efforts were not welcomed by those who profited from getting as many people as possible addicted to smoking. Big cigarette companies threatened her with lawsuits and made Mackay the subject of secret dossiers. A leaked internal document written by a trade organization identified her as "one of the 3 most dangerous people in the world." In public she was called "sanctimonious, dogmatic, meddlesome, puritanical, hysterical, prejudiced, and vehement." Mackay was even accused of having "subliminal, repressed, sexual frustration" because she could not bear to see the "position of a cigarette in relation to the male mouth." One U.S. smokers' rights group referred to Mackay as "a gibbering Satan."[6]

"I would say from about day three onward . . . I realized that trying to work with the tobacco industry was completely impossible," she said. The industry was constantly striving to attack her and discredit her professionally. During radio and TV debates, there was a "persistent niggling away."

More dramatic, in 1990 Mackay was held at gunpoint in Mongolia, and on a separate occasion the minister of health there admitted that his government initially thought she was an American spy. In fact, Mackay was the first Westerner from WHO to visit Mongolia, and she arrived on the same afternoon that the Russians were pulling out.

Mackay received death threats, gave slide presentations amid the sounds of explosions, and visited countries under martial law. And on top of all that pressure, her work was entirely unpaid for more than twenty years.

"There really wasn't any money," she says, almost as an afterthought. "There was no one to pay me. There was no career path or structure."

Yet despite this adversity, Mackay found the courage to continue. "Every time my spirits are sagging, all I have to do is be threatened with another lawsuit or a death threat, and I am up and running again," she said. Through it all, she has served as an inspiration for hundreds of new antitobacco advocates, and her efforts have brought change to millions of people. For example, in 1994 she convinced the prime minister of Cambodia to prohibit television advertising of tobacco during children's viewing hours as a first step, and made similar gains across the region. Altogether, she has advised governments of China, Indonesia, Japan, Laos, Malaysia, South Korea, Singapore, Taiwan, Vietnam, and others on tobacco-control policies and legislation. She played an instrumental role in developing the WHO's Framework Convention on Tobacco Control, which places signatory countries under an obligation to implement tobacco control policies and has been ratified by nearly all 192 WHO member countries.

In 2010, cigarette smoking was still the world's leading cause of death, killing more people than car accidents, AIDS, and drugs combined—causing one death every six seconds. But if there is a young person in Asia today who is persuaded not to start smoking, he or she probably has Mackay to thank.

GRACE UNDER PRESSURE

People have always celebrated the importance of courage. The word itself means "heart," from the French *coeur*, although we sometimes say *fortitude, bravery, gallantry,* or *will* to express the same concept. Many people believe that courage is the absence of fear, but this is not true. Rather, courage is the ability to act in spite of great fear or, as Hemingway memorably said, courage is the ability to act with "grace under pressure."

To fear we should also add risk, danger, intimidation, or ambiguity. People who exercise courage are aware—sometimes even terrified—of the weighty circumstances they are confronting. Yet they still find a way to march on. Physical courage is courage in the face of physical pain, hardship, death, or threat of death; moral courage is the ability to act correctly in the face of popular opposition, personal sacrifice, scandal, or shame.

Along with love, courage is probably world literature's most common theme. Prometheus ascended to the heavens and stole fire from the gods. Jason sailed through the Clashing Rocks. Theseus slay several bandits and the mighty half-man, half-bull Minotaur in order for his people to be free. The Bible tells us of David's unlikely victory over Goliath. These stories form a common thread, handed down through oral and written tradition. Their lesson is that no great advances are ever made without a healthy dose of courage.

In less allegorical terms, courage can be understood as a profound level of human balance and centeredness. It is an emotional commitment to what one is doing, to one's core values, or in the value of one's organizational mission. Courage is an emotional commitment because it frequently requires action that might not seem logical in terms of short-term payoffs. Objective reasoning might dictate staying silent, for example, or pursuing a path of self-preservation. But courage runs deeper.

In this respect, courage is part of what we frequently call character. People with courage are not easily swayed from their moral center, even in the face of great pressure, uncertainty, or opposition. Instead, they take action.

WHY IS COURAGE IMPORTANT FOR LEADERSHIP?

Courage has been and continues to be a critical factor in human affairs. Without the uncommon fortitude of leaders like Teddy Roosevelt, Mohandas Gandhi, and Nelson Mandela, the world would be a much different place in which to live. Roosevelt bravely led a cavalry unit up San Juan Hill in the Spanish-American War, but as president, he showed a different kind of courage. His bold efforts to take on the powerful corporations and Wall Street trusts in 1903–1904 led to key regulatory reform. Gandhi spent most of his adult life protesting the treatment of Indians by colonial Britain. His perseverance and nonviolent methods led to Indian independence in 1947 and inspired generations of future activists. Nelson Mandela spent twenty-seven years in prison but never abandoned his struggle for equal rights in South Africa. He was the key figure in the antiapartheid movement and in 1994 became the first democratically elected president of South Africa.

Courage is not reserved for heroic public figures alone, however. It is something that each of us should aspire to practice. In fact, the most important acts of courageous leadership are the smaller, quieter episodes that touch us every day.

How often does a fear of standing out inhibit your ability to do the right thing? In public, we ignore acts of cruelty or helplessness. In the workplace, we may close our eyes to unjust, unethical, and even illegal behavior such as talking behind backs, sexual harassment, or even stealing in order to avoid personal involvement or difficult confrontations. We are reluctant to stand up to others with the simple word *no*. Instead, we tell ourselves, "It's not my problem," or, "What can I do?"

At the organizational level, this timid disposition can be fatal. Without courage, a culture of conformity ensues, and entire systems get mired in groupthink. People resist facing up to reality and are unable to make tough but necessary decisions. They impede the flow of ideas, entrepreneurialism, or innovation.

"One of my biggest pet peeves is when people don't speak up and tell others what's on their mind," said Greg Greene, executive vice president and chief administrative officer at Ryder.[7] "Whenever I talk to Greg [Greg Swienton, Ryder's CEO], he knows he's going to get my honest opinion and not a lot of sugar because I've been on the other side too many times. A lot of times people have great ideas, or they notice an important angle that the top decision makers overlooked. But when people stay silent and just follow in step, that's all lost. The whole company suffers."

Courageous leaders keep organizations and other groups from falling into this trap. They are willing to handle certain demands when the rest of us can't. They speak up and let others know their opinions. Good leaders also encourage debate and are not afraid of hearing ideas that might undermine their own way of thinking.

Leaders Must Handle Adversity

Harvard Kennedy School professor Ron Heifetz has often said that to lead is to live "on a razor's edge."[8] In other words, leadership means facing a multitude of competing voices, values, and passions. It means exposing oneself to the possibility of cynicism, institutional inertia, ridicule, denial, and outright attack. Leaders must face down powerful interest groups that champion the status quo, while other groups fight just as hard for radical change. One CEO asked us, "Who am I supposed to listen to? The employees? The customers? The shareholders? Which shareholders: short-term traders or long-term investors? The company's founder? Unions? Public interest groups? Members of my community? These voices are always barking loud, and they almost never bark together."

At the same time, unexpected external events have a way of crushing even the best of well-laid plans. Financial markets collapse, and economies slide into recession. Natural disasters call for a shift in resources and distract a leader's attention. And in an age of global interdependence, events that were once isolated now affect us all. A civil war or terrorist attack in one part of the world has a ripple effect that quickly reaches other nations.

Leaders need courage in order to handle this adversity. Without it, they will fail to live up to the demands of the situation. They might retreat into a corner, immobilized. Or they might take a quick and easy fix. Courage enables leaders to carry on. It acts as an emotional needle, a moral compass. In times of great pressure, courage provides them with a sense of stability and direction.

Judith Mackay faced this type of adversity during much of her career: lawsuits, threats, cynicism, and the daunting truth that she was operating entirely on her own. There was no career path in activism against big tobacco companies in Asia. Activism had no structure, no pay, and success was highly uncertain. The easiest thing to do would have been to let it go. Confronted with immense personal sacrifice and little to no prospect of recognition or gain, she could have gone back to work at a hospital or in private practice. She could have enjoyed a quieter, more comfortable life.

We asked her why she didn't. "I don't know. Maybe I was a little crazy," she answered in her self-deprecating way. "But if you had seen all the patients who were suffering . . . there was nobody stopping it, and I felt determined."

In the 1980s and 1990s, Mackay had the courage to take on the powerful tobacco industry in Asia when no one else would. And her enduring will to champion the antismoking movement there has given others the necessary comfort zone to join ranks and eventually take her place. With millions of dollars flowing in from the Bloomberg Initiative, as well as important new legislation and the World Health Organization's Framework Convention, newer and younger antismoking advocates are well positioned to make even bigger gains. Her trailblazing leadership paved the way.

In the private sector, an exemplar of grace under pressure is Michael Capellas. His leadership drew public attention in 1999, when he became CEO of Compaq as the company was getting crushed by Dell and feuding with its former ally Microsoft. This was the heyday of the dot-com craze, when traditional companies like Compaq were under the hammer to come up with new and better revenue streams on what seemed like a daily basis (we're not sure this trend has dissipated, actually). Capellas repaired the strained relationship between Compaq and Microsoft and made the two companies key strategic partners.

His next move was to steer Compaq's acquisition by Hewlett-Packard. Agreeing to sell the company you run to another entity is never easy. In fact, a cabal of vested interests usually resists such a move with every breath it has. To make matters more difficult, HP was suffering internal crisis at the same time negotiations were going on. HP's CEO, Carly Fiorina, was in the process of being ousted by the company's board of directors, which itself was dealing with turmoil amid several ethics charges and accusations of illegal corporate spying. Capellas weathered this storm, delayed a proxy battle, and successfully saw the acquisition through.

From there he became CEO of MCI in 2002. Prior to his arrival, MCI had been known as WorldCom, but the company was forced to change its name in the wake of the toxic scandal left by Capellas' predecessor, Bernie Ebbers. (Ebbers was sentenced to twenty-five years in prison for corporate fraud and has been called one of the most corrupt CEOs in history.)[9] His legacy to Capellas and the rest of the MCI clan was an $11 billion accounting fraud liability, not to mention a corporate reputation that had sunk low enough to make Tony Soprano seem like a stand-up guy.

Still, Capellas was up to the challenge. He hired MCI's first ethics officer, launched an anonymous hot line for employees to report code-of-conduct violations, and led MCI out of bankruptcy and to the eventual acquisition by Verizon for a premium. He almost made it look easy.

When asked where his courage comes from, Capellas said that much of it could be traced to his family and upbringing. As a child, he was plump and blind in one eye, and when he wanted to play linebacker on the high school football team, his coach told him he "wasn't tough enough," Capellas remembers. "From that moment on, I always wanted the toughest job."[10]

His mother was a nurse and his father was a gritty army man who fought to push the Germans out of Italy in World War II. His Greek father also worked in the same steel mill for thirty years. "My dad had an unbelievable work ethic," Capellas said, clearly influenced by his father's strong sense of character.[11] When asked if he ever makes mistakes amid all the pressure, Capellas answered, "Oh yeah. And it's very simple: when you get more worried about personal PR in the marketplace and worry less about what really matters, that to me is a lack of courage."[12]

When it comes to operating under pressure, few other people can match the experience of Richard Clarke, the former U.S. national coordinator for counterterrorism and a thirty-year government veteran. He rose up the ranks to become President Clinton's terrorist "czar," a role he continued to hold in the subsequent Bush administration. On 9/11, he was the person who ran the White House situation room meeting immediately after the attacks on the World Trade Center and the Pentagon.

"I was at a meeting about three blocks from the White House when the first tower was hit," Clarke told us.[13] By the time he entered the West Wing, the second tower was burning too. President Bush was in Florida, so Clarke burst into Vice President Cheney's office, where he found Cheney and Condoleezza Rice, the president's national security advisor. "It's an al Qaeda attack and they like simultaneous attacks," he told them. "This might not be over."[14]

Minutes later Vice President Cheney was evacuated to a bunker, where Rice would soon follow. Meanwhile, Clarke was chairing an emergency videoconference with senior government officials who were scattered across Washington: Donald Rumsfeld, secretary of defense; George Tenet, director of the CIA; Air Force four-star general Dick Myers; and Cheney and Rice, among others. Everyone was yelling frantically on phones and grabbing papers. "Let's begin," Clarke announced. "Calmly. We will do this in crisis mode, which means keep your microphones off unless you're speaking. If you want to speak, wave at the camera. If it's something you don't want everyone to hear, call me on the red phone."[15]

We asked Clarke to tell us what it was like to lead in that situation. *Intense* was the word he used. "It was obviously very intense." Even setting aside the extraordinary circumstances of 9/11, the daily pressure on cabinet-level officials is palpable, he said. "You don't necessarily feel it in each moment, but you feel it with the job." There is no escaping it, he told us. The number of people and the resources that each cabinet secretary is accountable for leaves no other choice. "To lead at that level, you need to possess a lot of qualities, and courage is right near the top. You've got to make tough decisions quickly. A lot of very smart people can't handle the heat."

Another intense environment requiring courageous leadership is America's prison system. Needless to say, inmates are there unwillingly, often for violent crimes. With this in mind, we decided to talk with Brian Fischer, commissioner of the New York State Department of Correctional Services, to hear about his experience. Fischer oversees the state's entire prison system: fifty-nine thousand inmates, thirty thousand workers, and sixty-seven correctional facilities. Previously he was the warden at Sing Sing, a maximum security prison located about thirty miles up the Hudson River from New York City. For his leadership there, he was selected the National Warden of the Year in 2006.

Sing Sing has a storied past. During the nineteenth century, prisoners were forbidden from making any sound whatsoever, and torture was common. Suicide and death from malnutrition were also quite frequent, and those who were "sent up the river" to Sing Sing were never expected to be seen alive again. The electric chair was introduced in 1891, and over six hundred people were executed by electrocution at Sing Sing through the years.[16]

Although prison reform has changed how prisoners are treated today, Sing Sing is still a dramatic place. Fischer described to us his first visit and initial impression with these words: "It was scary. It's an old, old facility—in 2000 we had our 175th anniversary. It had the Death House. The Rosenbergs were executed there. There's this long history. No two prisons are alike, and Sing Sing is built on a hill that goes up from the river. You enter and you always feel as if you're walking up. It's like an uphill effort—walking up physically and emotionally to conquer it, over many stairs."[17]

His description of the inside was just as harrowing. "I see the place as one of depression, isolation. These are people who are not necessarily bad people; they've just made terrible mistakes. And it's depressing when you realize the loss of so much. They use drugs. It's isolating. Being there means you are no longer part of a family; you have no phone; you are by yourself. They feel lonely, regimented, ignored. There is yelling, crying, you're all by yourself and you have to internalize that. There's a quietness, an eeriness."

Leading a group of people under these extreme circumstances is no easy task. Social conflict at Sing Sing can literally become a matter of life and death as inmates and gangs jockey for power. As warden, Fischer dealt with adversity every day.

"One afternoon there was a homicide in Sing Sing," he told us. "It happened in the yard. About three hundred offenders were in the yard, and when an incident like that occurs, you know anything can happen. So immediately we had a lockdown, so there could be an investigation. But we had to keep everybody outside to keep them from destroying evidence. We locked down the cell block, and left everyone out who was out."

Fischer walked the galleries, explaining what had happened. The inmates were not happy. It was the middle of summer. It was "a hot, hot day," Fischer recalled. "Both inmates and guards were dripping with sweat. Tempers were short." Fischer ordered some cold water and snacks to give to them. "It was necessary for me to be seen at the incident rather than somewhere else. I had to show that I had their back as well. It solidified my role as CEO, if you will, of the facility." Fischer realized that despite the obvious tension, he needed to keep his head high and demonstrate to everyone why safety concerns dictated that they all wait.

Courageous leaders like Clarke and Fischer operate under extremely difficult conditions. They accept adversity as an inevitable part of leading other people in high-stakes situations. This does not mean that they are immune from fear, nervousness, mistakes, or shame. Rather, they rely on their emotional centeredness, strong sense of commitment, and accept the risk that unpleasant side effects like these might occur in order for everyone to keep moving ahead. While you could say that anyone who works as a counterterrorism official or prison warden probably has a pretty strong stomach, to a certain extent all leaders must be able to withstand adversity if they hope to succeed.

"My advice to a new warden who suffers a setback is to look forward," Fischer said. "Take a deep breath. What was occurring? You need to focus on reality. You have to be calm, but decisive and proactive."

Leaders Must Be Willing to Take Risks

Without courage, new ideas or ways of doing things never get started. It's too easy to let the status quo knock them down. Art, music, innovation, unconventional political thinking—all of these are met with scorn and widespread skepticism. John Lennon's aunt (and guardian) famously told him, "The guitar's all very well, John, but you'll never make a *living* out of it."[18] Most people cave in to this kind of pressure for approval. The easier path is the one that is well worn. Yet without individuals who are willing to accept risk, real breakthroughs are never made.

In 2000, entrepreneur William Angrick cofounded Liquidity Services, an Internet company that operates several auction Web sites, and as its CEO and chairman he helped take the company public in 2006. Liquidity Services is a bit like an eBay for big industrial corporations and government agencies that want to quickly unload extra goods, usually to smaller businesses. In 2010 the company recorded $500 million of revenues and was named to the Forbes List of 100 Best Small Companies in America for the third consecutive year.

Liquidity Services is a great success story, but getting there wasn't easy. Angrick, then thirty-two years old, had quit his job and decided to start the company with nothing more than his modest savings, a couple of partners, and an idea. It was a bootstrap beginning all the way. Angrick and one of his cofounders even shared a 300-square-foot studio apartment near their Washington, D.C., office.[19] Not very many people believed they would succeed.

"When we were looking for seed capital for our company, eighty people told us no," Angrick told us.[20] "It was one setback after another. You have to be fearless as a leader and accept uncertainty. You need to let failures be a learning process."

Angrick and his partners weren't deterred. They believed in the value of the business they were creating even when others didn't. Angrick was a three-sport letterman in high school and later a champion boxer at Notre Dame. He told us that many of the lessons he learned in sports were ones he relied on when facing the naysayers. For him, the experience of athletic competition was an important factor in developing courage. "You know you have to pick yourself up. You can't have any shame in failure," he said. "If you are exposed to failure early in life, that helps you prepare for leadership."

Without Angrick's willingness to risk his time and financial security, Liquidity Services never would have gotten off the ground. The same can be said for almost any other great company, from Apple to Honda Motor Company all the way back to Procter & Gamble, which was founded by two immigrants—a candlemaker and soapmaker—in 1837.

Although most people don't start their own companies, courage is still a critical leadership trait. In fact, courage is often just as important at large companies in order to counter complacency and groupthink. Without it, people stick to outdated routines and settle for the status quo.

With this in mind, how many of us have the courage to directly challenge the senior leadership of our employers? Many of the best leaders we know encourage their subordinates to question assumptions and stand up for what they believe in, even if their views are in direct conflict with the leader's. Yet the percentage of employees who actually do this, even when encouraged, is low. Most people, most of the time, are unwilling to put their own skin on the line.

Not so with Lieutenant Colonel Paul Yingling. Yingling graduated from Duquesne University in 1989 and was commissioned as a second lieutenant through U.S. Army Reserve Officers Training Corps. During the 1990s and 2000s, he was a rising star in the military. He did a tour in the Gulf War and later deployed to Bosnia as part of Operation Joint Endeavor. From there he returned to the United States and completed a master's degree in international relations at the University of Chicago, then taught at West Point. He also graduated from the Command and General Staff College and School of Advanced Military Studies at Fort Leavenworth, the military's elite leadership development program.

By the time the Iraq War began, Yingling was an executive battalion officer. He did two tours in Iraq, helping to train Iraqi security forces and its civil defense corps, among other duties. His career trajectory was rising fast.

But then Yingling did what some would label a curious thing. Disenchanted with the way in which the U.S. military had been conducting the war in Iraq, he published a critical article, "A Failure of Generalship," in the army's main newsletter, *Armed Forces Journal*. In it, Yingling likened U.S. efforts in Iraq to what had occurred in Vietnam. Each event, he argued, revealed an obvious inability to handle insurgent forces. Current leadership thinking did not live up to the demands of the day. Unless the military changed, Yingling said, it would not be able to fulfill its mission. "As matters stand now, a private who loses a rifle suffers far greater consequences than a general who loses a war," he wrote in a direct stab at both the top military brass and the congressional oversight used to identify and promote them. In the article, Yingling went on, "The intellectual and moral failures common to America's general officer corps . . . constitute a crisis in American generalship."[21]

Going public with these comments, especially in an organization as steeped in tradition and hierarchy as the U.S. Army, did not go unnoticed. Later that year (2007), General David Petraeus was called back from his post as U.S. commander in Iraq to chair a board that oversaw the army's promotion of one-star generals. Many observers, including senior defense officials, viewed this move as a shake-up in the way that the military operated its talent review system.[22] Several people also saw a direct link to Yingling's earlier letter. One journalist wrote: "In part owing to articles by several creative officers—Chiarelli, Lt. Col. John Nagl, and especially Lt. Col. Paul Yingling—the critique of the promotion system has been percolating for the past year or so in defense-policy circles of both parties. The winds are blowing; the ground is shaking."[23]

After Colonel Yingling completed his third tour of duty in Iraq in 2009, he took up a post as a professor of security studies at the George C. Marshall European Center for Security Studies in Germany, and in 2010 he was challenging military leadership again. He published another article, this time criticizing the lack of accountability that U.S. national security decision makers had for the true cost of armed conflict. He called for a return to the military draft and a reassertion of Congress's original constitutional role in deciding how and when America goes to war.[24] The *New York Times* wrote: "In a national security debate often filled with fuzz words, equivocation and not-for-attribution quotes, Colonel Yingling has boldly taken on an issue that has been simmering for years, one that most politicians and policy makers in Washington are happy to avoid."[25] While it seems unlikely that the United States will return to a military draft any time soon, it is safe to say that efforts by leaders like Yingling are at least turning heads.

This ability to challenge authority is important. Whether on the battlefield or in the boardroom, leaders must be prepared to take action, even unpopular action, when their organization's values are at stake. In fact, organizations and institutions with the most rigid hierarchical cultures are usually the ones that are most in need of someone like Yingling to step up and courageously lead.

In Chapter Three, we discussed another military leader who criticized his superiors, General Stanley McChrystal, who was removed from his command in Afghanistan after making remarks about members of the Obama administration. These two cases are different. McChrystal's remarks consisted of several personal attacks that were made behind the backs of President Obama, Vice President Biden, and other senior officials. Yingling's criticism was of the military system. He refrained from any personal attacks and published his remarks openly for everyone to see. McChrystal's behavior amounted to insubordination and demonstrated an inability to control his emotions. Yingling's letter, by contrast, was a reasoned, transparent, constructive effort to help his organization improve. By acting with leadership courage and integrity, Yingling fostered healthy debate. McChyrstal's lack of emotional intelligence risked leaving his followers with the impression that he was unpredictable and that top military leaders were not operating in sync.

Several decades earlier, another leader had the courage to take on government officials at the highest level, in this case with her entire organization's future on the line. Katharine Graham became president of the *Washington Post* when her husband, Phil, killed himself in 1962. Her late husband's were big shoes at the paper to fill. Phil Graham had been a former president of the *Harvard Law Review*, clerk to Felix Frankfurter, and by all accounts was a charismatic genius. Many people in fact expected Graham to sell the newspaper. Although her father had owned it, running a business wasn't seen as a woman's job at the time. (In 1962, only one woman had ever led a Fortune 500 company.) Boardrooms were men's clubs, and according to Ben Bradlee, who later signed on as managing editor, most of her friends and colleagues "secretly wanted her to sell."[26]

Graham didn't. Instead, she entered this men's world undaunted, committed to a public service ideal that her father had handed her. For Graham, a free press and truthful, first-rate journalism were the bedrock of democracy, and she wasn't about to place that responsibility in anyone else's hands.

It was not easy. In fact, Graham was terrified. "I thought I was this peasant walking around among brilliant people," she later admitted in an interview.[27] In a separate account, she said, "I was paralyzed with fear at first. It was like being the new girl in school. You're disoriented. You don't know what your role is. The first time I ever asked a question at one of our private editorial lunches, I thought I'd die."[28]

One of her biggest challenges was deciding how to deal with the Watergate scandal in 1972–1973. Early evidence surrounding the Watergate break-in did not show any direct link to the White House, and most of the press did not think that a cover-up story had legs. At the time of the 1972 election, of twenty-two hundred regular reporters in Washington, no more than fourteen were covering Watergate.[29] After the election, the story dried up almost altogether.

The *Post* persisted, seemingly alone, and the Nixon administration fought back. Ownership rights over several of the company's most profitable television stations were officially challenged, putting the company's financial health in question, and personal threats were volleyed as well. Graham later wrote that she endured "an unbelievable two years of pressured existence. It was painfully obvious they were out to destroy us."[30] During this period, the *Post* was also in a fragile financial position. As the Nixon administration issued licensing challenges, the company's stock price fell from thirty-eight dollars a share to sixteen dollars. "Another publisher than Katharine Graham might have succumbed to pressure and taken her reporters and editorial writers off the story," wrote historian Arthur Schlesinger Jr.[31] "She has the guts of a cat burglar," Bradlee used to say.[32]

To her credit, Graham endured, making journalistic history. The Post Company went on to become one of the most profitable and prestigious news organizations in the world. During Graham's tenure as CEO from 1963 to 1991, the company's revenues increased from $84 million to $1.4 billion. From the time the company went public until Graham stepped down, its stock price had an increase of 3,315 percent (the Dow increased 227 percent during the same time).[33]

FINDING COURAGE

True courage is a relatively rare human trait. We all wish that we possessed more of it, yet achieving this goal often proves elusive.

It is also difficult to determine who among us actually is courageous. With the benefit of hindsight, we easily recognize heroic acts among larger-than-life figures who change the course of history, such as Martin Luther King Jr. and the student in Tiananmen Square who faced a row of tanks. Making this determination before the fact, however, and under less dramatic circumstances, is more difficult. This is especially true in the more nuanced realm of everyday life. How can we know if future leaders are equipped to exercise courage before the storm even hits?

It's not an easy question. We have been asking successful leaders and academic experts the same thing for years. Most of them point to character or give vague answers about upbringing and genes.

When we posed this question to Richard Clarke, he said, "It might have something to do with what you've been through. We always talk of 'the greatest generation,' the generation that went through the Great Depression and World War II. Maybe you think to yourself, 'What's the worst thing that could happen if I do the right thing?' If you've been through what they have, not a lot."

When asked how to assess a candidate's courage and truthfulness, Michael Capellas offered: "Instincts take you a long way. If it feels right, it generally is. When you first have a conversation, do you get a sales pitch or do you have a candid conversation?"[34]

Our own work and research reveal that each of these leaders is right. Courage is an important part of character, and one's upbringing and personal experience often form the basis for future acts. We've also learned that conversations can tell a lot about a person's potential to tackle adversity and handle risk. The trick is asking the right questions and knowing where to look. During our executive assessment process, we combine traditional interview techniques and 360-degree referencing with other tools that are designed to probe the following three indicators:

1. Is she committed to core values and centered emotionally?
2. Can she navigate uncertainty?
3. Does she have patience?

Commitment to Core Values

Having a clear moral center is a good predictor of courage. Leaders like Katharine Graham, who believe fundamentally in the value of their organization's long-term mission, are less likely to lose direction when the winds of temptation or adversity start blowing in. By contrast, individuals whose moral compass has no true north are easily set off course. When trouble arises, they take the first lifeboat and let others deal with a sinking ship.

These character issues are bigger than courage itself, of course, and are directly related to our discussion of integrity in Chapter One. After all, courage without integrity leads to recklessness, even catastrophe. With this is mind, assessing a candidate's level of courage requires gauging ethical awareness as well. This is one of the most difficult aspects of the assessment process, yet it must not be overlooked.

Navigating Uncertainty

Many people erroneously cling to the notion that problems are easily classifiable because they believe we live in a world of black or white. In fact, we live in a world of gray, and leaders face tough ethical dilemmas on a regular basis. They need courage to accept this and to move forward knowing that in all likelihood, no perfect state or solution will emerge at the end. Along these lines, effective leaders realize that they cannot right every wrong and will not win every battle.

With this in mind, we probe executive candidates to see how they view the world. If they see too much of it through a black or white lens, a flag goes up. These people are usually quick to fasten on to the safe or familiar answer. They deal poorly with complexity and might have trouble making hard decisions.

One way to gauge a candidate's capacity to navigate ambiguity is to ask her to describe a situation in which she initiated a tough idea, stance, or vision. It's not so much the outcome we're concerned with but how she dealt with the situation. Did she make a reasonable attempt to assess the risks and rewards? Did she deal well with the negative reaction? Could she manage the pressure? In the end, did she possess enough gumption to reach a decision and stick with it? If so, this is an indication that the individual possesses the courage to deal with shades of gray.

In addition to asking candidates what they have done in the past, we present them with our own hypothetical case studies that force them to make a tough decision. In the cases, we are careful to attach unpleasant consequences to any resolution, which ensures that candidates feel some real tension. We also provide a way out of the scenario. Usually this involves an authority figure, delay, or some other kind of red herring. A person who lacks the stomach for pressure will usually seize this exit opportunity. A candidate with courage is able to move forward with confidence in her decision. She accepts the trade-offs as an inevitable part of leading and is careful to give each side its due attention.

Interviewing others about a leader is also revealing. We suggest talking with as many references as possible: subordinates, peers, partners, customers, and the candidate's boss. Probe to find out if the leader involves others in decision making or makes snap decisions. Ask the referee directly if the candidate is comfortable in highly ambiguous situations. Does the leader create structure in this kind of environment, or is his or her behavior all over the map?

Patience

We're not sure if people are patient because they have courage or whether they have courage because they are patient. We're not even sure it matters, but we do know the two go together. Patience is an integral part of courage in a couple of ways. First, it allows individuals to weather a certain amount of adversity. We all know people who have a very low tolerance for circumstances outside their comfort zone and blow up at the first moment of uncertainty. This is a sign that they might not be able to operate under pressure.

A lack of patience might also be an indication that someone is unwilling to accept personal sacrifice, even when it's the right thing to do. Imagine a person who gets unusually steamed by a traffic jam after a car accident, for example, because he must endure another fifteen minutes of waiting for the paramedics to arrive. How is he likely to act in a professional situation when more than a quarter-hour of his personal time is at stake?

Again, we are back to the intersection of courage and integrity. Does a candidate have the patience to endure a little bit of sacrifice because doing so is morally correct?

Finally, a person who does not have patience is likely to act carelessly, even recklessly. People whose natural tendency is to act hastily rather than face pressure are more likely to make costly mistakes.

Like integrity, courage is a difficult attribute to test. Simulating the kind of pressure that a candidate might feel in a genuine situation posing trade-offs and personal sacrifice is not easy to do with a hypothetical vignette. It is possible, however, to determine how a person thinks about a certain scenario that might call for courageous leadership. Does she see the trade-offs? Does she think of the decision in terms of personal risk versus the organization's overall needs? How does she balance these opposing interests? Does she take a patient approach? Or does she quickly state that there is a right or wrong answer? Most trade-offs that call for courageous leadership require a measured approach. When Paul Yingling decided to offer constructive criticism of army leadership, he didn't rush out and do it. Instead, he took time to write the article and had others review it before publication.

With these thoughts in mind, we offer the following hypothetical situation:

> You are a senior manager in a large real estate development company. Your company owns and develops commercial office towers and shopping malls.
>
> Three days ago, your boss told you that you are receiving a big promotion. You will be in charge of a $40 million project to develop a golf course. This project is of particular interest to your boss, and you know that if you do a good job, you will be rewarded with another promotion.
>
> For the past couple of days, you have been performing extensive due diligence to get up to speed on the project. As you learn more, however, you fear that this project is not in the best interest of the company. Several cost overruns seem likely, and the price of real estate near the site has dropped precipitously. Moreover, your company has no experience with golf courses. Up until now, your boss has been in charge, and you are convinced that it is a pet project of his.
>
> You plan to discuss this with him as soon as possible. Before then, however, at a weekly staff meeting, your boss raises the golf course issue. Even more surprising, the president of the entire company is at the meeting.

During the meeting, your boss says, "I want everyone to know that Kathryn is being promoted! She will be running our important new golf course development project!"

Everyone starts to clap. Even the president is interested. He says to you, "Congratulations. When do you get started?"

What is your reaction?

This could potentially be a highly difficult situation for the candidate. She is going to be feeling a lot of anxiety. Her promotion might also be on the line. Moreover, after the meeting, everyone in the company, including the president, is going to think that she is in charge of the golf course project. The longer these steps continue in motion, the more difficult it will be for Kathryn to do anything to slow down the project or refuse the assignment if these are options that she is considering.

Some candidates are tempted to speak up right away. They feel the need to clear the air. The fact that they have some serious misgivings about the project, added to the public nature of the meeting (and the president's presence), compels them to raise an objection.

Unless the president asks any more specific questions, taking this path is probably a poor decision. As we mentioned in our discussion of social savvy in Chapter Two on empathy, making her boss look bad here is not likely to yield a positive result. The meeting might turn into one of confusion, and this will not be good for anyone.

Instead, we look for candidates who can articulate an answer that touches on several of the important themes of courage. Does she have patience? Does she become flustered or keep her cool? Does she think she can handle the pressure of the meeting and then subsequently deal with the complicated, and perhaps tense, overall situation? Does she realize that not all problems can be solved instantly? Indeed, most difficult decisions involving personal trade-offs usually take time to settle.

In addition, can she recognize that maybe she is wrong? The golf course project might not be a black-or-white situation. Maybe there are other reasons for completing the project that she has not considered.

Finally, how do her own career and promotion figure into this? Are they worth risking? How will she decide? What kind of calculus does she use to weigh all of these different variables?

Again, we can't know from this vignette how a person would act in an actual situation, during a live meeting and with her promotion and career truly on the line. But a candidate who can articulate an answer that highlights these aspects of courage—patience, resisting a black-or-white approach, and having a reliable moral compass for tough dilemmas—is more likely to act courageously when the stakes are real. We then verify what she said with the results of our 360-degree interviews with former and current bosses, subordinates, customers, strategic partners, and peers. We want to be sure that there are no major disconnects between how she said she would act in this tough situation and how others have actually witnessed her act in previous situations.

As *you* think back on the hypothetical situation, what do you think is the best response?

Passion

Have you ever wondered what it's like to lose a billion dollars? If so, just ask Jeff Bezos. After being named *Time* magazine's Person of the Year in 1999, the founder and CEO of Amazon.com had an especially hard eighteen months. Many observers questioned whether his company could even survive.

First came fallout in March 2000 from the dot-com craze. For the previous five years, investors had been throwing money at start-up companies with no viable plan for turning a profit. When the market bubble burst and tech stocks plummeted,[1] Internet companies that had been valued in the billions of dollars disappeared seemingly overnight. Among the many to go were several backed by Amazon, including Pets.com, Living.com, and Kozmo.com. Bezos later lamented, "We were investors in every bankrupt, 1999-vintage, e-commerce startup."[2]

But it wasn't just the flash-in-the-pan start-ups that suffered. Stock prices plummeted across the board, and Amazon was no exception. In December 1999 Amazon was trading as high as $106 per share on a split-adjusted basis. By April 2000 the company's stock was less than $70 a share, and a year-and-a-half later it had sunk all the way to less than $6.[3]

Bezos's entrepreneurial star power certainly took a hit as well. Was he a brilliant tech wunderkind or just another bright-eyed CEO whose vision could never be translated into profit? More troubling was the market's perception of Amazon itself. Many experts in the financial community said that the company's days were numbered. Forrester Research president George Colony called Amazon.com "Amazon.toast," and an article in *Fortune* announced, "Amazon.com? Try 'Amazon.bomb'!"[4]

There was ample reason for worry because Amazon was bleeding cash. By the end of 1999, the company recorded a third-quarter loss of $197 million on revenues of $356 million. Compared to the same period a year earlier, sales had grown by 130 percent, but losses had risen by 437 percent. In the fourth quarter of 1999, the company lost $323 million—an increase of 700 percent over the prior year. In 2000, its losses ballooned to a walloping $1.4 billion. Since founding Amazon in 1994, Bezos had argued that the most important objective for the company was to get big fast; short-term profits didn't matter as long as the company added scale. But Amazon's ability to get big fast was increasingly outmatched by its penchant for accumulating red ink.

Faced with this crisis, something had to give, and in January 2001, the company laid off 15 percent of its workforce. The Seattle community, home to Amazon headquarters, was demoralized. Inside the company, too, spirits sagged. Employees who had managed to hang on to their jobs now pulled out their résumés. Without a new sense of urgency, a new plan, the company seemed destined to follow the path of so many other dot-com busts. For many observers, Amazon's great experiment with online book sales seemed to be coming to an end.

Amazon.com, of course, did not end. In fact, it rebounded and eventually thrived. Amazon restructured its business model, slashed expenses, and moved from being a specialty retailer to a vast online shopping portal with distribution (through a web of international partnerships) to nearly every country in the world. Profits soared, and stock prices rocketed to all-time highs. By 2010, Amazon was America's biggest online retailer, and one of the country's largest companies, with more revenue than Nike or McDonald's.

As for Jeff Bezos, his reputation as a pioneer of e-commerce became firmly established. He was frequently cited as one of the great business leaders of the turn of the century, mentioned in the same breath as Steve Jobs and Bill Gates.

What accounts for his extraordinary success? Even more important, how did he take Amazon from nothing, to Wall Street darling, to near financial ruin, and then back to the top again? Where did this resilience come from?

To be sure, no single factor explains it, and Bezos would be the first to admit that he's had plenty of help along the way. As a leader, he possesses many admirable traits, including vision, intelligence, creativity, and daring. But another trait has contributed as much as or more than these others to his success: Bezos is a man of extraordinary passion. Even in the darkest days, when Amazon was the subject of doubt and ridicule, Bezos stood firmly behind the company's plan. When skeptics scoffed and claimed that Amazon's aim at e-commerce advantage would never match traditional booksellers like Barnes & Noble—that consumers need to hold books, see them, thumb the pages, browse the stacks—Bezos never wavered for a second from his vision. He was steadfast in his belief that online book sales would eventually win. In fact, his passion is arguably the most important reason that Amazon.com succeeded. More than anyone else in the e-commerce segment, he exhibited the perseverance and determination to see his original idea through, and he practically invented an entire industry along the way.

Passion is an essential attribute of effective leadership in any field, and the perfect "book end" (pardon the pun) for our discussion here. Indeed, an individual may possess all the smarts and good judgment in the world; she might be of the highest integrity; she might be brimming with vision and social savvy. But without passion, she doesn't stand a chance to be a great leader.

WHAT IS PASSION?

A lot of people equate passion with charisma, but the meaning goes much deeper. *Passion* describes something fundamental about an individual, about his or her underlying needs. By contrast, charisma is a rather superficial quality; it doesn't necessarily reflect what a person holds inside. Charismatic individuals can be quite persuasive, bold, even intoxicating. Many of them are excellent leaders. But their charm and polish can also mislead. Moreover, we can instantly name several effective leaders—people like Michael Bloomberg, Henry Kissinger, Hollywood director Ron Howard—who are clearly driven and passionate but far from charismatic. The truth is that some very successful people have a fire burning inside them that the rest of us never see.

The passion we are referring to describes a person's drive. For example, we often hear the phrase, "He puts a lot of passion into his work" or "She has enormous passion." Usually this means that someone displays plenty of emotion or determination. Passion is a quality that *all* effective leaders have, although they possess and express it in different ways. Sometimes this passion is obvious and comes out in bursts of enthusiasm and emotion. But it can also be less visible, like a powerful inner engine that impels a leader forward. It is possible for a person to have a lot of passion—"to feel passionately" about something—without providing blatant clues. In terms of leadership, then, a key question is: What kind of passions counts? Which drives are important?

Harvard Business School professors Paul Lawrence and Nitin Nohria describe four distinct human drives that they say are active in organizational life: the drive to acquire, learn, bond with others, and defend.[5] Similarly, Daniel Pink argues in *Drive* that three innate psychological needs—autonomy, mastery, and purpose—are tied to individual motivation and success in the workplace.[6]

In our experience working with CEOs and other top leaders, two fundamental drives are at the heart of leadership passion: the drive to achieve and the drive to learn or master.

Drive to Achieve

The drive to achieve is part of our basic human nature. It includes the drive to acquire resources, recognition, status and social position.

Evolutionary logic explains how we came to be this way. Early humans faced tough conditions and scarce resources. Those who did not possess the drive to collect food, improve living conditions, and compete for suitable mates did not survive. Their genes did not pass on by means of natural selection. By contrast, those who did possess this penchant for competition and status survived.

Thousands of years later, that drive still resides within each of us. We instinctively understand that certain benefits attach to socio-economic status. We see it in our fascination with lists (the Fortune 500, the Billboard 100, the dean's list, the honor roll, the ubiquitous "top ten"). This drive for status explains why we covet BMWs, posh corner offices, and Ivy League degrees; why we admire (and sometimes obsess over) all-star quarterbacks, Pulitzer Prize–winning writers, and celebrities who are a fixture on prime-time TV.

The drive to achieve is also commonly referred to as ambition. Ambition is a tricky concept in leadership circles. We hear the word almost daily, yet many people who care about leadership are reluctant to talk about it. This is probably because of the self-serving connotation that is often attached to ambition. We think of individuals such as Hitler, Stalin, and Genghis Khan—all of them ambitious—and turn our heads away in disgust. A fear exists that ambition can't be distinguished from hubris. Modern day criminals, like the financier-felon Bernard Madoff, scare us into believing that effective leaders can't have anything in common with their destructive breed.

An egalitarian streak in modern society also restrains us from admitting how much we want to get ahead of the next person. Publicly it seems wrong to celebrate a natural desire to beat out others, especially if those others do not share the same advantages or resources. It rubs against our notion of fairness.

Yet ambition is real, and we all know it. We are being dishonest if we pretend that some of our most revered leaders were not driven by ambition. George Washington, Winston Churchill, and Benjamin Franklin all shared this trait in spades. Abraham Lincoln is rightly celebrated for having been a noble man, but he was also enormously ambitious. According to his law partner and friend, William Herndon, "His ambition was a little engine that knew no rest."[7]

Moreover, how can we provide a genuine accounting of humankind's greatest accomplishments without giving ambition its due? Did the giant explorers of history—Magellan, Columbus, and Amundsen—devote their lives to danger out of charity? Did they do it for fun? Can we say with a straight face that legendary builders like Bernini, Carnegie, Vanderbilt, and Rockefeller were devoid of any individual longings for fame? Of course not.

The truth is that top thinkers have recognized ambition since early in human history. Aristotle described the great-souled man as one who possesses a certain magnanimity (*megalopsuchia*), or desire to receive an accurate assessment of his worth. Plato spoke of *thymos*, or spiritedness. Hobbes used the word *vainglory*. Alexander Hamilton wrote in the *Federalist Papers* that the love of fame is "the ruling passion of the noblest minds," and Nietzsche referred to man as "the beast with red cheeks."[8] All of these historical figures noted that people are driven by a strong need for achievement, status, and recognition.

In terms of leadership, a competitive fire is often necessary to overcome obstacles and propel oneself to the top. Ambitious people channel their natural drive to achieve into hard work and a devoted sense of mission. It keeps them focused, energized, resilient, alive.

We see it in the life of Jeff Bezos. From an early age, he was an overachiever. In high school, where he was the class valedictorian, he wrote a term paper entitled "The Effect of Zero Gravity on the Common Housefly," which won him a visit to NASA.[9] Some people reported that he showed an easygoing facade, but behind it lay a relentless work ethic. "He was always a formidable presence," said one classmate. His girlfriend, herself an overachiever (a recipient of a scholarship to Duke University and later a Rhodes scholar), said, "Jeff always wanted to make money. It wasn't about money itself. It was about what he was going to do with the money, about changing the future."[10]

After high school, Bezos went on to Princeton, where he studied electrical engineering and graduated summa cum laude in 1986 with a 3.9 grade point average.[11] In his senior year, he turned down job offers with Intel, Bell Labs, and Andersen Consulting to go work for a start-up called Fitel.[12] From there he went to Bankers Trust and then to a hedge fund, D. E. Shaw, where he quickly moved up to senior vice president. But Bezos was itching for something different, something bigger.

Not quite four years later, after Bezos had started Amazon and seen its annual revenues reach $1 billion, the world got a glimpse of just how passionate he could be. John Cassidy, in his book on the dot-com era, wrote, "The scale of Bezos's ambition was stunning. Some commentators said he wanted to create an online Walmart, but that was an understatement . . . Bezos wanted to dominate the entire online shopping market."[13] Bezos himself revealed this audacious streak during an interview with the *New York Times*. His words were like the brash declaration of a general ready to conquer the world: "Sixteen months ago, we were a place where people came to find books. Tomorrow, we will be a place to find anything, with a capital 'A.'"[14]

Don Hewitt, the late creator and executive producer of *60 Minutes,* shared this competitive fervor. Hewitt became sole director of the *CBS Evening News* at age twenty-six and worked with television icons such as Bill Paley, William Murrow, and Walter Cronkite. When Kennedy and Nixon participated in the first televised presidential debate, Hewitt was the man running the show. His crowning achievement was *60 Minutes,* which he created and nurtured as executive producer for thirty-six years. On the air continuously since 1968, the show has won more than seventy-five Emmy Awards and is the most successful program in television history. Among those who know the TV business, Hewitt is a legend.

What a lot of people don't know is just how competitive Hewitt could be. Barbara Walters said, "Don may have been one of the most competitive people I've ever known,"[15] and this held true throughout his long career. There was the time, for example, when he was running the studio and had field reporter Bill Downs listening to him through a headset. They were covering Richard Nixon's vice-presidential campaign. All the networks were huddled around the candidate, when Hewitt suddenly had an inspiration: stick the headset on Nixon's head before he could realize what was happening. "Bill thought I had lost my mind, but he did what I told him. He took off his headset and stuck it on Nixon's head, handed him the mike and told him, 'Walter Cronkite and Ed Murrow want to talk to you.'"[16] If you had been watching ABC or NBC, you wouldn't have heard Cronkite or Murrow; you'd just have seen what appeared to be Nixon having a one-sided conversation with a CBS microphone.

On February 4, 1959, a plane crash in New York's East River left the networks scrambling. A tugboat strike meant there was no easy way to get near the wreckage. Only one boat, from New Haven, Connecticut, was in the vicinity, and reporters from all three networks converged in the wheelhouse to interview the captain. When the captain told Hewitt who owned the boat, Hewitt phoned his studio and told them to take action. Minutes later, the captain hung up his telephone and said, "Okay, which one of you guys is Hewitt? The boat is under your charter. What do you want me to do?" Hewitt immediately answered that he wanted the guys from the other networks cleared from the decks.[17]

Hewitt was more aggressive still during Nikita Khrushchev's visit to an Iowa farm later in 1959. Early one morning, Hewitt found an NBC remote truck parked on a dirt road near the farm, with the keys still in it. What to do? He hijacked the truck and hid it in a nearby cornfield. NBC never had a chance—not with Hewitt on the scene.[18]

Millard "Mickey" Drexler, chairman and CEO of clothing giant J. Crew, shares the same salty determination. During the 1990s, Drexler was chief executive of Gap. Under his stewardship, the company grew from a relatively small chain of private and public labels into a $14.5 billion powerhouse. With ad campaigns featuring iconic stars like Whoopee Goldberg and Spike Lee, the brand became synonymous with American pop culture, and sales revenue soared.[19]

But then Drexler made a series of bad decisions. In the face of competition from Abercrombie & Fitch and even Walmart, he tried to steer the company away from its signature basics toward a more trendy aesthetic.[20] The move failed, and when Wall Street lost confidence, the Gap fell into an extended funk. Drexler's relations with board members became fractious, and in 2002 he was fired.

He might have given up. By then, Drexler had become a very wealthy man (he cashed in over $350 million in stock options upon leaving the Gap).[21] But he was angry; the dismissal left Drexler raw. The way he saw it, he had built the Gap from nothing to a multibillion-dollar juggernaut. His competitive streak wouldn't permit him to just walk away and retire, so he focused his attention on a new project and poured $10 million into a 22 percent share of struggling retailer J. Crew, with an eye toward making the company much better. J. Crew was majority owned by private investment firm Texas Pacific, but Drexler became CEO. Jim Coulter, a partner and cofounder at Texas Pacific, admitted to initial doubts about whether someone with Drexler's wealth still had the fire to tackle a turn-around—until he saw Drexler go to work. "Does he have the energy and passion?" Coulter said. "He loves it. I call him up, and he'll be worried about 48 things, and then I'll ask how he's doing and he says, 'I'm having so much fun.'"[22]

Some people might call Drexler's competitiveness and dedication extreme, perhaps bordering on obsession, but the world is full of aspirations that die for a lack of ambition. How many times have you come up with a new idea, only to let go of it a few days or weeks later? Leaders pursue their dreams with indomitable spirit. They unleash their drive to achieve in ways that sustain them through the hard work necessary to excel and get ahead.

For many years, a certain mythology held that leaders are uniquely talented, that their success is due to special gifts. Fewer people believe that now. Today more and more experts agree that achievement stems from determined action. In *Outliers,* Malcolm Gladwell made famous a study by Anders Ericsson called the "10,000-Hour Rule": that people who are excellent and expert at anything—science, sports, a musical instrument—get that way only after years of intensive practice. They work harder than their peers. Whatever the discipline, the magic number for achieving expertise seems to be about ten thousand hours of concentrated practice.[23] (Child prodigies simply start working or practicing much sooner than most others.) Less important are innate skills or blind chance. The old axiom that success in life is 80 percent perspiration and 20 percent inspiration holds true. Leaders, just like artists and athletes, get better with determined practice.

Take Sprint-Nextel CEO Dan Hesse, who prior to taking over the helm at Sprint-Nextel in 2007, had been at AT&T for twenty-three years, rising to president and CEO of AT&T Wireless, the largest wireless provider in the United States at the time. He has been named Most Influential Person in Mobile Technology by *Laptop* magazine, Wireless Industry Person of the Year by *RCR* magazine, and Executive of the Year by *Wireless Business and Technology* magazine, among many other awards. Hesse received a master's degree in science from MIT, an M.B.A. from Cornell, and an undergraduate degree from Notre Dame.

With a pedigree like that, you might think that he was destined for success. But Hesse has a different explanation. He said that he resolved to open doors at an early age. "I wanted an internship at AT&T, but when I was in grad school AT&T only interviewed at Harvard and Wharton. They didn't come to my school," Hesse explained to us. "But I had a sister who lived in Boston. So I told her to go by the placement office at Harvard Business School and pick up a pamphlet and whatever materials they had." His sister helped out and picked up an application for AT&T's Manager Development Program. He filled it out and sent it to the company. "A couple of weeks later a guy at the company called me," Hesse recalled. "He said, 'How'd you get this application? We don't recruit at Cornell.'" Hesse told him the story, and the recruiter immediately told Hesse to hop on a plane. With that kind of ambition, the recruiter wanted to see him right away.[24]

Drive to Learn and Master

Ambition isn't the only form that passion takes, and not everyone is driven by the same need for achievement or status. Some are driven to learn, to build, to master, and this can be an equally powerful motivator for those who will lead.

In evolutionary terms, an innate drive to learn makes obvious sense. Over tens of thousands of years, survival of the fittest meant survival of those who were equipped with curious minds. Our earliest ancestors had to venture out of caves and master the environment. They had to farm and build and then tackle problems of social organization. All of this required an innate drive to learn.

Today we see this drive at work on every newborn's face. Within days of birth, babies are curious, reaching for objects, aware of unusual shapes. Before long, they are forming sounds and exploring. And if there was any doubt, every parent is surely aware of even a very small child's drive to learn: "Why is the sky blue?" "Why is there a moon?" "Why do we breathe?" In fact, studies of highly gifted children show an intense and obsessive drive to learn, which experts refer to as a "rage to master."[25]

Many leaders tap into this natural instinct and develop it. What they release is great passion. They channel an incredible amount of inquisitiveness into their work, and the results are often staggering.

Sarah Wessling, a high school English teacher in Johnston, Iowa, was named the 2010 National Teacher of the Year, having been chosen from 6.2 million teachers in the United States. In the classroom, Wessling refers to herself not as the teacher but rather as the "lead learner" because, she says, it more accurately reflects who she is. We asked her why she thinks she is such an effective leader in the classroom. "My students would say that one of the first things that they notice is how passionate I am," she told us. "I'm not putting on a show. It's not a fiction. I love to learn, and I love to be transparent about that. I love to share that passion with my students. I am a self-proclaimed geek about a lot of things. And I'm not ashamed about that. I'm happy about it. I'm proud."[26]

K. R. Sridhar, founder and CEO of Bloom Energy, grew up in India and later moved to the United States, where he earned a master's in nuclear engineering and a doctorate in mechanical engineering. NASA asked him to develop equipment that would allow people to live on Mars. Essentially they wanted him to come up with a way to use solar power and Mars water to produce oxygen for humans to breathe and hydrogen to run vehicles. This experience enabled him to conceptualize a new approach to energy production here on earth.

Bloom Energy's central innovation is a new fuel cell, the Bloom box, which Sridhar and others believe will revolutionize the energy industry in much the same way that the personal computer did away with the centralized mainframe. The Bloom box works like a small power plant that can power anything from a single home to an entire city. The single-home variety is about the size of a loaf of bread. Although lack of scale makes the private unit uneconomical for now, larger models are already being used by industrial customers like eBay, Microsoft, Amazon, and Google, and Sridhar's company has been backed by at least $300 million in venture capital funding.

To hear Sridhar tell the story is to be struck by a man brimming with passion. "What I'm building now is not just a company. I'm building an ecosystem," he told us. He wants to revolutionize the way in which people generate and consume energy. His new fuel cells offer a cleaner and more efficient alternative to current sources. The cells can also be operated independent of a centralized grid, a critical factor for undeveloped countries that lack infrastructure. If it works, this technology might bring jobs and economic growth to billions. "This is my motivation for everything," Sridhar says.[27]

Passion is important to lead effectively in any field. Nicholas Zeppos, the eighth chancellor of Vanderbilt University, channels his passion for learning into his work in academia. Earlier in his career, Zeppos practiced law in Washington, D.C., then joined the faculty at Vanderbilt Law School before moving on to other academic and administrative posts within the university. In 2008, he was appointed chancellor.

Zeppos makes no secret about his desire to learn and help improve the lives of others. In fact, he claims that it was something he realized at a very young age. He described his Greek upbringing as teaching him to be gritty, resourceful, and scrappy as a way to enrich his life. "I believe in people's potential," he told us.[28] "That's who I am. I believe in helping to create lifelong learning for every student. In a small way, I can really make that happen now, and it's exciting."

Part of the drive to learn and build also includes a desire to bond with others. Leaders like Zeppos seek partners with whom to collaborate. They approach relationships with enthusiasm, appreciation, and fun. For example, Zeppos once approached a group of high school seniors who were taking a tour of Vanderbilt's tree-covered campus on a cold, rainy day. Although Zeppos was late for a meeting with a university dean, he stopped and told the shivering guests, "Don't worry, guys, this is as cold as it gets around here. And believe me, it's twenty degrees colder at Harvard right now." Everyone smiled, especially the parents.

People who lead with passion and enthusiasm create positive energy. They attract followers and act as catalysts for the formation of highly motivated teams.

Lance Armstrong, as most people know, is a cancer survivor and the greatest professional cyclist in history. He won the Tour de France a record seven times between 1999 and 2005. He is also the founder and chairman of the Lance Armstrong Foundation (LAF), a non-profit organization dedicated to people affected by cancer. LAF has launched several programs and products under the LIVESTRONG name, including the yellow bracelets seen on many wrists.

What most people don't realize is that Armstrong started his foundation before he was a celebrity. He was diagnosed with testicular cancer (which had spread to his abdomen, lungs, and brain) in 1996 and formed LAF in 1997. His first Tour victory was in 1999, nearly three years later.

"When Lance first approached me, I had never heard of him," said Doug Ulman, chief executive officer of LAF.[29] Ulman was inspired, however. As a fellow cancer survivor, he was drawn to Armstrong's passion. "To me what makes him a great leader is that his reasons for founding this organization were based entirely on his own experience and an authentic desire to help other people."

To be sure, Armstrong's cycling success and celebrity have been major factors in his foundation's visibility. But this isn't what drives his work or inspires his employees. Plenty of celebrities bounce in and out of charitable projects. LIVESTRONG relies on something more substantial. What makes Armstrong's leadership so compelling is that it is tied intimately to his personal story. This was the basis of his leadership before he won the Tour de France, and it is likely to sustain his leadership long after his riding days are over.

Ulman told us: "I don't think you can put a value on that. That's what people relate to. No other cancer survivor is going to win the Tour seven times. But right now some cancer survivor is walking to the top of the street to the mailbox, or running a mile, which they never thought was possible in the hospital. . . . It's his passion for really transforming the way the world fights cancer which is most significant."

Former New York City fire chief Nicholas Scopetta channeled his personal passion and mission into a career in public service. For many years he worked with children and other vulnerable groups, including as president of New Yorkers for Children, a nonprofit group that he founded in 1996 that works closely with the city's child welfare and foster communities. Scopetta told us that he traces all of this leadership back to the experiences that he had as a child.

The son of Italian immigrants who struggled to get by in Manhattan during the Great Depression, he was handed over to public care at the age of four. He moved around a lot and eventually ended up with his brothers in a foster home in the Bronx called Woodycrest—a "big old Gothic building," Scopetta recalls.[30] "A stone's throw from Yankee Stadium."

Scopetta remembers following Joe DiMaggio from a distance like so many other starry-eyed kids who grew up at that time. DiMaggio's roots also had special meaning for Scopetta. "I learned he was a child of immigrants, very poor, who went on his own when he was young and hired himself out to play with neighborhood teams for five dollars a day. That was my connection," he said.

That formative experience in New York's foster care system, Scopetta told us, left a big impression. "It basically saved my life and gave me a sense of direction, although I didn't fully know it at the time," he said of the city's efforts. As an adult, and with this as his reference, Scopetta sought out leadership opportunities dedicated to public service.

While we all inherit certain instincts and drives as part of our human nature, what we do with our instincts goes a long way toward defining our leadership passion. Early childhood experiences matter. Effort matters. Finding out what we love to do matters. Staying true to our values and principles matters. "Many of today's leadership experts conclude that leaders can't be made," Scopetta explained. "But they start with basic ingredients and they are then formed by life experiences. By the time you're in your twenties you have a pretty good foundation to the kind of leader you are." For Scopetta, that kind of leadership has involved breathing hope and opportunity into other people's lives and showing the confidence to stick with them through good times and bad. Whether as a fire chief, president of a nonprofit that serves the welfare and foster care communities, or other public positions, Scopetta has consistently found a leadership role that flows from his life experience and passion.

This is another reason that self-awareness is so important for leadership. Leaders who are able to align their natural drive and ambition with a clear sense of who they are as individuals and what matters to them at the deepest level are the people most likely to channel their leadership in productive ways.

According to former Medtronic CEO Bill George, "Many people have natural leadership gifts, but they have to develop them fully to become outstanding leaders."[31] Part of this development includes learning how and where to leverage one's innate passion. It means discovering how to unlock one's energies. "Your life stories give you the passion to lead. That's where you find your passion."[32] By life story, George means the way in which a person frames her experiences, goals and talents. It refers to the voice that a person gives to the beliefs, values, and motivations that she most cherishes.

Nobel Prize winner Albert Schweitzer was born into a middle-class family in the late nineteenth century. He was extremely bright, hard working, and well liked, and he became an accomplished organist, pianist, and historian. As a young adult, Schweitzer enjoyed the company of some of Europe's best minds and was a patron of Paris café society.

In 1905, at age thirty, he announced to his family and friends that he intended to enter a seven-year program to study medicine. He wanted to become a medical doctor and treat the people in the jungles of west central Africa. At that time, age thirty was more like forty or forty-five today, and Schweitzer was entering the most productive period of his career. Moreover, the jungles of Africa were considered unsafe, bizarre, a place for savages. Those who knew Schweitzer were not happy with his decision. "My relatives and friends all joined in expostulating with me on the folly of my enterprise," he wrote. "I was a man, they said, who was burying the talent entrusted to him."[33]

Schweitzer ignored those pleas not to go off to Africa in order to pursue his personal passion. After raising funds, he moved to Africa with his wife and founded a hospital in Lambaréné (now Gabon). His work there saved thousands of lives, inspired countless more, and Schweitzer became famous. He subsequently worked with Albert Einstein and Otto Hahn to fight nuclear testing, and was made an honorary member of the Order of Merit by Queen Elizabeth II. He received the Nobel Prize in 1952.

Later in life, Schweitzer reflected on his leadership success. "Success is not the key to happiness," he said. "Happiness is the key to success. If you love what you are doing, you will be successful."[34]

A QUESTION OF BALANCE AND INTEGRITY

In our experience, individuals who exhibit a balance of passions are the ones most likely to succeed. In other words, in the end, the right question is not who is the most ambitious or the most driven to learn and bond with others, but rather whether a particular individual is ambitious or socially driven enough. Does she exhibit a healthy balance in the drives to achieve, learn, and grow? When it comes to passion, does an individual's behavior allow the expression of each of these? This is the sign of a strong leader.

People who are dominated by one particular drive often fall short as leaders. Consider ambition. All of us know people who are wildly ambitious, and this drive can carry them a very long way. Their extraordinary focus on achievement and status might translate into a stellar grade point average, for example, and then a plum first job. It might even propel them quite far into a successful career.

But at some point, exhausting all of one's energy in the pursuit of status gains is a recipe for disaster. If we starve ourselves of our innate need to learn and grow in the name of ambition, we can turn into narcissists. Leaders must retain that central element of a balanced character. Along these lines, we have come full circle from the first chapter of this book, because a person who gets absorbed in his own ambition and does not possess integrity will not succeed. He will not become a great leader. Like the legendary Greek figure Icarus, whose unbridled passion impelled him too close to the sun, a leader who possesses ambition but no character will eventually get burned by hubris and greed.

ZEROING IN ON LEADERSHIP PASSION

Why do some people seem to be more passionate than others? Part of the reason is surely genetic. Humans are diverse. We show variability in height, personality, intelligence, athleticism, and numerous other traits. It would be surprising if differences in passion did not, at least to a certain extent, belong to a similar rank. For example, Jeff Bezos had to be dragged out of a kindergarten class because he didn't want to stop learning. Not every child experiences this same level of fascination.

Environment no doubt plays an important role as well. Where and how we are raised affects the way we think and behave. Some cultures and groups encourage expression; others discourage it. Some embrace competition and celebrate individual achievement; others are more collectivistic. Even within a particular culture, context takes the raw material of our inheritance and gives it texture, form, and shape.

Nevertheless, after working with leaders and studying this topic for many years, we are convinced that passion is something that lies within everyone's individual reach. Each of us has the ability to unlock our unique passion. In fact, great leaders demonstrate this. They are able to tap into the power of their deepest aspirations.

One of the keys to doing so is emotional intelligence, or a keen sense of self-awareness. Individuals who know themselves well and have a broad range of diverse experiences are most likely to find and direct their energies in focused, transformative ways. People with high emotional intelligence are also better equipped to temper their ambition and maintain a healthy balance.

Together passion and emotional intelligence run hand-in-hand. Armed with emotional intelligence, a potential leader is less likely to aimlessly strike out in pursuit of a career. The source of his inner strength can be understood and channeled. Like a biologist in possession of a powerful microscope, he can analyze his most basic interests and determine where to apply them to achieve the most productive gain.

The good news is that it is never too late to find one's passion. Sam Walton didn't open his first Walmart until he was forty-four, and KFC's Colonel Sanders didn't franchise his first restaurant until age sixty-five (using money from an early social security check). Nor should difficult circumstances be an excuse for inaction. Ambitious people find a way. Prior to writing her first Harry Potter book, J. K. Rowling was diagnosed with clinical depression, and she wrote it as a single mom on welfare. You don't have to be fresh out of university and armed with a trust fund to follow your passion. In fact, the reason most people fail to find their passion is that they do not look inside themselves and persevere long enough to yield results.

In terms of finding passion in others, most organizations look for high energy and enthusiasm, of course. Candidates who possess an inner fire are at the top of every recruiter's list.

Our approach is to dig beneath the surface to determine where that fire comes from. We want to make sure the candidate's passion will last. Too often interviewers mistake feigned high energy and a polished style for something more substantial, but a real drive to achieve or grow transcends any one-hour act.

During the assessment process, we also want to confirm that a candidate isn't in it just for himself. Effective leaders have balance. They must show that their ambitions are grounded and that their interest in the job doesn't stop at earning a substantial salary.

Here are a few questions that we like to use to kick-start the conversation when we interview executive candidates:

- What aspects of this job do you think you would most like? Which would you want to change or eliminate? Why?
- What would you like to achieve in this job?
- How is this organization, in particular, able to help you achieve your goals?
- What connection does the job you are seeking have to your current position?
- What kinds of jobs did you have when you were growing up?
- What was your first job?
- What aspect of work is boring to you?
- What motivates you?
- Who do you think has the best job in the world? Why?
- If you had it all to do over again, what career would you choose?
- How important is it to draw a line between your professional and your personal life? What are the pros and cons of some overlap?

While some of these questions may seem simplistic, the responses that individuals give reveal a lot. When interviewing for a leadership position, passionate candidates demonstrate that they have put a lot of thought into their answers. They are able to speak convincingly about the way in which the organizational mission and their personal passion are intertwined. For example, a candidate might bring up something about her personal background that is central to her leadership purpose today, similar to the way Nicholas Scopetta or Lance Armstrong might mention foster care or cancer, respectively. Using the detail of one's life story to show why the job matters on a visceral level is important. A passionate candidate will explain how this life story feeds into the demands of the job for which she is interviewing. Perhaps it's a matter of helping others as a way of expressing one's personal experience in foster care and the values that experience helped to shape. Others might be driven to run a medical device manufacturer as a way of releasing a dual passion of improving health care and a lifelong fascination with science. The truth is, we all have life stories. We all have our own unique set of experiences, values, goals, and aspirations. The difference is that passionate leaders know how to tie this to their leadership mission. For them, passion and the job description are almost one and the same.

We once interviewed a CEO candidate who told us, "My whole career . . . wait . . . my whole life seems to have been leading me to this job, this moment in time." We can't say we're strong believers in fate, and so initially we were skeptical. Was this a well-rehearsed line? Was he trying to game the interview process? Or was he for real? As we spent more time with him, we discovered he was for real.

Within seconds, before we even had a chance to start asking questions, he went on the offensive. He wasn't rude and wasn't trying to control the process; he was simply enthusiastic. He talked about the overall strategy and positioning of the company relative to other major players in the industry. With an impressive grasp of details about the company (some board members confided after the interview that even they didn't have this level of knowledge), he explained how the company's strategy was likely to suffer in the long run, particularly given recent acquisitions and technological advances made by competitors.

Turning the tables, he became the interviewer and started asking *us* questions about potential strategic options. What if we were to establish a joint venture with Company X to establish an early beachhead in the Chinese market? he asked. Do we have the bandwidth to upgrade our technological platform? He said, "I suspect we will need it if we continue to grow at the same pace, and hopefully we can grow even faster." Notice how he used *we* instead of *the company*, projecting confidence that he was already part of the team.

Not satisfied with gleaning a better strategic and technological understanding of the company, he then probed with savvy and genuine interest about sensitive cultural issues within the organization. Other CEO candidates thought these issues were too "soft" or "personal" to talk about in an interview. Not him. "Let me be frank," he said, "I have heard some not-so-flattering things swirling around about the culture of this organization." The candidate, having done his due diligence, had already spoken to several former executives who had left the firm to join competitors. He learned that while the company had great talent and a strong balance sheet, a silo mentality pervaded the company. Besides damaging morale and a sense of team spirit, this mentality also precluded the sharing of new ideas across geographical boundaries, he discovered. Growth and innovation were stifled.

The candidate talked about experiences he had had in two of his past jobs where he was on what he called a "personal silo-busting mission." The first time was a complete failure, he admitted. We were somewhat surprised but quite pleased that he volunteered a personal story about a failure. Usually we have to ask repeatedly before a candidate shares any story of defeat.

"I tried to strong-arm people in different divisions to work together, which was a nightmare. People resisted at every turn and dug their heels in even deeper. I learned that you can't make people want to work together; you have to show them the benefits of sharing and joining forces." He then explained to us that he suspected that this organization had a similar problem and that the approach he just explained could also work here. He was careful to say that he knew he didn't have all the answers and that he would likely have to make adjustments along the way. But it was clear to us that he had thought deeply about how his past experiences, personal passion, and the leadership requirements of the job made him the right candidate for the position.

Another passionate leader we met is John DeLucie, head chef of the Lion, in New York City, and the Royal, in Miami Beach, Florida. After opening in spring 2010 in Manhattan's West Village, the Lion spent the year as one of the most coveted reservations in town. Regulars included Cameron Diaz, Lenny Kravitz, and Jennifer Anniston. We asked around, and opinion differed as to why the place was such a big success. Some said it was the stoic doorman and trendy location. Others said the dark, decadent lounge. Still others noted the old-style Parisian salon, with framed art covering the walls. We suspected that it had more to do with the kitchen, with the sheep's-milk cavatelli and lobster pot pie—which is why we wanted to speak with DeLucie.

We weren't interviewing him for a leadership position, of course; we just wanted to learn more about the top leadership job in a restaurant—the head chef. After a few minutes with DeLucie, we wished that he had been an actual candidate because he was so authentic and fun. Our conversation amounted to DeLucie explaining his career path, to which he connected a long line of experiences, lessons, and personal values to what he most wanted to accomplish as a chef. He was brimming with energy and had plenty of ideas about what it takes to succeed in the competitive Manhattan restaurant market. In short, DeLucie exhibited all the signs of a person with enormous leadership passion.

First, there was the way he described his background. DeLucie grew up on Long Island and like a lot of other young people, for many years he didn't know what he wanted to do. He said that he was "miserable" during much of his twenties and hopped from one job to another. He tried sales, advertising, a stint as headhunter for the insurance industry. DeLucie did well, but he wasn't happy. At night he'd go home and console himself by strumming his guitar. "In my twenties I realized I wasn't tapping into things that made me feel fulfilled. I realized that I wanted to motivate people, I wanted to push them and be a part of something exciting and new. It took me a long time to figure out all that."

In 1990 he signed up for a class, The Master Chef, at the New School. There were eight or nine people in his class, and all of them, he says, were there for the same thing: to try something different, to break out of the routine, to grow. For DeLucie, the experience was particularly catalytic: "*This was cool*, I thought. It's all about the team. You've got the vegetables, I've got the protein . . . let's go! Let's crank out ninety meals in this little kitchen!"

One of his earliest jobs was working the grill for lunch at a place across from Bloomingdale's, near the intersection of Sixtieth Street and Third Avenue. "I got my head handed to me on the first day," DeLucie told us. "My boss pointed to the fryer and said, 'You work over there.' I had to make the same damn calamari caesar salad about a hundred times a day. I had to fry it, and it was all covered in flour and milk. At the end of lunch, I looked as though *I* had been fried."

Reading those words, you might think that DeLucie was bemoaning his earlier incarnation as an unappreciated apprentice. But when he told the story to us, he had a big grin on his face. For him, it was all part of getting better at something that he loved. "The cool thing was, I was between two guys—the pizza guy and the sauté station. It's like playing basketball. You had to get in there and score thirty points. The pressure was on, fatigue set in, but there was no way I wasn't going to do it."

While most of his other New School classmates had had enough after a year or two, DeLucie kept plowing forward, learning tricks of the trade from a variety of mentors, gaining recognition, and eventually finding his own niche as a chef. Early on he was at the French restaurant Luxe, working for executive chef Rick Laakkonen. "Nothing got past him," DeLucie recalled. "That's when I saw that you had to be uncompromising in the product, as well as in the selection of your cooks, because you're only as good as your team, and you can't cook every dish alone." Fifteen years later, at the Waverly Restaurant, DeLucie remembered that lesson when a reviewer from the *New York Times* showed up. "They came in," DeLucie told us, "and my first impulse was to push my assistants out of the way and cook everything myself, but I backed off. I had to trust my guys."

DeLucie's story struck a chord with us because we have met hundreds of otherwise passionate leaders who were unable to step back and adopt this kind of detached posture under pressure. The natural tendency is to rush forward even harder. This is a common weak point for many passionate leaders, and it can have a devastating effect on one's support team. But DeLucie, to his credit, exhibited enough self-control at the Waverly to avoid this trap.

After Luxe, DeLucie became a sous chef at Nick and Tony's and then worked for Steve Hanson at the Blue Water Grill. He landed his first gig as head chef at Night and Day, "for a debonair French guy" who was known for operating hangout joints rather than world-class kitchens. "It wasn't gastronomic, but I didn't care. I assembled a great team and loved the food that I was making. We had this great grilled pizza flatbread." Later he moved to Al Forno in Providence, Rhode Island; Bridgehampton Café in the Hamptons on Long Island; and then back to Manhattan to Oceana (under Rick Moonen), the Waverly, and finally the Lion.

Throughout DeLucie's incredible journey from salesman to celebrated chef, he followed his passion. Once he discovered what he truly wanted to do, he never wavered, and he never held back. Each step along the way, from cooking school to head chef, was merely another progressive opportunity to channel his energies toward bigger things. Like the other leaders described in this chapter, DeLucie exhibits a healthy competitive streak, as well as a strong desire to grow and master his industry. He was not shy in telling us of his entrepreneurial dream to be in charge of a few more restaurants. But also like the best leaders, DeLucie's passions are balanced. He hasn't allowed his success to let him get carried away. When he spoke of the future, he kept referring to his past. He said that trendy restaurants come and go, and owners are always looking for that elusive silver bullet in the form of the next big hit. But to be successful, DeLucie told us, a chef can't stray too far from his roots. "In New York it's either an enormous hit or you fail. That's why the food in the city becomes very much the same—people don't want to take chances. For me, I always revert to my childhood. I don't need to be fancy. I don't push forward; I look back. What did I eat as a kid? What do I like? Other people try to get too fancy. You've got to know who you are if you want to succeed," he said.

It's hard not to be impressed by DeLucie's passion, but what sets him and other leaders apart is the way in which their strengths are balanced with so many other traits. The greatest leaders exhibit all seven leadership attributes. To truly excel, one, two, or even a few are not enough. A candidate who possesses passion, along with the other six essential attributes, is most likely to make a strong and lasting impact on any organization.

A Better Way to Choose Leaders

Without a doubt, it is difficult to pick good leaders, and the reason why can be broken down into two areas: the what and the how. The *what* aspect refers to the particular qualities to seek in a potential leader. Should the person be empathic, smart, forward thinking, creative? Which attributes are most important? Once this question has been settled, the next hurdle is determining whether a candidate possesses the requisite traits. This is the *how*. Is the quality hidden? Is it measurable? Is the candidate bluffing? How can you fairly and accurately compare two or more candidates?

In the first seven chapters, we described the essential attributes of effective leadership: integrity, empathy, emotional intelligence, vision, judgment, courage, and passion. At the end of each chapter, we also provided techniques for determining whether a person possesses that particular attribute. Together, these end-of-chapter sections provide a snapshot of the overall leadership assessment process.

This final chapter contains a more complete description of how a robust leadership assessment assignment works in organizations. We take you behind closed boardroom doors to show what decision makers look at when trying to decide between two stellar candidates, both with highly accomplished track records and a knack for making things happen. How do boards choose one candidate over another? How does a CEO become aware of a rising star in the organization early in his or her career? How does your boss know if you have what it takes to succeed at the next level, in a role radically different from the one you're in now? We also show how the best organizations help rising stars reach full leadership potential. Executive assessment and leadership development should always be tightly linked. CEOs don't care about an executive assessment report; they care about developing leaders. And the assessment is the essential first step that guides the entire leadership development process.

In world-class organizations, leadership assessment is used as both a means to make better leadership choices and as a road map for grooming rising stars. It is now time to tie all of this information together.

· · · · · · · · ·

We once met a man named Michael (not his real name) who was the president of a major division of an international medical equipment manufacturer. The division had annual revenues of several hundred million dollars and would have been clicking on all cylinders were it not for one particular product group. The group was poorly managed and an underperformer according to both company and industry standards. Michael, along with other senior executives at the company, determined that the leader of that product group had to be removed from the position, and they started a search for a replacement. Michael contacted a talent advisor from a large international executive search firm, explained the open position to her, and discussed what kind of candidate the company needed.

A week later, Michael and the advisor met to discuss a few potential candidates. One of the candidates (we'll call him Richard), Michael later told us, jumped out at him. "He had great experience in the industry, a track record of turning around underperforming business, and already had relationships with several of our largest customers," Michael enthused. Moreover, the search firm had conducted extensive background referencing, and all signs were positive. Richard was results oriented, friendly, well liked, and driven.

Michael interviewed Richard for two hours, and everything he learned left a positive impression. The two men discussed the industry. They talked about mutual acquaintances. They reviewed Richard's work history and many accomplishments. One episode in particular caught Michael's attention: Richard was able to sell a large piece of business to a customer with whom Michael had had absolutely no success, despite years of effort.

"That was the clincher," Michael admitted. "I was definitely convinced that he was the right guy."

The company hired Richard, but only six months later it was clear that this was a mistake. Richard was skilled at bringing in new business, just as Michael had predicted, but several problem areas emerged. In particular, he failed to develop and communicate a coherent vision for his product group. Many of his subordinates were left in the dark and had little idea how their day-to-day jobs helped the company achieve its strategic objectives. When morale slumped, Richard reverted to what he knew best: he gathered everyone in his group for emergency off-site meetings and gave them a motivational sales pitch that many viewed as obtuse, even condescending. "Does he think I am a client?" one subordinate later admitted to thinking. Richard showed a severe lack of empathy and emotional intelligence. He was unable to read his audience and anticipate their needs or likely reaction, much less adjust his leadership style in a way that resonated.

Why did this happen? How could the hiring mistake have been avoided?

Michael fell into some classic leadership selection traps when evaluating Richard. First, Michael was unduly swayed by Richard's ability to talk convincingly about his past triumphs. Although it is certainly important to understand a candidate's professional record, most senior-level executives have had years to rehearse for this type of interview.[1] Candidates expect to be asked about their successes (and failures), and it is not all that hard for them to come to the interview prepared with three or four impressive stories to tell. In Richard's case especially, given his charm and impressive selling skills, delivering a polished pitch must have been easy. Michael also placed disproportionate weight on Richard's story about bagging a coveted customer. Naturally this story impressed Michael, but in the overall scheme of things, the story didn't represent much in terms of Richard's ability to lead in the new position.

This brings us to the most common assessment mistake, and one that Michael committed: failing to determine whether a leader can succeed in a fundamentally new and challenging position. The problem with the way in which most leadership candidates are evaluated is that the process is essentially backward looking. People like Michael spend inordinate amounts of time going over a candidate's résumé and credentials: they ask about prior successes and failures, they ask others how the candidate performed, and so on. But this backward-looking investigation has limited predictive value when trying to determine a candidate's likely success in a different position.

HOW TO CONDUCT A FIRST-RATE LEADERSHIP ASSESSMENT ASSIGNMENT

Richard's case is not unusual, and after one or two misfires like this, most CEOs and boards of directors are anxious to make sure that it doesn't happen again. They want to learn how to make informed leadership selection decisions.

Getting Started

The first step in this process is putting together a list of potential candidates, usually with the help of a top executive search firm. These firms typically do a good job helping organizations assemble a pool of candidates with the right background and experience. We need to be clear here, because we mentioned that a candidate's prior experience and success shouldn't unduly influence the assessment of her ability to lead in a more challenging position. While this is true, a solid track record is still the right starting point. In order to put together a list of candidates, we must start somewhere, and narrowing the candidate pool based on education, experience, skills, and training is the logical first step. Experience matters a lot when it comes to finding the right leader. As we discussed in Chapter Five, experience gives individuals the opportunity to learn, grow, and reflect, all of which are necessary for making increasingly complex executive decisions. That a candidate should have familiarity with the relevant industry also makes a great deal of sense. After all, it would be hard to imagine a successful professional basketball coach who didn't have experience in the sport, a university president without a history in academia, or a CEO of a high-tech company who didn't understand the underlying technology. To be sure, smart people are fast learners, and a small percentage of leaders have successfully taken on challenging roles with little or no direct experience. But this is the exception, not the rule.

This point recalls the disastrous performance of John Sculley, the former Pepsi executive who was hired as CEO of Apple Computer in 1983. "I came in not knowing anything about computers," Sculley said. After ten painful years and countless ill-advised strategic decisions (most notably a failure to partner with Intel so that Apple's software could run on Intel's microprocessors), Sculley was fired by the company's board in 1993. In a 2010 interview, Sculley openly admitted, "Looking back it was a big mistake that I was ever

hired as CEO." Sculley confided that he just didn't have the technical expertise to run Apple.[2]

Once a pool of candidates is assembled, organizations often
engage an external leadership assessment professional. This is the
point at which we are often invited to enter the process. When organizations call on us to help them identify the right leader, they typically have three or four candidates already in mind. At this juncture,
we sit down with the CEO, board member, and human resource
executive who are leading the search, and we discuss the candidates
and position. We focus on a number of questions—for example:

- How much overlap is there between each candidate's current job
  and the one for which he or she is interviewing?
- What are the major challenges that the new person is likely to
  face in the organization?
- To whom will the candidate report?
- Who will be on the candidate's team?
- What resources will he or she have?
- How do you expect the job to evolve?
- How much time is available to learn new skills?

We also want to learn more about the organization's culture.
This is important for ensuring that we identify the candidate who is
the best fit for the organization, on top of his or her leadership potential and skills. Along these lines, at this stage in the discussion, many
executives want to make sure that we recommend a candidate
with the right "personality" or "style." This can be a tricky issue.
For starters, *personality* is an extremely vague word. In our experience, when executives discuss personality, no two of them use the
word to mean exactly the same thing. For some organizations,
the "right" personality means someone who is highly driven. For
others, it means someone who operates with grace under pressure,
or who is even-tempered, or who is transparent and candid. Often

these qualities aren't personality types at all, but rather character attributes. Incidentally, these attributes are all tested for in our leadership assessment model, such as grace under pressure (courage), even-temperedness (emotional intelligence), tenacity (passion), and transparency or candor (integrity). These latter (character) attributes always matter, regardless of corporate culture.

The other reason that personality is a bit of a thorny issue is that personality type is not an accurate predictor of leadership potential. This statement comes as a surprise to many of our clients, particularly those who are used to assessing executives using the latest personality assessment tool. A misconception continues to persist that individuals with a charismatic personality, for example, are more likely to be effective leaders than those who have a more taciturn or reserved personality. But research does not support this conclusion.[3] In fact, management expert Jim Collins indicates that a charismatic personality can even be negatively correlated with leadership success. In *Good to Great*, he uses the term "Level 5" to describe the highest level in a hierarchy of executive capabilities. Level 5 leaders were at the helm of all eleven exceptional companies that he identified—companies that outperformed the general stock market by nearly seven times over a fifteen-year period.[4] Importantly, these leaders were not the high-profile, larger-than-life personalities who occupy the public's imagination. Instead, Collins writes, "Self-effacing, quiet, reserved, even shy—these leaders are a paradoxical blend of personal humility and professional will. They are more like Lincoln and Socrates than Patton or Caesar."[5]

Similarly, many people use the word *style* without clearly expressing what they mean. For some, leadership style is a label for the same attributes listed above, such as a person who operates with transparency. Others use it to mean a nurturing or participative approach. For others, the word might refer to a person's willingness to roll up his sleeves and dive into the details of a job. When it comes to leadership effectiveness, however, trying to make an inference based on one's "style" carries the same difficulties as personality type. Research on the relationship between style and executive success is mixed at best.[6]

More important than having a particular style is the ability to adapt one's style to meet different circumstances and demands. Former Medtronic CEO Bill George writes that in today's fast-moving environment, leaders must "adapt their style to fit the immediate situation. There are times to be inspiring and motivating, and times to be tough about people decisions or financial decisions. There are times to delegate, and time to be deeply immersed in the details. There are times to communicate public messages, and times to have private conversations."[7] In other words, a successful leader must wear a variety of hats. This does not mean that a leader should be inauthentic or try to emulate others. What it does mean is that successful leaders know how to stretch their skills and behavior in different ways. This ability to do this requires a high degree of social savvy, empathy, and emotional intelligence, for the reasons explained in Chapters Two and Three in this book. (Appendix B provides a guide to how these and other attributes work together.) These are precisely the kinds of skills that Richard in our example lacked. An assessment process that favors one style over another is comparatively superficial and less likely to yield accurate results.

Nevertheless, engaging in a discussion with senior management about any personality or style concerns that they might have can be an important part of the candidate selection process. As assessment specialists, we want to understand as much as we can about the organization's culture. Often this requires probing a CEO or human resource executive to determine what he or she means exactly by a "style" or "personality" that is consistent with the position. If the organization's culture is described as autonomous, hard-charging, the "eat-what-you-kill" type, for example, and the candidate will be constantly feeling pressure to perform, this is valuable information for us. At the other end of the spectrum, the culture might be more team oriented and focused on consensus building. Some organizations have a disciplined or conservative culture; others are more free-wheeling and open to radically different ideas. Some emphasize work-life balance, while others are known for grueling hours and short weekends. Whatever the case, it is important for us to understand these nuances and differences before beginning the individual assessment process. Armed with this knowledge, we are equipped not only to recommend the candidate who demonstrates sufficient leadership potential, but also the one who is the best organizational fit.

Conducting the Assessment (Getting to Know the Candidates)

Once the specifications for the position are clear, and the initial candidates are chosen, we meet individually with each of them.[8] These meetings take place at the organization's office or at a neutral location. This is our opportunity to get to know each candidate and to assess his or her leadership potential. To do so, we use a combination of approaches and techniques. We work with the organization to determine precisely which assessment tools make the most sense. The important issue is to get agreement at the start as to which assessment tools to use, which might include 360-degree referencing, simulations and case studies, direct observation in group settings, traditional behavioral interviews that focus on past accomplishments, and specially created hypothetical scenarios that test a candidate's leadership potential. This last technique is critical because it is forward looking. Unlike a typical interview question that asks candidates to discuss what happened in the past, these hypothetical situations present candidates with unfamiliar and challenging leadership situations. No amount of preparation or interview savvy will enable a candidate to fudge her answer or game the interview process.[9]

Instead, we have an opportunity to watch how she thinks on her feet and learn how she would likely approach a leadership challenge if she were hired for the position. Does she exhibit the kind of ethical awareness needed to lead the organization in unpredictable circumstances? Does she demonstrate empathy and emotional intelligence? Does she possess the kind of disciplined, analytical thinking necessary to make complex business decisions? To underscore the importance of this approach, imagine the answers we would get if we probed candidates on these leadership attributes using a traditional backward-looking question. Imagine if we asked, "Do you believe in transparency and integrity in the workplace?" "Tell us about a complex business problem that you were able to solve," "Are you capable of admitting mistakes or dealing with your blind spots?" Comparatively speaking, these are softball questions. A savvy interviewer will have prepared good answers well in advance. And even then the answers are not necessarily indicative of how she will react to a challenge that she has never seen before. Backward-looking questions simply do not provide a complete picture, despite the fact that some pundits cling to the belief that the past is the best predictor of future success. This is true only to the extent that the future position is the same as the old one, which is rarely the case when an individual gets promoted or recruited to an entirely new organization.

Providing Feedback (Don't Let the Reports Sit on a Shelf and Collect Dust)

Our approach overcomes the limitations of traditional interviews, and based on the results, we prepare a leadership potential profile. This profile summarizes the candidate's assessment across each of the seven essential attributes described in this book and benchmarks these results against other best-in-class executive leaders around the world. From this, we are able to compare candidates' overall potential not just against each other but also relative to other leaders. This is quite valuable for organizations that want to see if they have the caliber of talent needed to surpass (or at a minimum, just keep up with) top competitors.[10]

In our final feedback session, we also take into account the organizational culture and other job specifications discussed earlier in the process. The result is a summary recommendation, including an objective, data-driven profile of each candidate's overall fitness for the position.

Finally, because we are able to measure a candidate's leadership potential across several attributes, our evaluation also provides the organization with valuable information regarding potential trouble spots in the event that a particular candidate is hired. Most seasoned boards and realistic executives understand that there is no perfect leader. With this in mind, they appreciate knowing about potential red flags ahead of time. Using this information, they can take steps and avoid being blindsided by an unanticipated trouble spot down the road. For example, if our assessment shows that a candidate generally possesses strong leadership potential, but sometimes has difficulty with complex social dynamics, the organization can provide special assistance in the event that the candidate is hired. Indeed, in this type of situation, we are often asked to recommend and work closely with specialized coaches who can bridge the gap. Other times we help select, or even help create, a particular type of executive education program. Or we may assist the organization with choosing a mentor from within the organization who will get the new person comfortable with the unfamiliar social structure. Linking the assessment process with an ongoing, robust leadership development program is something that the best organizations undertake.

In addition to the assessment report and analysis that we provide to organizations, we provide feedback to individual candidates. From both the organizational and individual candidate standpoint, this kind of feedback is important regardless of which candidate is ultimately selected.

USING LEADERSHIP ASSESSMENT TO SUPERCHARGE LEADERSHIP DEVELOPMENT

Let's return to the case of Michael and his medical equipment man-ufacturer. After the painful episode with Richard, senior manage-ment did not want to make the same mistake again. This time they wanted another point of view to confirm that Richard's replacement was in fact the right person to hire. So they engaged us to conduct an objective leadership assessment of three new candidates, one of whom ("Kevin") was ultimately selected.

Not stopping there, however, the company decided that it wanted to get a much better grasp of the leadership potential among its senior ranks. For succession planning purposes, the company took a more long-term view and determined that it needed to know the extent of its ready-now, near-ready, or rising-star talent. Ready-now successors are immediately ready to step into the new executive role being considered. For example, during CEO succession discus-sions, many boards like to say, "If our CEO was hit by a bus, would we have any ready-now successors to take his or her place?" Near-ready successors are one to three years away from being able to step into the role being considered. And rising stars are three to five or more years away from stepping into the role being discussed.[11]

Assessing its talent early on, the company further reasoned, would be an excellent way to foster a culture of leadership develop-ment across the entire organization and send a positive signal to the outside world, which is exactly what happened. Before long, many external candidates learned of the company's reinvigorated focus on leadership development and secretly began to make inquiries. The HR director later confided to us that the number of external appli-cants had increased threefold since the company had become more serious about leadership development and career advancement.

The company's efforts are representative of how this kind of initiative begins at many organizations. It also serves as a perfect example of how leadership assessment can be used to supercharge a successful overall talent development program. What follows is a summary of how it worked in this company's case (with all names changed to protect anonymity).

The CEO and head of HR took the lead from the beginning. Getting the CEO's involvement was critical in order to let other members of management know that they should take the initiative seriously. The right tone has to be set at the top for an organization to develop a culture that embraces leadership development. Otherwise managers on the front line, concerned about hitting hard revenue targets and securing new clients, for example, might initially view a new leadership development exercise as soft and not meaningful. When the CEO gets behind it, however, others fall in line. In this organization, the CEO and head of HR selected four or five individuals whom they thought would constitute the most appropriate focus group for the assessment initiative.

At first, the "guinea pigs," as they called themselves, were not pleased. Not knowing what to expect, they didn't see the assessment project as a great opportunity but as a distraction from their jobs. They grumbled and moaned, saying, "I don't need a test . . . I've been here for sixteen years," or "I have an M.B.A. from Stanford . . . I know about leadership." This initial resistance was typical of what we see at many companies. Frank, transparent communication to explain the process and the many benefits is an important first step. We often advise the CEO to send a personal note to each candidate explaining what to expect.

The assessment professional also plays a key role in helping to put the candidates at ease during the entire assessment and feedback process. In fact, if this is done correctly, a strong connection emerges between the assessment professional and the candidate, particularly after constructive development advice is dispensed.

In virtually every situation, participants eventually warm up to the process, which is what happened in this case. In fact, after they got into the actual assessment interview, many of them wanted more. The interactive hypothetical scenarios in particular were something they truly enjoyed (which is very typical too). Many of them made comments such as, "I was a little nervous at first, but this is pretty neat. It's sort of like the debates we used to have in my most interesting M.B.A. classes," or, "You know, this kind of situation just seems so *real*. It could happen tomorrow," or, "That was the fastest two hours of my entire week." For them and others, the one-on-one interaction was totally unlike anything that they might have imagined in terms of a "test." They immediately recognized the applicability, and each of them wanted feedback. "How do I stack up against other leaders in my field?" they wanted to know. "What did you notice? How can I become a better leader?"

From this small group of four, the word spread. And as the assessment process expanded, the resistance early participants showed gave way to a more positive reaction. People started to view the project as a critical part of their own leadership development. Instead of seeing it as a test, they began to see it as an opportunity. Moreover, an invitation to participate was seen as a badge of honor, a source of pride—an indication that the organization was considering them for bigger challenges.

From the organization's point of view, there were many obvious benefits. The first was a much deeper, robust understanding of the company's bench strength in several key areas. Senior leaders immediately had a clear picture of the specific strengths, weaknesses, and potential trouble spots for each key member of their teams. On a larger scale, this is exactly what occurred after Peter Löscher took over as CEO of Siemens in 2007. As we discussed in Chapter Five, as part of his repositioning strategy at Siemens, Löscher launched a leadership assessment of the top four hundred people in the company, which he correctly believed was needed before he could successfully execute his bold, new strategy. The results were integrated with a new management review process.

Löscher and the managing board were then able to make much more informed executive decisions.

Similarly, in the case of Michael and Kevin, the leadership assessment process gave them valuable, actionable information. They were able to ascertain that all but one of their senior executive team members were in the right role given their respective strengths.

Once this step was complete, Kevin did a bit of "job sculpting," to ensure that the scope, requirements, and authority of each remaining position were in sync with an individual's abilities and potential. This stretched everyone, but without stretching anyone too thin. The stage was set for them to develop and grow in their jobs while not burning them out.

This process also recalls the example of Mike Krzyzewski that we highlighted in Chapter Two. In order to maximize the chemistry and overall performance on the men's Olympic basketball team, Coach K leveraged the strengths of each player. He put each player in the right role and tweaked his respective responsibilities. Coach K's ability to recognize and manage the group's bench strength was a key element in Team USA's gold medal success in the Olympics. Coach K only had a dozen or so athletes to gauge, and he spent hours with them every day. Assessing the leadership potential of a large group of corporate professionals, who are in different places at different times, and each with different resources and responsibilities, is a more complicated endeavor.

Another major benefit of the assessment performed for the medical equipment manufacturer was the custom-tailored feedback that every individual received. After participating in the interview, everyone was able to get honest, objective feedback, or what we like to call "feed forward."[12] For some, it was the first time that they had received direct, constructive feedback about their leadership skills and potential.

The assessments also helped the rising stars zero in and focus on the small handful of personal development issues that needed the most work. Without the assessment, many would not have known where to target (or even begin) their efforts. One executive admitted to us that he had twelve action items to focus on in his last HR-created developmental plan. "It was way too much and too tactical. I ended up blowing off the whole list and accomplished nothing."

The net effect on Kevin's group was a noticeable improvement in performance. In a departure from the past, the group did not lag behind other units, but instead excelled. Performance reviews showed an improvement in eight of the ten areas that were measured for purposes of calculating professional bonuses, including teamwork, cross-selling, and customer satisfaction. The company reported that group morale also increased dramatically. Because individuals knew that management cared about their development, they became more invested in their jobs as well as the overall organization.

There was also a more subtle, but very important, benefit for Kevin. With a succession plan and the right leadership development initiatives in place, he too was more likely to move up. After all, most organizations are reluctant to promote a leader unless senior management, or the board in the case of CEO succession, is confident that a successor can seamlessly replace him. They don't want to leave a key position empty or understaffed. By developing the people beneath him, Kevin was also giving himself a career boost. And once his promotion came, he could rest more easily knowing his division would be in good hands. Often a leader's legacy is shaped and cemented by how well the organization performs after he or she leaves. This is particularly true for the top spot of CEO.

Finally, from the CEO's point of view, the business unit finally had a plan to develop leaders from within. They no longer had to turn to outsiders on an ad hoc, emergency basis. Although senior management realized that bringing some outsiders onboard kept the company from becoming insular, they also knew that this practice was risky. Historical research shows that filling top positions from the inside is a less risky choice, particularly when the company isn't floundering.[13] Once a leadership assessment and development process was put in place, however, the former danger was mitigated.

WHEN AND HOW TO BEGIN

From an organizational standpoint, assessing high-potential leaders is the first step toward building a strong leadership bench. This part of the process allows an individual to honestly evaluate and understand his or her bundle of strengths and developmental opportunities. Using this information, the individual can then focus on the two or three areas that need the most work over the next year. Over time, the individual has the opportunity to sharpen many leadership attributes and enjoy cumulative success. In other words, in order to maximize leadership potential, both the assessment and development pieces must be tightly linked.

In terms of timing, it is wise to begin the process relatively early in one's career. The most effective CEOs we have seen are those who started to focus on personal leadership development by the time they were thirty. Equinox Fitness CEO Harvey Spevak told us, "We start developing leaders almost immediately. People who show promise at the individual fitness club level soon find that they are leading several locations, or even an entire region. At each increasing level of responsibility, weak spots emerge, but we're right there helping them reflect and giving them support. Building our leadership pipeline in this way has proven to be a major advantage as we grow nationally and into new markets, like yoga and personal training. We rarely have to rely on outside talent because we do such a nice job developing it in-house."[14]

Another key to a successful leadership development process is making sure that assessment reports do not sit on a shelf and collect dust. An action plan should be set in motion right away. For example, consider the following profile summaries. These are typical of what an organization might do after an initial, trial assessment:

> John showed a lot of analytical horsepower, but he lacked confidence and didn't fully connect with others. Instead, he used a cookie-cutter approach when communicating with colleagues, customers, and in front of groups, and he frequently came off as rigid. In short, John didn't do a good enough job of trying to understand what made others tick; he needed to better leverage his empathic ability. To address this challenge, John recruited a mentor from inside the organization who was known for her ability to relate well with a wide variety of constituents. With John present, we helped the mentor understand John's development need and how other leaders had effectively used mentors in a similar situation.

> Susan was a hard-charging, experienced professional with a relatively narrow band of expertise. She was the person the boss called on if a task absolutely had to get done in a short time frame and on budget. Her challenge, however, was that she found it hard to stray outside her comfort zone. Like John, Susan was smart, but she didn't approach tough challenges from multiple viewpoints or solicit the input of others. To improve in this area, she used an external coach. The coach helped her see the value of proactively approaching others on her team and throughout the organization, before rolling out a solution. The coach even offered tactical advice regarding when and how to approach others. After a while, Susan began to probe complicated issues from multiple angles; she showed others that she cared about their ideas, and she was able to get needed buy-in.

> Tony had a brilliant creative mind, and generated lots of interesting ideas, but when it came to execution he was too slow. He tried to "boil the ocean," as the expression goes.

Tony's leadership assessment revealed that he lacked enough courage to pull the trigger and make tough decisions. Instead, he often let projects linger, or didn't assert himself vigorously enough to get sufficient resources to carry his ideas into practice. To deal with this development need, the organization sent Tony to a specialized executive education course that we recommended. The course was not the generic, open-enrollment variety, but rather one that focused on developing courage as a skill. With practice, Tony became more confident, and he learned to adopt a useful internal calculus for approaching difficult challenges and making faster decisions.

Simon was a midlevel rising star. Although he had never been flagged for character issues, his leadership assessment showed that he didn't have a particularly high level of ethical awareness. Combined with his strong ambition and concern for personal achievement, this represented a caution sign. Without further attention, Simon might have been setting his organization (and himself) up for trouble down the road. Additional 360 referencing was conducted to probe this issue further, and Simon was also given some honest feedback during the assessment process. This is a sensitive area for any professional or organization. But often a little extra work early on can thwart a real ethical breach later, when the temptation and stakes are higher.

As these examples show, there are many leadership development options that an organization can choose from. The challenge is picking the right ones. Once a critical mass of individuals has gone through the assessment and feedback process, the organization can discern some important developmental themes and commit resources in just the right way. It might learn that a core group of employees needs work with complex social dynamics, for example. As a result, the organization can custom-tailor its leadership development activities to meet these specific needs. Note how different this is from merely sending a large number of executives to a more generic, off-the-shelf executive education program. Besides the high cost, this option won't focus on the growth issues that are most critical for the organization's attendees. Indeed, for them, a general management program or other open enrollment course might be entirely misguided. In fact, many executives have confided to us that they attended these programs for the opportunity to say that they participated in a top-tier program, even though, in retrospect, they aren't convinced that they actually learned much. But they did enjoy showcasing their new credentials by hanging their "Executive Education" diplomas on their office walls.

A better development approach uses the assessment results as a prescription and road map for more specialized, custom-tailored activities. For example, among the sample summaries provided above, all of the individuals showed significant analytical skills. They were all strong thinkers and driven professionals. At the same time, each also came up short in the area of strategic thinking and innovation. Using this information, an organization could build a robust leadership development plan that might include some or all of the following:

- Creation of highly customized internal executive education programs by cherry-picking strategic management professors from top business schools
- Action learning programs where rising stars work on actual corporate challenges and new innovative projects under the supervision of external executive education faculty and internal mentors
- Rotation programs that give rising stars broader knowledge of the organization, for example, a stint in China or in a new function like finance, strategy, or marketing

- Mentoring programs, where rising stars meet with and confidentially discuss with seasoned executives within the company new strategic ideas, possible solutions, and how to get internal buy-in of these ideas
- External coaching to work on the specific and highly specialized needs of the rising stars, like communicating an entirely new vision or innovation in a succinct, meaningful way to constituents
- Shadowing opportunities where rising stars are afforded the opportunity to work side by side with senior executives in the company to learn firsthand what works and why it works
- Fresh job opportunities and challenges created for high-potential leaders even if the position is entirely new to the company
- The creation of a special, cross-functional task force or committee for rising stars that encourages them to share ideas and solve broader corporate-wide challenges with other rising stars who have different backgrounds
- Serving on external committees and boards to broaden the perspective of the rising star beyond his or her corporate walls
- Internal summits where rising stars meet among themselves to voice concerns, discuss future challenges, share insight, and build relationships with one another, which has the benefit of building the informal networks needed to get things done more efficiently in the organization

One company that truly understands and leverages the link between assessment and development is Allianz SE, based in Germany. Allianz is among the world's largest insurance and financial services providers, with 2010 revenues in the range of $100 billion. In order to advance to the highest levels of management at the company, individuals must participate in a formal leadership assessment process. In particular, leaders and senior professionals are evaluated according to key, predefined competencies, common to the whole Allianz Group, and part of a career development center (CDC), which is basically a management review structure that was put in place in 2008 to assess, monitor, and develop the Group's top talent. "We do CDCs in all our countries and in all entities," explained Werner Zedelius, Allianz SE board member in charge of human resources. "So for the company in Korea, there will be a CDC in Korea. The same would apply in India or the United States or Spain or Germany."[15] The CDCs extend to functional practice areas and global business lines, as well as to the top executive team in the company's Munich headquarters. As of 2010, over three thousand senior professionals were included in the company's assessment database. "For a selected group of executives, this process is also accompanied by an external assessment specialist," Zedelius told us, "and the candidate gets the usual 360-degree review from subordinates, peers, and bosses. Depending on the level, it's more intense and always ends in the structure of the CDC."

Because all executives worldwide are assessed according to the same template, Allianz has a clear, continuous picture of its leadership depth across the organization. Consequently, as part of the CDCs and for succession planning purposes, it can place individuals within a grid to highlight which ones have the potential to move up or sideways. This process enables senior management to anticipate any potential leadership gaps before they occur and then do something about it. It also gives them a realistic, up-to-date snapshot of their ability to execute key strategic initiatives given the talent in key jobs.

In addition, Allianz uses the CDC process as an integral part of its overall leadership development efforts. The company takes information obtained from its assessment results to customize both individual and group initiatives. At the individual level, this means tailoring personal development agendas that address any deficiencies indicated by the assessment model. If the assessment process unveils a development need in the area of emotional intelligence, empathy, or social savvy, for example, this is addressed through executive coaching, mentoring, and other local activities.

Assessment results also enable professionals and their bosses to work together to make sure that there are open feedback, targets, and clear expectations. "We expect that everybody has a personal development plan based on results out of the CDC," Zedelius told us. "This is another advantage of the structured assessment approach. Some critical discussions need to take place for people to move ahead, and this process leads to a more regular, transparent exchange between individual managers and others in the organization who are responsible for evaluating and supporting them. At first we had to learn how to give tough, honest feedback and support, and it wasn't easy. Now we're getting pretty good at it." Altogether this well-coordinated effort ensures that Allianz is developing individuals locally who will have the ability to lead on a global scale.

On a more general level, the company uses its assessment process as a way of funneling the most qualified leaders of the organization into critical development programs. For example, over a period of months, these senior leaders must go through a special development program at the Allianz Management Institute, located just outside Munich. The curriculum there includes customized leadership workshops and seminars that the company has developed with the help of some of the world's leading business schools and experts. Program content is highly practical, reflecting actual business challenges facing Allianz.

"This has worked out very well for us," Zedelius explained. "It's a big opportunity for the people. Participants in these programs have to work on concrete topics and present them back to the board. It's a very good exercise to widen their horizon to get them to better understand Allianz from a totally new perspective, from an elevated, helicopter view. It also stretches and strengthens them as leaders."

As the experience of Allianz shows, linking the assessment process with custom-tailored development initiatives is a powerful approach to grooming leaders. In fact, in the best organizations, these elements are tightly intertwined. Organizations that follow this approach benefit from a larger and deeper talent pool. They also consistently choose better leaders for key roles; develop solid succession plans; rely less on riskier, external talent searches; witness increased internal morale; strengthen their competitive advantage; and become a desirable destination for high-caliber professionals who seek an organization with the reputation for a strong commitment to leadership development.

But where does an organization start? It can seem overwhelming to a CEO who reads about companies that have built formidable leadership development brands over the last several decades, including General Electric, Procter & Gamble, and Johnson & Johnson. One CEO admitted to us, "I want to do the right thing. I want to invest in my people and help them grow, but I have no idea where to start, and I can't afford to spend as much as GE. I know GE is good, but frankly I'm tired of hearing about them!" There's a very simple answer to that dilemma. First, the CEO should not aspire to be GE. He should focus on the specific leadership development activities that make sense for his organization, based on aggregated feedback from assessment reports and analysis. This will likely be a small slice of what GE focuses on, and that's okay. Second, where does it all start, how can the CEO get the ball rolling?

It all starts with a reliable assessment of leadership potential. We urge organizations of all shapes and sizes to focus more closely on the seven attributes that truly matter: integrity, empathy, emotional intelligence, vision, judgment, courage, and passion.

* * * * * * * * *

The seven leadership attributes also form the right starting place for readers everywhere who are ready to begin choosing better leaders. Now that you understand the fundamental attributes—the basic building blocks—of leadership, what they mean, and why they are important, the next step is up to you. In the Introduction we made the point that we can't always blame our leaders for failing us. We too need to shoulder some of the responsibility. After all, we are the ones who promoted them through the leadership pipeline. Now that you have a better idea of how the best organizations zero in on promising talent, of what is discussed behind closed boardroom doors before new promotions are handed out, we hope that you are well positioned to zero in on real talent and make effective choices when selecting leaders.

In a more personal way, we hope you will begin to think about leadership, including the leaders most important to you, in a new light. When it comes time to elect your next mayor, for example, we hope you will look beyond her charm, her background, or her debating skills. Does the candidate demonstrate empathy? What is her level of ethical awareness? Does she have the courage to make tough decisions? It is not possible for each of us to evaluate candidates in a comprehensive, one-on-one interview. But we can start asking better questions in public debates. And we can certainly be more astute listeners during these debates. We can better separate substance from spin. We can influence journalists to focus on the most important matters when they go to press. We can use social media and online communication to shape discussion in a way that is more closely tied to leadership potential. We can approach the evaluation of our future leaders with more sophistication. And we can do this with less anxiety and confusion by remembering the leadership framework described in the previous chapters.

Similarly, using the insights in this book, every reader should be able to make better talent-related decisions in his or her organization. When hiring new people, figuring out who to promote, or appointing a leader of a new team, we can cut through distraction and focus on emotional intelligence or judgment, for example, and put considerations of a candidate's educational background or personality to rest. We can be wary of canned answers to predictable, backward-looking questions. Whether it's hiring a new supervisor, a new basketball coach, or a new university president, the same fundamental building blocks of leadership all come into play.

Finally, we have also explained why self-assessment based on the seven essential attributes is so important for personal development. Leaders who know themselves well, their respective weaknesses and strengths, are equipped with the knowledge they need to practice, stretch, reflect, and grow. They know where to direct their development efforts. They understand the areas in which they are likely to excel and where they may struggle at first. They seek advice and counsel when they need it. They use mentors and coaches to gain focus and clarity. Using the insights in this book, we hope you too will seek out and tackle complex new challenges. The journey itself will help you become a better leader.

Appendix A

Commonly Used (and Misused) Leadership Terms

In our experience, even the most qualified executives are prone to describe leadership in vague and imprecise terms. For example, during CEO succession projects, we often deal with corporate directors who say, "We need a leader with charisma." Or, "Does she have the decisiveness to handle this position?" Or "Does she have leadership presence?" Unfortunately, rarely is there any common understanding of what these words mean or how they are related to effective leadership.

With this in mind, we have compiled this glossary. Note that many of these words are misnomers. Others are so ambiguous that they invite instant confusion. Some are important skills, but they flow from more basic traits. We have broken these commonly used (and misused) terms apart to show how they relate to a leader's fundamental characteristics. Adopting a shared vocabulary will help all of us have more productive leadership conversations.

• • • • • • • • •

Ambitious Ambition is part of passion. It is important for leadership but must be balanced with integrity. See Chapter One.

Analytical Analytical skill is the ability to visualize, articulate, and solve complex problems and is part of judgment (see Chapter Five). Note that among a group of individuals, the one with the best analytical skill is not necessarily the member of the group with the best judgment. Strong analytical skill facilitates good judgment, but does not guarantee it.

Assertive Someone who is assertive may or may not be a good leader. A leader needs courage, but this is not the same as assertiveness. A person who is assertive needs emotional intelligence and empathy to recognize the effect that she has on others and to moderate her behavior accordingly. See Chapters Two and Three.

Authoritative The concept of authority is distinct from that of leadership. Many authority figures (police chiefs, heads of state, CEOs, prison wardens) are poor leaders, while many people with almost no formal authority (for example, Gandhi) are quite effective as leaders. Along these lines, an authoritative style or personality by itself is not a good predictor of leadership effectiveness. Sometimes the word *authoritative* is used to mean "capable of making decisions," which is a part of judgment (see Chapter Five) and important for leadership. But another meaning for the word is "bossy" or "heavy-handed," which can be an impediment to effective leadership.

Broad-minded It is important for a leader to be open to new ideas; this is a sign of emotional maturity and is a part of emotional intelligence. See Chapter Three.

Calm-headed Acting with composure and controlling one's emotions is important for leadership. This is an aspect of emotional intelligence. See Chapter Three.

Caring Most people probably agree that having a caring leader is desirable. But the word is a little too vague to have meaning as a predictor of leadership. A leader with integrity respects the rights of followers. Similarly, a leader with empathy understands the emotional needs of followers. These two attributes capture the essence of caring that is important for leadership.

Character (strong) Strong character is essential for effective leadership, although the term is too broad to lend much help in terms of assessing a leader's potential. More helpful is attention to specific aspects of character—qualities like honesty, integrity, courage, patience, and self-control. Honesty is part of integrity, patience is part of courage, and self-control is part of emotional intelligence. See Chapters One, Three, and Seven.

Charismatic When people say someone is charismatic, they usually mean the individual is self-confident, magnetic, influential, almost larger than life. The word comes from the Greek *kharisma,* which means divine gift, and there is a certain heroic aspect to the concept that many scholars and laypersons alike find appealing. Examples of charismatic leaders are Moses, Muhammad, and Martin Luther King, Jr. More recently, corporate leaders such as Jack Welch and Steve Jobs belong to this group. But charismatic individuals can destroy as well as build; Adolf Hitler and Jim Jones are in this category. For this reason, charisma is not a good predictor of leadership effectiveness. Rather, it is important to look at more fundamental attributes that might give rise to charismatic behavior, such as vision or passion. The existence of integrity will also help followers distinguish between someone like Martin Luther King Jr., whose magnetism created long-term value, and Hitler, who was not an effective leader because his leadership was destructive. Finally, many truly effective leaders are not charismatic (think of Bill Gates and Michael Bloomberg). In fact, Bloomberg went to public speaking class soon after running for mayor of New York City.

Clever The word *clever* is usually used to refer to a person who is mentally quick or quick-witted. It is also used to describe someone who has practical ingenuity. Mental quickness can enhance leadership, depending on what the leader is quick at doing. For example, quickly sizing up which issues are important and which information is needed to solve a problem is an essential part of good leadership judgment (see Chapter Five). Similarly, practical ingenuity or resourcefulness is somewhat similar to strategic thinking skills, another element of judgment. However, simply being fast is not necessarily helpful. Some decisions take time to evaluate and should not be rushed.

Communicator A leader cannot be effective without good communication skills. Communication skills flow out of more fundamental attributes, including empathy (Chapter Two), vision (Chapter Four), and emotional intelligence (see Chapter Three). Passion is important here as well. The message from a leader who is genuinely passionate about what he or she says comes across with sincerity and punch. These attributes can be developed over time, which implies that communication skills can become sharper and more persuasive over time as well.

Competent Competent is too general a term to provide much guidance when assessing leadership ability. Competent at what? At making decisions? (Judgment) At seeing the big picture? (Vision) At dealing with other people? (Empathy) It is important for a leader to demonstrate that she meets a minimum threshold for all attributes in our model.

Confident Confidence is attractive to followers and helps leaders face adversity and tough decisions. Confidence itself is not a fundamental building block of leadership, however. Rather, it is a by-product of more fundamental attributes, such as courage, high emotional intelligence, and good judgment. Confidence that flows from these attributes contributes to leadership effectiveness. Confidence that arises without a solid basis, however, can lead to costly mistakes and the impression of arrogance. It might also mask a lack of other critical attributes. No one should follow a leader, especially a confident one, who lacks judgment or integrity. An individual's confidence can grow as he or she masters each of the seven attributes in our model.

Increased confidence in turn allows individuals to further enhance certain attributes—being more courageous and having good self-control, for example.

Crisis manager Good crisis management skills flow from several fundamental attributes. A leader who is adept at handling crises possesses good judgment (see Chapter Four), courage (Chapter Six), and strong social savvy (see Chapter Two).

Cunning In some cultures, cunning is considered to be a positive leadership attribute, akin to cleverness and resourcefulness. In other cultures, the term has a more negative connotation, indicating someone who is clever, perhaps even a strong strategic thinker, but with questionable integrity.

Decisive Leaders have to make tough decisions. It is critical that they also have the capacity to make good decisions. Decisiveness without overall good judgment is not conducive to effective leadership. See Chapter Five.

Delegator All effective leaders know how to empower followers and delegate work. One of the quickest ways for an otherwise good leader to get derailed is by micromanaging or overcrowding his or her own agenda with tactical items. Leaders must focus on the big picture and see how the pieces fit together. This requires an ability and a willingness to delegate. Of course this also requires that leaders have confidence in their team, which shouldn't be a problem if they have used our seven attributes to make hiring and promotion decisions. Good delegating skills flow from judgment (see Chapter Five) as well as social savvy (see Chapter Two).

Diplomatic A leader needs social savvy, which includes an ability to handle complex interpersonal dynamics in a diplomatic way. Individuals who possess strong empathy (see Chapter Two) and emotional intelligence (see Chapter Three) are likely to meet this test. It is an important leadership skill. The best leaders are able to dampen potential social conflict before it has a chance to erupt into something truly disruptive.

Ethical A leader must have strong ethics to be effective. This is part of integrity and is discussed at length in Chapter Two.

Experienced Experience is important for leadership, but the kind of experience and a leader's ability to reflect on her experience are more important than a set number of years. This topic is discussed at length in Chapters Five (on judgment) and Three (on emotional intelligence). Depending on the context, leaders may also need a certain amount of relevant domain expertise in order to succeed. For example, a chief financial officer needs to understand finance; a chief technology officer needs strong training in his or her respective field. This requirement is not as stringent for the most senior, generalist leadership positions. For example, effective U.S. presidents have included former soldiers, teachers, lawyers, and farmers (it is interesting that the two trained in business, Herbert Hoover and George W. Bush, score low marks for their leadership). In all cases, however, individuals need relevant general experience—at making decisions and mistakes, learning, reflecting, communicating, directing a budget—in order to excel.

Firm Firmness does not provide an indication of leadership potential. At best, it might be a proxy for decisiveness or authoritativeness, which are also problematic leadership labels. Even less desirable is the kind of firmness that indicates an inability to reflect, accept criticism, adjust course, or listen, all of which can lead to disaster. Followers may assume at first that a firm leader knows what he is talking about. After a while, however, the leader will lose support if he doesn't back up his style with fairness and sound decision making.

Forward looking Good leaders are forward looking and inspire followers with big, imaginative ideas. This is a part of vision and discussed in Chapter Four. Sometimes the term *forward looking* refers to a leader's ability to see the whole chessboard and think strategically several moves ahead. This is a part of judgment and is discussed in Chapter Five.

Honest Honesty is important for leadership and part of integrity. See Chapter One.

Iconic A handful of leaders have developed such a strong reputation that their very names command loyalty and respect. Nevertheless, *iconic* is not indicative of leadership potential. It does not make sense to say, "Sarah should work to be more iconic," or, "We need to assess whether Terry is iconic."

Imaginative Imagination is important for leadership and part of vision. See Chapter Four.

Inclusive Bringing others together as part of the decision-making process is a strong sign of emotional intelligence. It helps align everyone around common goals and makes them feel as if they are part of the process. Still, inclusiveness, as well as collaboration, must be carefully balanced with decisiveness. A leader who is too inclusive or collaborative may delay making necessary strategic trade-offs or decisions.

Influential Effective leaders are good at inspiring, motivating, and influencing others. For example, a leader must be able to motivate employees and influence outside actors. This ability flows from strong passion, vision, and empathy. See Chapters Seven, Four, and Two.

Innovative Innovative thinking is a complex leadership competency that draws on several leadership attributes. It requires the imagination to conceive of a new vision, the judgment to ensure this vision is practical and can be implemented, the empathy to anticipate how others will react to the new idea and to garner their support, and the courage to stick with a plan despite inevitable bumps in the road. Because innovation draws on so many of the attributes, it is a rare quality among many leaders. See Chapter Four for an extensive discussion of innovative leaders.

Inspirational Good leaders must be able to inspire their followers. The ability to inspire is part of vision. See Chapter Four.

Intelligent There are many types of intelligence that are important for leadership. Emotional intelligence is discussed in Chapter Three. Social intelligence, which requires both emotional intelligence and empathy, is discussed in Chapter Two. Sometimes cognitive ability is referred to as practical intelligence. Our discussion of judgment in Chapter Five, including an ability to frame issues, quickly size up important information and relationships, and think strategically, demonstrates why this is critical for good leadership.

Intuitive Some leaders seem to have a strong "gut feel" or intuition when it comes to making decisions. This is another way of saying the leader has good judgment, which itself is the product of a diverse range of experiences and systematic reflection about each of these experiences (for example, what worked in the past and what did not).

Leadership aura (or presence) *Strong leadership aura* is a phrase that many board members use to describe what they most desire in a CEO. Usually what they mean is someone who has many or all of the seven attributes in this book and as a result is composed, confident, and well balanced. For example, courage, emotional intelligence, and passion give leaders the kind of presence that is usually implied by leadership aura. Also, good judgment raises the bearing that a leader gives off to others. See also *composure; confidence.*

Loyal Loyalty is an admirable human trait, but somewhat confusing as a leadership descriptor. Sometimes people use the word *loyal* to convey a sense of integrity. For example, if a leader is loyal to his word or to his employees, this implies that he follows up on his promises and keeps his commitments, despite personal cost. Someone who stays loyal during difficult times also demonstrates courage. Both integrity and courage are essential leadership attributes (see Chapters One and Six). But a person can have conflicting loyalties, as in commitments to different constituent groups. Viewed in this light, simply knowing if a leader is loyal won't reveal much about this person's leadership effectiveness. To answer this, we would want to gauge his or her level of integrity and ethics. See Chapter One.

Mature Maturity flows from emotional intelligence (see Chapter Three), particularly self-awareness and self-control, as well as experience (see the discussion of experience in Chapter Five).

Moral See *ethical.*

Motivating Effective leaders are good at motivating others. This ability flows primarily from vision and empathy, and also from passion. See Chapters Two, Four, and Seven.

Participative Several researchers have distinguished between a participative versus a directive leadership style or democratic versus autocratic. Participative and democratic styles are more interpersonally oriented, and many observers agree that contemporary conditions necessitate a movement in this direction and away from hierarchical, directive styles. Participative leadership skills are essentially good relationship skills. In this sense, they flow from strong empathy (see Chapter Two) and emotional intelligence (see Chapter Three).

Patient Patience, discussed in Chapter Six, is connected with courage and is important for leadership.

Perfectionist Some leaders demand high quality and standards. This is a positive quality, but when it is carried to an extreme, to the point of demanding perfection, it can have negative consequences and undermine a leader's effectiveness. A perfectionist can easily get bogged down in unnecessary tactical or operational activities and details rather than keeping focus on higher-level strategic issues.

Persuasive Good leaders inspire and persuade their followers. They do so with vision (see Chapter Four) and strong social savvy (see the discussion of empathy in Chapter Two), and by constructing a strong case for their decisions (see Chapter Five).

Positive Few people would dispute that having a positive leader is a good thing. As a leadership predictor, however, it is not a very descriptive or useful term. More important are the fundamental attributes that create a positive attitude and energy between leader and follower, including empathy (see Chapter Two) and passion (see Chapter Seven). Authenticity (described as a part of passion in Chapter Seven) is important here because people who align their personal values and life stories with an overall leadership purpose tend to come across as committed, engaged, optimistic and energetic.

Presence See *leadership aura.*

Reliable Followers look for a leader they can trust to uphold commitments, make good decisions, and get things done. This is a part of integrity and judgment and discussed in Chapters One and Five, respectively.

Resilient Resilience, or the ability to bounce back from adversity, is based on a combination of emotional intelligence and passion. It requires the capacity for reflection and learning connected with strong emotional intelligence, as well as the passion and determination to keep going, despite inevitable setbacks.

Resourceful Resourcefulness is part of good judgment (see Chapter Five). Leaders who are resourceful know how to get the most out of what they have. They focus on what's important, discard the extraneous, and combine assets in an efficient and productive way. They use their strategic thinking skills to look ahead and predict how best to leverage future resources. This is an important part of leadership.

Risk taker Risk taking is viewed quite differently depending on culture. In our experience, a leader's propensity for risk taking is not very helpful in terms of predicting leadership effectiveness. On the one hand, progress and innovation depend on a willingness to take risks. On the other hand, excessive risk taking amounts to recklessness. A leader who possesses the courage to make hard choices and act boldly, while also possessing the good judgment to calibrate this risk taking, is the kind of leader who is poised to succeed.

Self-assured See *confident.*

Self-confident See *confident.*

Sensitive The word *sensitive* means different things to different people. A person who is so sensitive that he cannot accept criticism demonstrates a lack of emotional maturity and will not be an effective leader. Nevertheless, an appreciation of or sensitivity to the needs and emotions of others is critical for leadership. This is synonymous with good empathy (see Chapter Two).

Solid character See *character.*

Steady Effective leaders possess steady character, in the sense of being reliable (see Chapter One) and possessing a balanced (that is, composed and self-controlled) emotional makeup, meaning strong emotional intelligence (see Chapter Three).

Strategic Good strategic thinking is a part of judgment and discussed at length in Chapter Five. It stems from an individual's ability to see the whole chessboard, to make wise and timely decisions, to understand the context, and to anticipate the unintended consequences of one's decisions.

Subdued Middle managers in many cultures believe that a subdued personality contributes to outstanding business leadership, while in other cultures, this attribute has a negative connotation. The GLOBE Project, an eleven-year study involving 170 researchers in more than sixty countries, determined that the same view holds with respect to attributes such as "cunning" or "class conscious." In our experience, someone with a subdued personality may or may not be an effective leader. The same can be said for someone with an extroverted or animated personality. What distinguishes effective leaders from ineffective ones are the seven fundamental attributes in this book.

Supportive Leaders should be supportive but not coddling. Followers want to feel as though leaders are there for them and can be counted on. Without this, there can be no trust. Leaders with strong empathy (Chapter Two) and integrity (Chapter One) meet this test.

Team builder Team-building skills flow from several more fundamental attributes, including empathy (social savvy) (Chapter Two), judgment (Chapter Five), and passion (Chapter Seven). See *diplomatic; good communicator; motivator.*

Tenacious Someone who perseveres even in the face of adversity. This is an aspect of passion, and important for effective leadership. Tenacious leaders are equipped to overcome inevitable obstacles. Without tenacity, individuals are likely to give up too easily or wallow in mediocrity.

Transformational/transactional For many years, theorists have focused on the purported benefit that charisma, or personal magnetism, has for those who lead. What experts have learned is that this quality is a double-edged sword: some charismatic individuals are quite effective, and others can be narcissists whose leadership (as in the case of Hitler) destroys. Research has also revealed that charisma is not easy to identify in advance. Given these shortcomings, in the 1970s and 1980s scholars began to expand on the concept of inspirational power associated with effective leadership. In 1978 James MacGregor Burns distinguished between transformational and transactional leadership. Transformational leadership incorporates many of the elements associated with a charismatic person, including confidence, good communications skills, magnetism, and vision. Importantly, transformational leaders are said to appeal to the highest ideals of their followers. They inspire us to transcend self-interest and work toward lofty goals such as peace, justice, or community building. An example of this kind of leader is Franklin D. Roosevelt, who used his inspirational communication skills to achieve social reform. Transactional leaders, by contrast, are said to rely more on bargaining and an appeal to followers' self-interest. They use incentives and threats to engage in mutually beneficial exchange. Both styles have been shown to be effective in certain situations. The trouble with the transformational/transactional dichotomy, however, is that it isn't very useful when trying to assess leadership potential. Instead, these terms are better reserved for evaluating an overall body of leadership well in the past. To capture the kind of qualities that might give rise to transformational leadership, it is better to focus on the attributes highlighted in this book.

Trustworthy It is critical for leaders to be trusted by their followers. Trustworthiness flows from integrity (see Chapter One) and overall leadership competence, which is a function of all of the attributes discussed in this book. For example, a leader who consistently demonstrates good judgment will inspire trust in others because followers will have faith in his decision-making capability.

Appendix B

The DNA of Leadership Competencies

Change Agent

- *Empathy:* Must be able to quickly and accurately analyze how different constituents will react to proposed changes and then custom-tailor his or her argument to resonate with each of these constituents, all with different agendas and motivations, in a convincing way
- *Emotional intelligence:* Very open to new ideas and always questioning his or her own approaches and the status quo
- *Courage:* Must be able to present radically new ideas to the masses and plow forward despite what will surely be resistance from powerful, entrenched constituents

Growth Catalyst

- *Vision:* Particularly imaginative in thinking of novel opportunities for the organization
- *Judgment:* Will make consistently wise decisions about which growth opportunities make the most sense for the organization, and steer clear of unproductive initiatives
- *Passion:* Will stay focused on growth and push forward even during the most difficult times

Confident

- *Judgment:* Has the ability to make sound decisions in complex, ambiguous situations
- *Emotional intelligence:* Is highly self-aware and in control, and as a result projects an image of being comfortable in his or her own skin
- *Courage:* Has a strong moral center and is able to stand up for important values or goals

Charismatic

- *Passion:* Wears passion on his or her sleeves. The troops sense the passion and are naturally drawn to the leader and his or her ideas.
- *Empathy:* Knows how to construct a story that strikes a chord across a variety of stakeholders; does not have a one-size-fits-all approach.

Great Communicator

- *Empathy:* Similar to the charismatic leader, with a keen sense for the underlying agendas and motivations of an audience and the ability to tailor an appropriate approach
- *Emotional intelligence:* Has a deep self-awareness and can connect with others in a highly personal way
- *Vision:* Inspirational
- *Passion:* Sincerely believes in, and is enthusiastic about, the story she conveys

Global Perspective

- *Empathy:* Able to accurately size up and connect with individuals with radically different styles, backgrounds, and personalities
- *Emotional intelligence:* Open to performing activities in fundamentally new ways, even though the old way may have worked just fine domestically
- *Judgment:* Able to cut through complexity and large amounts of new data to focus on the most important issues

Resilient

- *Courage:* Willing to take bold chances even if there is a clear chance of failure
- *Emotional intelligence:* Engages in serious reflection when setbacks occur, which they always do, and makes necessary adjustments
- *Passion:* Will not let setbacks deter him or her from charging forward
- *Judgment:* Is able to prioritize, tinker, and recombine existing resources in new ways; makes the most out of a seemingly dire situation

Tenacious

- *Passion:* Highly committed to achieving goals no matter what the sacrifice
- *Courage:* Does not become immobilized when faced with tough obstacles

Turnaround Artist

- *Judgment:* Able to make tough decisions with limited resources; knows when to say no to requests that are superfluous or unproductive
- *Empathy:* Understands how others will likely react to major cuts and change in strategic direction and preemptively addresses these concerns

Keep the Ship Sailing Steady and Smooth

- *Judgment:* Makes decisions with a clear understanding of the organization's overall vision
- *Courage:* Is not afraid to turn down new requests from powerful constituents (customers, shareholders, special interest groups) who want the organization to do something different

Innovator

Innovators are rare because they require high doses of virtually all of the fundamental attributes.

- *Vision:* Highly imaginative forward-thinking; views complex situations from multiple angles
- *Emotional Intelligence:* Always keeps an open mind and brings others into the loop to solicit fresh ideas and constructive criticism; this serves the dual purpose of contributing to the original idea and making others feel that they have contributed to the solution
- *Courage:* Willing to take bold chances and venture into highly ambiguous, poorly defined situations
- *Passion:* Not easily deterred even though he or she will surely face a seemingly endless array of naysayers and setbacks in the attempt to bring this vision to life
- *Judgment:* Can effectively determine if the dream has the potential to be effectively implemented
- *Empathy:* Has the ability to determine the best way to communicate his or her vision to a wide variety of constituents, each with his or her own motivation, vantage point, and underlying agendas.

Notes

Introduction

1. The poll was conducted by the Center for Public Leadership at Harvard University and the Merriman River Group. "Poll Shows Americans Still Disappointed in Leaders," Center for Public Leadership, Kennedy School, Harvard University, Oct. 28, 2010.

Chapter One

1. D. Gergen, *Eyewitness to Power: The Essence of Leadership: Nixon to Clinton* (New York: Touchstone, 2000), p. 346.
2. P. Singer, *The Expanding Circle: Ethics and Sociobiology* (New York: Farrar, Straus & Giroux, 1981).
3. J. Moran interview with Jerry Storch, May 12, 2010.
4. T. Simons, *The Integrity Dividend: Leading by the Power of Your Word* (San Francisco: Jossey-Bass, 2009), p. 3.
5. Simons, *Integrity Dividend.*
6. J. Moran telephone interview with Dave Dillon, Aug. 21, 2009.
7. J. M. Kouzes and B. Z. Posner, *The Leadership Challenge,* 4th ed. (San Francisco: Jossey-Bass, 2007).
8. Kouzes and Posner, *Leadership Challenge,* p. 32.
9. Ryder, *2009 Annual Report.*
10. All Greg Swienton comments from J. Cohn telephone interview, Nov. 3, 2010.
11. Authors' interview with Greg Greene, Sept. 21, 2010.
12. S. Milgram, "Behavioral Study of Obedience," *Journal of Abnormal and Social Psychology,* 1963, *67,* 371–378.

13. B. McLean and P. Elkind, *The Smartest Guys in the Room: The Amazing Rise and Scandalous Fall of Enron* (New York: Penguin, 2003).

14. *Enron: The Smartest Guys in the Room* (Magnolia Pictures, 2005). Film.

Chapter Two

1. Unless otherwise indicated, all Jerry Colangelo comments come from J. Cohn telephone interview with him on Aug. 19, 2009.

2. D. K. Goodwin, *Team of Rivals: The Political Genius of Abraham Lincoln* (New York: Simon & Schuster, 2005), pp. 167–168.

3. D. Goleman, R. Boyatzis, and A. McKee, *Primal Leadership: Learning to Lead with Emotional Intelligence* (Boston: Harvard Business School Press, 2002), p. 49.

4. Several media and academic institutions maintain a video recording and transcript of this debate, including C-Span and the University of Richmond. The complete transcript is also available at the *New York Times*, October 16, 1992.

5 J. Cohn conversation with Mike Krzyzewski, Nov. 2010.

6. J. P. Donlon, "CEO of the Year," *Chief Executive*, July–Aug. 1999.

7. Donlon, "CEO of the Year."

8. Donlon, "CEO of the Year."

9. All Gary Kelly comments were related during J. Cohn telephone interview with Ginger Hardage, senior vice president of communication and culture at Southwest Airlines.

10. Author telephone interview with Ginger Hardage.

11. Howard Kurtz, "Howell Raines's Tenure: It Left a Nasty Mark," *Washington Post*, June 9, 2003.

12. J. Poniewozik, "Mutiny at the Times," *Time Magazine*, June 13, 2003, p. 49.

13. C. Johnson, "The Rise and Fall of Carly Fiorina: An Ethical Case Study," *Entrepreneur*, Nov. 2008. http://www.entrepreneur.com/tradejournals/article/187962046.html.

14. T. Webb, "BP Boss Admits Job on the Line over Gulf Oil Spill," *Guardian*, May 14, 2010.

15. The comments by President Obama were made during an interview for the *Today Show* that aired on June 8, 2010, and were covered

extensively by most major media outlets. A. Kornblut, "Tough-Talking Obama Seeking 'Ass to Kick,'" *Washington Post*, June 8, 2010.

16. Goleman, Boyatzis, and McKee, *Primal Leadership*, p. 31.

17. J. Cohn conversation with Jerry Colangelo, Mar. 2008.

18. S. R. Covey, *The Seven Habits of Highly Effective People* (New York: Free Press, 1989), p. 239.

Chapter Three

1. Author interview with Cosgrove at the Cleveland Clinic, 2009.

2. Goleman's definition of emotional intelligence is more expansive than ours. He defines it as the self-mastery, discipline, and emphatic capacity that allows leaders to channel their passions and build rapport with others. D. Goleman, "What Makes a Leader?" *Harvard Business Review*, 1998, *76*(6), 94. Although we agree that empathy is a critical element of effective leadership, we prefer not to lump it together with emotional intelligence. As an attribute, empathy stands by itself. Indeed, many leaders are quite empathic, but they still struggle to control themselves. For example, Bill Clinton scores very high in terms of empathy, while self-control issues have weighed him down.

3. See J. D. Mayer and P. Salovey, "What Is Emotional Intelligence?" in P. Salovey and D. J. Sluyter (Eds.), *Emotional Development and Emotional Intelligence: Educational Implications* (New York: Basic Books, 1997), p. 5; P. Salovey and D. Pizarro, "The Value of Emotional Intelligence," in R. J. Sternberg, J. Lautrey, and T. Lubart (Eds.), *Models of Emotional Intelligence* (Washington, D.C.: American Psychological Association, 2003). Part of the reason for the mixed opinion regarding the connection between leadership and emotional intelligence might be that most researchers don't know how to test for emotional intelligence in any consistent way that is tied directly to leadership performance (but see our discussion in the assessment section of this chapter regarding how to overcome this challenge). Those who disagree with Goleman's theory also have a problem with its emphasis on behavior or personality traits. Numerous studies have shown that these factors are not reliable predictors of leadership, or at least no more reliable than other

traditional tests, such as IQ tests. On this point, we also deviate from the core of Goleman's model; our definition of *emotional intelligence* is personality neutral, and our assessment method does not rely on any traditional type of personality test.

4. J. S. Nye Jr., *The Powers to Lead* (New York: Oxford University Press, 2008), p. 70.

5. S. Pinker, *The Blank Slate* (New York: Viking Press, 2002), p. 265.

6. W. Bennis, *On Becoming a Leader* (Reading, Mass.: Addison-Wesley, 1989), pp. 40, 53.

7. B. George, *True North: Discover Your Authentic Leadership* (San Francisco: Jossey-Bass, 2007), p. 71.

8. R. A. Heifetz, *Leadership Without Easy Answers* (Cambridge, Mass.: Harvard University Press, 1994).

9. J. Moran telephone interview with Bacardi, Nov. 12, 2010.

10. J. Bailey, "Approach Boss with Caution," *New York Times,* Jan. 19, 2007.

11. Bailey, "Approach Boss with Caution."

12. Bailey, "Approach Boss with Caution."

13. "The World's Best CEO Tirades," *Business Pundit,* Mar. 23, 2010, http://www.businesspundit.com/?s=the+world%27s+best+ceo+tirades.

14. D. Gilbertson, "Mesa Air's CEO Remains Optimistic on Future," *Arizona Republic,* Apr. 9, 2008.

15. M. Hastings, "The Runaway General," *Rolling Stone,* July 8, 2010.

16. M. Hastings, "The Runaway General."

17. "He meddled in the smallest matters of ballpark maintenance." Richard Goldstein, "George Steinbrenner Who Built the Yankees into a Powerhouse, Dies at 80," *New York Times,* July 13, 2010.

18. Goldstein, "George Steinbrenner, Who Built Yankees into Powerhouse, Dies at 80."

19. J. Cohn, phone interview with George Steinbrenner, Oct. 2007.

20. "Sports World Reacts George Steinbrenner's Death," *Newsday,* July 13, 2010.

21. T. Poletti, "Facebook CEO has a Richard Nixon Moment," *MarketWatch,* June 3, 2010; D. Nosowitz, "Mark Zuckerberg Gives

Awkward, Sweaty Interview at D8: Touches on Privacy and Scandal," *Fast Company,* June 3, 2010.

22. M. Helft, "Mark Zuckerberg's Most Valuable Friend," *New York Times,* Oct. 2, 2010.

23. Tenacity and passion are classified by some as personality character-istics. These are undeniably important for leadership success, as we point out in Chapter Seven (see also Appendix A).

24. C. Diehl, "Hearing the Right Notes from a Job Candidate," *New York Times,* July 24, 2010.

25. The evidence is quite convincing that development is significantly enhanced when individuals take charge of their own learning. See L. Dragoni, P. Tesluk, J.E.A. Russell, and I.-S. Oh, "Understanding Managerial Development: Integrating Developmental Assignments, Learning Orientation and Access to Developmental Opportunities in Predicted Managerial Competencies," *Academy of Management Journal,* 2009, *94,* 731–743; D. S. DeRue and N. Wellman, "Developing Leaders via Experience: The Role of Developmental Challenge, Learning Orientation, and Feedback," *Journal of Applied Psychology,* 2009, *94,* 859–875; G. M. Spreitzer, M. W. McCall, and J. D. Mahoney, "Early Identification of International Executive Potential," *Journal of Applied Psychology,* 1997, *82,* 6–29. The deep dive into cognitive processing by Dominick, Squires, and Cervone provides a partial explanation not only for when and how experi-ence is internalized, but how cognitive structure and process develops experientially. P. G. Dominick, P. Squires, and D. Cervone, "Back to Persons: On Social-Cognitive Processes and Products of Leadership Development Experiences," *Industrial and Organizational Psychology,* 2010, *3,* 33–37.

Chapter Four

1. Bono interview with Cynthia McFadden on *ABC News Nightline,* June 6, 2007. For a transcript, see the *Nightline* Web site: http://www.tran-scripts.tv/nightline.cfm.

2. "Schumpeter: Uncaging the Lions," *Economist,* June 10, 2010.

3. Walmart reportedly spent $4.6 billion on Massmart, an African retailer with 290 stores. R. Powell, "How to Invest in Africa with Cutting-Edge ETFs," MarketWatch, Oct. 21, 2010. Procter & Gamble opened a Pampers diapers factory in South Africa in 2009 and doubled its capacity in 2010. Press release, Aug. 4, 2010: http://www.pg.com/en_US/news_views/index.shtml. Unilever has placed a big emphasis on the African market for several years. D. Ball, "As Its Brands Lag at Home, Unilever Makes a Risky Bet," *Wall Street Journal,* Mar. 22, 2007.

4. M. Wines, "China Pledges $10 Billion to Africa," *New York Times,* Nov. 8, 2009.

5. "Schumpeter: Uncaging the Lions."

6. See A. Perry, "Battling a Scourge," *Time Magazine,* June 10, 2010.

7. "Q&A: Sudan's Darfur Conflict," BBC News Online, Feb. 23, 2010, http://news.bbc.co.uk/2/hi/africa/3496731.stm. Darfur is a region in Sudan that was the site of guerrilla conflict, civil war, and humanitarian emergency from 2003 to 2009.

8. Zimbabwe president Robert Mugabe was widely accused of interfering with the 2008 election process and other acts of corruption during his administration. As of 2010, Somalia was a failed state and home to several pirates who threatened international shipping off the Horn of Africa.

9. Bob Geldof is the Irish musician and activist who, with Midge Ure, formed the charity supergroup Band Aid in 1984 to raise money for famine relief in Ethiopia. Band Aid released the single hit, "Do They Know It's Christmas?" Bono was a participant in Band Aid, and the two men have worked together on several other projects.

10. "Brian Williams in Africa," *NBC Nightly News,* May 23, 2006. Video archive available at http://www.msnbc.msn.com/id/12916501/. Bono also described the difference this way: "If RED is a charity, ONE is about justice. ONE is the marching boots inside of what we do."

11. J. Moran telephone interview with David Lane, Dec. 9, 2009.

12. According to the ONE organization's Web site: http://www.one.org/international/, Nov. 2010.

13. Michael Elliott wrote that "Bono's support for the campaign was critical; he gave a patina of glamour to people who would otherwise have been dismissed as nice but deeply unfashionable." "Right Man, Right Time," *Time Magazine,* Mar. 4, 2002.

14. "Clinton Praises Bono," *BBC News,* Nov. 7, 2000.

15. "Clinton Praises Bono."

16. Author interview with David Lane, Dec. 9, 2009.

17. J. Pareles, "U2 in the Round, Fun with a Mission," *New York Times,* Sept. 24, 2009; "Burmese Dissident Is Freed After Long Detention," *New York Times,* Nov. 13, 2010.

18. D. Dyomkin, "U2's Bono Asks Russia's Medvedev to Help Beat AIDS," Reuters, Aug. 24, 2010.

19. Bono has been a finalist for the annual prize at least twice. S. Marley, "Nobel Peace Price Overlooks Bono for Bangladeshi Bank," Bloomberg, Oct. 13, 2006.

20. "Brian Williams in Africa."

21. M. Weiler and W. B. Pearce (Eds.), *Reagan and Public Discourse in America* (Tuscaloosa: University of Alabama Press, 1992), p. 57; F. W. Smith, "All in a Day's Work," *Harvard Business Review,* Dec. 2001, p. 57.

22. W. Bennis, *On Becoming a Leader* (New York: Basic Books, 2009), p. 188.

23. Author interview with John Maeda, 2010.

24. Author interview with Jeff Bezos.

25. J. Stein, "Steve Wynn," *Time Magazine,* Apr. 30, 2006.

26. T. Hayes, "Observers: Wynn Lofty Visionary," *Las Vegas Review-Journal,* Mar. 7, 2000.

27. O. A. El Sawy, "Temporal Perspective and Managerial Attention: A Study of Chief Executive Strategic Behavior," unpublished doctoral dissertation, Stanford University, 1983, Dissertation Abstracts International 44 (05A): 1556–1557. We are grateful to Kouzes and Posner for alerting us to El Sawy's findings. See generally J. M. Kouzes and B. Z. Posner, *The Leadership Challenge,* 4th ed. (San Francisco: Jossey-Bass, 2007).

28. Nixon was a student of history and possessed a strong capacity to understand the flow of historical events. As early as the 1950s, he talked of
visiting mainland China, and in the 1960s he raised the idea of building bridges to Peking even though it seemed to be firmly embraced
by the Soviet Union. Former presidential advisor David Gergen, who
worked for Nixon as well as three other presidents, wrote: "He was the
best strategist we have had in the Oval Office in the past three decades
and, arguably, since Woodrow Wilson. No one else in recent years has
come close." D. Gergen, *Eyewitness to Power: The Essence of Leadership:
Nixon to Clinton* (New York: Touchstone Books, 2001), pp. 56–57.

29. Gergen, *Eyewitness to Power.*

30. Nixon went to China in an election year. Many of his advisors thought
that given Nixon's strong anti-Communist record, a trip to meet personally with General Mao was an unnecessarily risky political move.
Nixon's reputation as a strong anti-Communist was established early
in his career. In 1948 he gained recognition when his investigation
for the House Un-American Activities Committee helped resolve the
Alger Hiss spy case, and later, as a senator, he continued to maintain a hardline stance. He famously called opponent Helen Gahagan
Douglas "pink right down to her underwear" when the two ran against
each other in the 1950 Senate campaign.

31. See L. Menan, "Chaos Under Heaven," *New Yorker,* Mar. 12, 2007.
In a review of Margaret MacMillan's book *Nixon and Mao: The Week
That Changed the World,* Menan writes that Nixon's trip to China in
February 1972 is an event that "has earned almost universal respect."
Four months after his China visit, Nixon visited Moscow for a summit with Leonid Brezhnev. The two signed ten formal agreements, an
antiballistic treaty, the interim Strategic Arms Limitation Treaty, and
a billion-dollar trade agreement. Many observers agree that Nixon's ability
to draw closer to China made the Soviet Union more open to negotiation.
American Experience: The Presidents, "Richard Nixon," PBS online at
http://www.pbs.org/wgbh/amex/presidents/.

32. K. Chang, "Obama Plan Privatizes Astronaut Landings," *New York
Times,* Jan. 28, 2010.

33. "Runway Opens at World's First Spaceport," *BBC News,* Oct. 23, 2010; "Virgin Galactic Successfully Tests VSS Enterprise," CNN.com, Oct. 16, 2010.

34. "Runway Opens at World's First Spaceport," *BBC News,* Oct. 23, 2010. Video archive available at http://www.bbc.co.uk/news/world-us-canada-11611630.

35. Joseph Pelton, director of the Space and Advanced Communications Research Institute at George Washington University, is among those who have offered a cautionary note. In 2007 he said, "There's still skepticism as to this being possible in terms of a viable business plan. Can it succeed? Yes, there is a business potential there, but will the space agencies be willing to let go and redefine their roles so that business enterprise can move forward?" Pelton thought that the answers to these questions wouldn't be known for another decade. Brian Wingfield, "To Infinity and Beyond," *Forbes,* Mar. 29, 2007.

36. J. Moran telephone interview with Chris Connor, Feb. 2010.

37. H. Gardner, *Leading Minds: An Anatomy of Leadership* (New York: Basic Books, 1995), p. 9.

38. In 2001 Gergen became the director of the Center for Public Leadership at Harvard Kennedy School.

39. Gergen, *Eyewitness to Power,* p. 221.

40. J. Moran telephone interview with Philip Francis, Oct. 12, 2009.

41. J. Cohn telephone interview with John Maeda, June 2008.

42. We thank Roger Martin of the Rotman School of Business for taking time during a trip to New York during summer 2010 to help us understand why these qualities are so important.

Chapter Five

1. Data are from Siemens, *2010 Annual Report to Shareholders.*

2. E. Lichtblau and C. Dougherty, "Siemens to Pay 1.34 Billion in Fines," *New York Times, Dec.* 15, 2008.

3. J. Ewing, "Siemens' Culture Clash," *BusinessWeek,* Jan. 29, 2007.

4. Unless otherwise indicated, all Peter Löscher comments are from J. Moran telephone interview with Löscher and Nicolas von Rosty on Nov. 4, 2010.

5. J. Moran interview with members of executive team during a visit to Siemens headquarters in Munich, Germany, Nov. 17, 2010.

6. Governance experts such as Jeffrey Sonnenfeld of Yale University; noted author and business advisor Ram Charam; Warren Bennis of University of Southern California; and Dayton Ogden, head of CEO Succession Services at Spencer Stuart, to name a few, agree that when boards of directors become more involved in talent management and succession planning, overall performance rises.

7. M. Gerlach and J. Hack, "Siemens Offers Blowout Dividend, 2011 Growth," Reuters, Nov. 11, 2010.

8. "Siemens: A Giant Awakens," *Economist,* Sept. 9, 2010.

9. John F. Kennedy was the youngest U.S. president elected to office, at the age of forty-three.

10. J. Moran telephone interview with Eric Wiseman, June 25, 2010.

11. J. Moran telephone interview with Dan Hesse, Apr. 12, 2010.

12. C. A. Garfield, *Peak Performers: The New Heroes of American Business* (New York: Morrow, 1986), p. 156. No lasting record of this quote exists in Einstein's collected writings. An alternative original source might be the sociologist William Bruce Cameron. In 1963, he wrote a book that contains the following passage: "It would be nice if all of the data which sociologists require could be enumerated because then we could run them through IBM machines and draw charts as the economists do. However, not everything that can be counted counts, and not everything that counts can be counted." W. B. Cameron, *Informal Sociology: A Casual Introduction to Sociological Thinking* (New York: Random House, 1967), p. 13.

13. J. Cohn interview of Peter Darbee at PG&E headquarters, San Francisco, July 2010.

14. "Most Innovative Companies," *Fast Company,* Feb. 17, 2010.

15. Bloomberg Business Exchange: General Dynamics. Accessed Dec. 2, 2010, at http://bx.businessweek.com/general-dynamics/news/.

16. General Dynamics, *2009 Annual Report.*

17. D. Hedgpeth, "At General Dynamics, Chief Leaves a Legacy of Nailing the Numbers," *Washington Post,* June 22, 2009.

18. J. Moran telephone interview with Nicholas Chabraja, Nov. 22, 2010.

19. Authors' interview with Nigel Spencer at Simmons & Simmons' London office, Nov. 3, 2010.

20. Fleischer is considered a rising star among Hollywood insiders. Nikki Fink reported in "Warner Brothers Wants Fleischer to Lead Gangster Squad," *Deadline Hollywood,* Dec. 2, 2010. In the article, Fink remarked that Fleischer was a "rising star" and beat out A-list directors Ben Affleck and Darren Aronofsky.

21. P. Travers, "Review: Zombieland," *Rolling Stone,* Oct. 2, 2009.

22. J. Moran telephone interview with Cris Conde, May 4, 2010.

23. J. Moran telephone interview with Chip Bergh, Aug. 2, 2010.

24. The company ended 2008 with record sales and revenues, and enjoyed near-record profits. With a healthy balance sheet, it was able to avoid the tailspin that afflicted many of its peers.

25. A. Swift, "Western & Southern Financial Group: A Smart Approach," *American Executive,* Mar. 1, 2010.

26. Author interview at Western & Southern headquarters, Dec. 22, 2010.

27. "About Us," 2011 Western & Southern Web site, 2011.

28. J. Cohn telephone interview with Scott Davis, Sept. 15, 2010.

29. R. Martin, *The Opposable Mind: Winning Through Integrative Thinking* (Boston: Harvard Business School Press, 2009), pp. 26–27.

30. Both of us have extensive experience preparing case studies at Harvard Business School and at the Chief Executive Leadership Institute, which is now at Yale University.

Chapter Six

1. J. M. Burns, *Leadership* (New York: HarperCollins, 1978), p. 39.

2. All quotes are from J. Moran's telephone interview with Mackay on May 5, 2010, unless otherwise noted.

3. Due to lack of legislation, international tobacco companies engaged in behavior that had been outlawed in the United States for years, such as advertising on television and directly to children. According to a 1996

article in the *Washington Post*, British American Tobacco was one of the most egregious companies. "Three nights a week, for instance, it transforms the Nightman Disco in Beijing into a free-floating advertisement for its 555 brand. Slender Chinese women in blue tops, miniskirts and boots all emblazoned with the 555 logo greet people at the door, handing out free cigarettes." G. Frankel and S. Mufson, "Vast China Market Key at Smoking Disputes," *Washington Post,* Nov. 20, 1996.

4. A. Ahlman, "Antismoking Advocate for the World: Dr. Judith Mackay," *Angels in Medicine,* Feb. 21, 2004.

5. With the fall of communism and huge tobacco liability settlements in the United States, international tobacco companies moved aggressively into Asia during the late 1980s and 1990s. In 1996, for example, the *Washington Post* reported that more than 350 million smokers existed in China, more than the entire population of the United States, and that it was one of only six countries in the world where cigarette consumption was steadily rising. Moreover, with little or no tobacco control regulatory framework in place there, these tobacco companies believed that Asia was the key to significant future profit. "Tobacco companies see it as the grand prize, the place where they can recapture and far outstrip the sales volumes they are losing in the West." G. Frankel and S. Mufson, "Vast China Market Key at Smoking Disputes," *Washington Post,* Nov. 20, 1996.

6. L. Fitzpatrick, "Asian Heroes: Judith Mackay," *Time Magazine,* Nov. 5, 2006.

7. All of Greg Greene's comments are from the authors' interview with him at Ryder headquarters, Miami, Florida, Sept. 21, 2010.

8. R. A. Heifetz, *Leadership Without Easy Answers* (Cambridge, Mass.: Harvard University Press, 1994), chap. 6.

9. *Time* magazine named him the tenth most corrupt CEO in history. "Top 10 Crooked CEOs," *Time Magazine,* June 9, 2009.

10. S. Hamm, "Compaq's Rockin' Boss," *BusinessWeek,* Sept. 4, 2000.

11. Hamm, "Compaq's Rockin' Boss."

12. "Making the Tough Decisions," *Directorship,* Sept. 1, 2007.

13. Until otherwise noted, all Richard Clarke quotes are taken from J. Moran telephone interview with Clarke, Apr. 5, 2010.

14. R. A. Clarke, *Against All Enemies: Inside America's War on Terror* (New York: Free Press, 2004).

15. Clarke, *Against All Enemies.*

16. D. Brian, *Sing Sing: The Inside Story of a Notorious Prison* (New York: Prometheus, 2005).

17. Ethel and Julius Rosenberg were American communists who were executed at Sing Sing in 1953 for conspiracy to commit espionage. This was the first execution of civilians for espionage in U.S. history. "Fifty Years Later, Rosenberg Execution Is Still Fresh," Associated Press, June 17, 2003.

18. E. Partridge, *John Lennon: All I Want Is the Truth* (New York: Viking Press, 2005), p. 35.

19. "Beyond Their Years," *Entrepreneur,* Nov. 2003.

20. J. Moran interview with William Angrick, Nov. 10, 2010.

21. P. Yingling, "A Failure in Generalship," *Armed Services Journal,* May 2007.

22. A. S. Tyson, "Petraeus Helping Pick New Generals," *Washington Post,* Nov. 17, 2007.

23. F. Kaplan, "Promoting Innovation: Can Gen. David Petraeus Fix the Army's Broken Promotion System?" *Slate Magazine,* Nov. 21, 2007.

24. P. L. Yingling, "The Founders' Wisdom," *Armed Forces Journal,* Feb. 2010.

25. M. Gordon, "Bring Back the Draft," *New York Times,* Feb. 4, 2010.

26. B. Bradlee, *A Good Life* (New York: Simon & Schuster, 1995), p. 253.

27. Katharine Graham interview on the *Charlie Rose* show, Feb. 5, 1997. For video archive and transcript information, see http://www.charlierose.com/view/interview/3031.

28. S. McBee, "Katherine Graham and How She Grew," *McCall's,* Sept. 1971, p. 130.

29. R. Gerber, *Katharine Graham: The Leadership Journey of an American Icon* (New York: Portfolio, 2005), p. 145.

30. Gerber, *Katharine Graham,* p. 146.

31. A. Schlesinger Jr., *The Imperial Presidency* (Boston: Houghton Mifflin, 1973), p. 265.

32. Gerber, *Katharine Graham,* p. 131.

33. Gerber, *Katharine Graham.*

34. "Making the Tough Decisions," *Directorship,* September 1, 2007.

Chapter Seven

1. The Nasdaq stock market declined 78 percent from a level of 5048 (its all-time high on March 11, 2000) to 1114 on October 9, 2002. Nearly $5 trillion of equity value was erased during this decline. *Wall Street Journal* historical stock data.

2. J. Quittner, "The Charmed Life of Amazon's Jeff Bezos," *Fortune,* Apr. 15, 2008.

3. *Wall Street Journal:* historical stock price data on AMZN.

4. J. Useem, "Dot-Coms: What Have We Learned," *Fortune,* Oct. 30, 2000.

5. P. L. Lawrence and N. Nohria. *Driven: How Human Nature Shapes Our Choices* (San Francisco: Jossey-Bass, 2002).

6. D. Pink, *Drive: The Surprising Truth About What Motivates Us* (New York: Riverhead, 2009).

7. W. H. Herndon. *Herndon's Life of Lincoln* (Cleveland: Cleveland World Co., 1942), p. 304.

8. A. Hamilton, The Federalist No. 72 (1788); F. Fukuyama, *The End of History and the Last Man* (New York: Avon, 1992), p. 162.

9. J. Cassidy, *Dot.con: How America Lost Its Mind and Money in the Internet Era* (New York: HarperCollins, 2002), p. 136.

10. C. Bayers, "The Inner Bezos," *Wired,* 1999, no. 7.03, http://www.wired.com/wired/archive/7.03/bezos_pr.html.

11. Cassidy, *Dot.con.*

12. Bayers, "The Inner Bezos."

13. Cassidy, *Dot.con,* p. 259.

14. L. Kaufman, "Amazon.com Plans a Transformation to Internet Bazaar," *New York Times,* Sept. 30, 1999, p. A1.

15. "Remembering Don Hewitt," *60 Minutes,* Aug. 23, 2009. Video archive and transcript information available at: http://www.cbsnews.com/video/watch/?id=5260393n&tag=mncol;lst;1.

16. D. Hewitt, *Tell Me a Story: 50 Years and 60 Minutes in Television* (New York: Public Affairs Press, 2001), p. 53.

17. Hewitt, *Tell Me a Story,* p. 60.

18. Hewitt, *Tell Me a Story.*

19. M. Gordon, "Mickey Drexler's Redemption," *New York Magazine,* May 21, 2005.

20. Gordon, "Mickey Drexler's Redemption."

21. "Man in the News: Millard Drexler," *Financial Times,* Nov. 26, 2010.

22. "Man in the News: Millard Drexler."

23. M. Gladwell, *Outliers: The Story of Success* (New York: Little, Brown, 2008).

24. J. Moran telephone interview with Dan Hesse, Apr. 12, 2010.

25. E. Winner, *Gifted Children: Myths and Realities* (New York: Basic Books, 1996), p. 4.

26. J. Moran telephone interview with Sarah Wessling, May 13, 2010.

27. Author telephone interview, Aug. 2007.

28. J. Cohn interview with Zeppos in July 2010.

29. J. Moran telephone interview with Doug Ulman, Aug. 3, 2010.

30. J. Cohn interview with Nicholas Scopetta, New York, New York, July 2010.

31. B. George, *Authentic Leadership: Rediscovering the Secrets to Creating Lasting Value* (San Francisco: Jossey-Bass, 2003), p. 12.

32. B. George, speech at the Marshall School of Business, University of Southern California, May 8, 2008.

33. A. Schweitzer, *Out of My Life and Thought* (New York: Holt, 1933), p. 108.

34. *Happiness: Webster's Quotations, Facts and Phrases* (San Diego: ICON Group International, 2008), p. 14.

Chapter Eight

1. The formal name for interviews that focus on past performance and skill accumulation is past behavioral interviews or competency-based interviews.

2. "John Sculley on Steve Jobs, The Full Interview Transcript," in L. Kahney, *The Cult of Mac* (San Francisco: No Starch Press, 2004).

3. Ever since the German sociologist Max Weber used the word *charisma* to describe one of the ideal types of authority over one hundred years ago, experts have tried unsuccessfully to define exactly what it means or

the extent to which it contributes to effective leadership. See M. Weber, "Types of Authority," in B. Kellerman (Ed.), *Political Leadership: A Source Book* (Pittsburgh, Pa.: University of Pittsburgh Press, 1986). Most people generally use the term to mean personal magnetism or attraction, although there is little agreement about what the source of that attraction is. Some say it comes from a leader's communication style. Still others say it is an inherent trait or that it arises as much from the relationship with followers as from the individual leader alone, and Weber himself argued that charisma should be understood this way. Another source of disagreement is whether it is a personality type or a leadership style. Setting this ambiguity aside, experts such as Joe Nye argue that charisma is an important part of "soft power" and, depending on the context, a key to effective political leadership. J. Nye Jr., *The Powers to Lead* (New York: Oxford University Press, 2008). In the business world, some researchers have claimed that charisma is an advantageous motivational tool and sets good leaders apart. Others emphasize that it enables leaders to attract resources from outside the organization. F. J. Flynn and B. M. Staw, "Lend Me Your Wallets: The Effect of Charismatic Leadership on External Support for an Organization," *Strategic Management Journal,* 2004, *24,* 309–330. From this perspective, charisma (however defined) is viewed as contributing to leadership success. Yet numerous other experts, such as Jim Collins, have argued convincingly that charisma is a poor indicator of leadership ability. J. Collins, *Good to Great* (New York: HarperCollins, 2001), pp. 72–73. Rakesh Khurana is another academic who has been critical in this regard. He studied the performance of several companies that hired individuals with attractive, "heroic" images and concluded that this "irrational quest for charismatic CEOs" was usually a mistake. R. Khurana, *Searching for a Corporate Savior: The Irrational Quest for Charismatic CEOs* (Princeton, N.J.: Princeton University Press, 2002). See also Rakesh Khurana, "Good Charisma, Bad Business," *New York Times,* Sept. 13, 2002, p. A27. As a whole, research and opinion on this topic are inconsistent, inconclusive, and poorly defined.

4. Collins and his research team spent years looking at financial results to find companies that went from average or underperforming to

best-in-class for a sustained period. As he notes in his book, if a person had invested $1 in a mutual fund of these "good-to-great" companies in 1965, by 2000 the amount invested would have multiplied 471 times, compared to only a 56-fold increase for a general stock market fund. J. Collins, *Good to Great* (New York: HarperCollins, 2001), p. 3. Collins and his team identified a framework to explain what accounted for this extraordinary level of performance. The first factor in the framework was Level 5 leadership.

5. Collins, *Good to Great*, p. 13.

6. For decades researchers have tried to find a clear link between leadership style and performance. In the 1950s researchers at the Ohio State University developed the Leader Behavior Description Questionnaire (LBDQ). In one form or another, the LBDQ was widely distributed and used to make statements about leadership potential. P. G. Northouse, *Leadership Theory and Practice*, 3rd ed. (Thousand Oaks, Calif.: Sage, 2004). Similarly, in the 1960s, the Leadership Grid was developed by management theorists Robert Blake and Jane Mouton as a purported framework for assessing leadership potential. The Leadership Grid distinguishes leaders whose style demonstrates a concern for people versus those with a concern for results. More recently, many researchers have begun to talk about the effectiveness of leaders who rely on a traditionally masculine, assertive style versus a more stereotypically feminine style that emphasizes relationship building. This style approach to leadership contains the same problems with definition, context, and inconsistency that plague the "personality" branch of leadership. The result is largely an incoherent and inconclusive body of research. According to Gary Yukl, "The results from this massive research effort have been mostly contradictory and inconclusive." G. Yukl, *Leadership in Organizations*, 7th ed. (Upper Saddle River, N.J.: Prentice Hall, 2009), p. 75. For several years, Justin Menkes has studied the predictive power that a leader's style has for determining performance, and his conclusion is that, as with personality type, it is insignificant: "No personality type or interpersonal style is responsible for excellent performance." J. Menkes, *Executive Intelligence* (New York: HarperCollins, 2005), p. 174.

7. B. George, *Authentic Leadership: Rediscovering the Secrets to Creating Lasting Value* (San Francisco: Jossey-Bass, 2003), p. 14.

8. The best organizations are conscientious about detailing these requirements in a document that is typically called a specification sheet. This helps everyone agree, up front, on the job's unique requirements and the kind of leader the organization needs.

9. For an excellent overview of these kinds of questions see Menkes, *Executive Intelligence.*

10. We spoke to the CEO of a large media company that had just acquired a coveted target company. He confided, "At first I was extremely proud that we were finally able to get this done. For eighteen months, I knew that we needed their product to round out our customer offering. However, I soon realized that I had little idea of the caliber or quality of executives in the acquired company. It was a strange, helpless feeling. My stomach was in knots. My head of HR recommended that we assess them, which we did. Fortunately, most of them were as good as or better than I had hoped. But about 10 percent of them didn't measure up, and we had to let them go. Our company's success depends on it."

11. The degree of readiness depends on the role being considered. A rising star may be five years away from a very senior position, but near ready or ready now for a completely different, more junior, position.

12. This term was developed by superstar executive coach Marshall Goldsmith in his book *What Got You Here Won't Get You There* (New York: Hyperion, 2007).

13. Research shows that selecting outside CEOs is a more prudent strategy when a company is in crisis. In more stable times, an insider is a better choice. J. M. Citrin and D. Ogden, "What's the Best Route to the Top?" *Harvard Business Review,* Nov. 2010. http://hbr.org/2010/11/succeeding-at-succession/ar/2.

14. J. Cohn telephone interview with Harvey Spevak, Aug. 2010.

15. J. Moran telephone interview with Werner Zedelius, Dec. 2010.

Acknowledgments

This book would not have been possible without the help of countless people.

We are grateful to the scores of CEOs, executives, and other leaders who gave generously of their time when we were writing this book. Every one of the leaders we worked with and interviewed is a major contributor to the book, and the anecdotes and insights they offered were far more interesting than what we have been able to convey in the space here. To the extent that we were able to structure their ideas in a useful way, we owe thanks to our great editors at Jossey-Bass. Mary Garrett, Beverly Harrison Miller, and especially Karen Murphy did an excellent job of shepherding our manuscript from start to finish. No one else encourages both creativity and discipline simultaneously as well as Karen does. We are incredibly thankful for her insight, her patience, and her tough love.

The journey to this book has been long and exciting. Almost two decades ago, we met an important mentor, Jeffrey Sonnenfeld, at the exact same time, which, incidentally, was when we met each other. We were both research fellows at his Chief Executive Leadership Institute at Yale University. Sonnenfeld provided a valuable introduction to the world of executive education and unparalleled access to chief executives across the country. The opportunity to work with him and develop CEO seminars and conferences was like that of young, eager apprentices learning from a master craftsman. We were in awe that leading CEOs with their busy schedules would make time to come back, year after year, to Sonnenfeld's seminars. But Sonnenfeld had a knack for understanding what kept CEOs up at night, and we are grateful that he was our first mentor in the leadership domain.

• • • • • • • • •

Jeffrey Cohn: The Harvard Business School (HBS) provided a uniquely fertile environment to launch a career in leadership development, succession planning, and executive assessment. My experience as a research associate in strategy and finance, nearly two decades ago, afforded unfettered access to many of the world's top scholars as well as top executives. As a kid fresh out of graduate school I was way out of my league interviewing CEOs, but somehow survived. To ensure I stayed afloat, my friends, mentors, and bosses at Harvard always threw me a lifeline at just the right time. I am particularly grateful to Michael Porter, David Yoffie, Michael Rukstad, Michael Enright, Michael Edleson, Jay Lorsch, Scott Mason, David Collis, and Clayton Christensen. I am particularly grateful for the coaching, mentoring, and friendship of a now-deceased friend, Michael Rukstad. I miss you, Mike.

I would have never even known about the research associate program at HBS had it not been for Srinivasa Rangan, a former M.B.A. strategy professor of mine. I thank him for his career advice, which was the nudge I needed right when I needed it most. I also thank him for his constant intellectual stimulation and his continued friendship for the past two decades.

I have since kept in touch and worked closely with many faculty members at HBS. In particular, professor Rakesh Khurana and I have written articles together and advised senior executives and CEOs on critical leadership development initiatives. More than anyone else, he has helped shape my thinking on the many problems that can arise when companies overvalue charismatic leaders. He is also an excellent assessor of leadership potential and executive educator.

I thank Dominique Turpin, president of IMD, and Bernie Jaworski, a close friend, a wonderful tennis player, and perhaps the most gifted person alive when it comes to helping leaders assess their leadership potential, understand their developmental needs, and most important, bridge their development gaps in highly practical and ingenious ways. Richard Rumelt, the godfather of strategic thinking, has been a good friend and mentor to me for fifteen years. No one else has a sharper strategic mind than he does. David Teece, a friend and former boss, is maybe the only academic on the planet who feels equally comfortable in the classroom, the boardroom, and the courtroom, testifying as an expert witness in complex litigation cases. I sincerely hope just a bit of his wisdom and entrepreneurial magic has rubbed off on me as I've worked with him over the years.

From the ivory tower to the boardroom, Spencer Stuart is a world-leading executive search firm with unparalleled access to CEOs and board members around the world. It's hard to imagine any other professional services firm that has higher quality standards. I had the privilege of working at Spencer Stuart for several years alongside many gifted professionals, including Dayton Ogden, Jim Citrin, Nick Young, Joe Boccuzi, Lloyd Campbell, and Michael Anderson. I worked closely and learned from each of these people as we advised boards of directors on important CEO succession issues. I also thank Cathy Anterasian, Bob Stark, Justin Menkes, and Steven Blackman, who not only are good friends and mentors, but are also truly gifted in the area of assessing leadership potential.

Elkhonon Goldberg, a gifted, award-winning neuroscientist and friend, invited me to his Manhattan office one hot summer day. He offered this fascinating idea: "Jeff, I am telling you that people should exercise their brains like they exercise the rest of their bodies. Not only does this ward off dementia, it makes them smarter." I couldn't resist and asked what the best way is to exercise my brain. He had a simple answer. Write a book. So I did. Boy, was he right. Sure I've written several articles, but it was nothing like the exercise

I got when writing this book. So thanks, Elkhonon. And next time just tell me to go to the gym for some exercise. That would be a lot easier.

I would also like to thank some very special friends and colleagues for reviewing this manuscript and providing invaluable advice: Dean Roger Martin, Seth Shaffer, Perry Goldfarb, Mark Gabbay, Steve Fine, Ana Kaczmarek, and Richard Ellman.

And last but not least, I thank my family, especially my mother. She is the intellectual and emotional inspiration for everything I do, including this book. And although Dad is now retired and living the good life in West Palm Beach, his business mind and competitive spirit remains sharp as a tack, and he serves as an inspiration to me every day. And of course I thank my little brother, Danny, for all his support and advice. Now all grown up, he is a successful intellectual property attorney and promises to be a great leader himself in the near future.

• • • • • • • • •

Jay Moran: Several academic and professional mentors and colleagues in addition to Jeffrey Sonnenfeld provided advice and inspiration that helped fuel my career in the leadership field including John Ryan, Bill Carney, Martha Grace Duncan, and Tim Terrell, to name just a select few. Patrick Allitt unleashed in me an interest in history that has carried my fascination with leadership across many centuries.

Speaking of centuries, my years as a corporate lawyer seem almost that long ago. Back then Jay Harris and John McNamara showed me first-hand how to exercise effective leadership in order to complete billion dollar acquisitions, often late at night in conference rooms and without much sleep. Their friendship and coaching were invaluable, and I'm certain that everyone else who has followed in their footsteps has also benefitted. More recently, as the ideas expressed in this book began to percolate, several people at

Harvard were instrumental in helping to challenge and strengthen my understanding of leadership. They include Graham Allison, Richard Clarke, Bill George, David Gergen, Ron Heifetz, Joe Nye, Steven Pinker, Roger Porter, and Dean Williams. Special appreciation goes to Joe Badaracco and Barbara Kellerman for their extra time, advice, encouragement, and friendship.

Over the years, I have had the privilege to be a part of some of the best universities and executive education programs in Europe and the United States and to provide private consulting services to world-class companies. The people I have met have given me much more than they will ever realize. As a professor, it has been my good fortune to teach leadership to extraordinarily bright students who are willing to push ideas back at me, and my collaboration with various executive education programs has allowed me to absorb knowledge from middle managers and senior executives in a variety of fields. In my work as a professional assessment and leadership development expert, the opportunity to interview and assist so many bright and successful executives, from so many companies, has been a thrilling learning experience. This entire group of students, practitioners, and executives—many hundreds of them by now—has contributed to this book in ways that my words cannot adequately express. Time and again, they have galvanized my appreciation for leadership with fresh insights, tough questions, and real-life stories that defy simple categorization. The imprint of their collective experience and wisdom is all over the pages of this book.

Finally, I owe special thanks to my parents, Patrick and Jill Moran, for their unwavering support and encouragement. They continue to inspire me with their leadership every day.

About the Authors

Jeffrey Cohn is an advisor to business leaders around the world who has coached over a thousand executives and helped Fortune 500 companies develop CEO succession plans. After receiving a degree in economics from Vanderbilt and an M.B.A. from Tulane, Cohn worked as a research associate at the Harvard Business School, focusing on applied corporate finance and corporate strategy, as well as at the CEO Leadership Institute, which is now part of Yale University. At the institute, Cohn helped launch dozens of highly focused conferences based on his interviews of chief executive officers to better understand their pressing leadership issues. Cohn also served as a research associate at INSEAD to better understand how global companies successfully enhanced their corporate culture. Cohn was a principal at LECG, an upstart management-consulting firm based in Berkeley, California, and was a specialist in CEO succession planning and executive assessment at Spencer Stuart, a premier executive search and consulting firm. Cohn has coauthored several best-selling *Harvard Business Review* articles and case studies, including "Finding and Grooming Breakthrough Innovators" and "Growing Talent as if Your Business Depended on It." He lives in New York City.

Jay Moran is an expert in executive talent evaluation and leadership development and a professor of leadership and international business at IES in Barcelona. He works with large organizations to implement first-rate succession planning and talent management systems. He also works hand-in-hand with executive coaches and other professors and has helped design leadership development workshops and curricula at several of the world's leading business schools, including at the Chief Executive Leadership Institute (now at Yale). Earlier in his career, Moran worked as a corporate lawyer at King & Spalding and strategy consultant at Deloitte, and he leverages that experience today by assisting law firms and other professional services groups on important leadership assessment and development issues. He has a B.A. in economics, an M.B.A., a law degree, and a master's degree in public administration from Harvard University, where the focus of his study was leadership. He lives in Barcelona.

Index